THE
CREDENTIALED
COURT

BENJAMIN H. BARTON

THE
CREDENTIALED
COURT

INSIDE *the* CLOISTERED
ELITE WORLD
of AMERICAN JUSTICE

Encounter BOOKS

New York • London

First American edition published in 2022 by Encounter Books,
an activity of Encounter for Culture and Education, Inc.,
a nonprofit, tax-exempt corporation.
Encounter Books website address: www.encounterbooks.com

Manufactured in the United States and printed on
acid-free paper. The paper used in this publication meets
the minimum requirements of ANSI/NISO Z39.48–1992
(R 1997) (*Permanence of Paper*).

FIRST AMERICAN EDITION

LIBRARY OF CONGRESS CATALOGING-IN-PUBLICATION DATA

Library of Congress Cataloging-in-Publication Data

Names: Barton, Benjamin H., 1969– author.
Title: The Credentialed Court: Inside the Cloistered, Elite World of
American Justice / Benjamin H. Barton.
Description: First American edition. | New York: Encounter Books, 2022.
Includes bibliographical references and index.
Identifiers: LCCN 2021004437 (print) | LCCN 2021004438 (ebook)
ISBN 9781641772044 (hardcover) | ISBN 9781641772051 (ebook)
Subjects: LCSH: United States. Supreme Court—Officials and
employees—Selection and appointment—History.
Judges—Selection and appointment—United States—History.
Classification: LCC KF8748 .B277 2022 (print) | LCC KF8748 (ebook)
DDC 347.73/2634—dc23
LC record available at https://lccn.loc.gov/2021004437
LC ebook record available at https://lccn.loc.gov/2021004438

1 2 3 4 5 6 7 8 9 20 22

CONTENTS

～

CHAPTER ONE

INTRODUCTION

The Rise of Our Cloistered Elite Court

Those who followed the Supreme Court confirmation processes of Merrick Garland and Brett Kavanaugh likely concluded that the country has never been more divided on what makes a good Supreme Court Justice. Kavanaugh's hearings and processes were among the most divisive and brutal in the history of the Court. Kavanaugh at least had a hearing. Obama nominee Merrick Garland was announced dead on arrival in the Senate, and he did not even get a chance to make his case.

The roil in the Senate is, of course, just a reflection of the political reality that the Supreme Court and the selection of Justices has become a preeminent political issue. As with many other trends, Donald Trump made this subtext the text in his first presidential campaign. Trump released a list of twenty-one potential nominees (almost all Federalist Society choices and rock-ribbed conservative originalists) ahead of the election in an effort to win over Republican voters who might have otherwise objected to other aspects of Trump's campaign and lifestyle. Candidate Trump loved to trot out the specter of multiple Hillary Clinton nominees as a critical reason why Republicans, evangelicals, libertarians, and others should vote for him. He wasn't exactly subtle—consider this quote, from a 2016 rally in Cedar Rapids: "If you really like Donald Trump, that's great, but if you don't you have to vote for me anyway. You know why? Supreme Court Judges. You have no choice, sorry, sorry, sorry."[1]

The tactic worked well in 2016. In the immediate aftermath of the release of the infamous Access Hollywood audiotape, Franklin Graham advised his followers to stick with Trump: "Hold your nose and go vote," he said. "You have to decide which one of the two [presidential candidates] you would trust to appoint justices that are going to protect our religious freedom as Christians."[2] 2016 exit polls showed that Trump voters were especially likely to have considered the Supreme Court a deciding factor in their vote.[3]

Yet despite deep political divisions, Americans have unwittingly come to a different sort of consensus on Supreme Court Justices. This consensus is reflected in the remarkably similar educational, professional, and geographic backgrounds of recent appointees. Here are the backgrounds of three recent nominees listed anonymously and in no particular order. See if you can tell who is who:

NOMINEE ONE grew up in an upper-middle-class family and was the child of two lawyers. He attended an exclusive suburban private high school and graduated with a distinguished record. He then attended Columbia University as an undergraduate. He went straight from Columbia to Harvard Law School where he graduated *cum laude*. Nominee One was awarded a prestigious Marshall Scholarship to study at Oxford and eventually received a doctorate in Philosophy from Oxford. Nominee One clerked for a distinguished judge on the D.C. Circuit and then went on to clerk on the Supreme Court. After the clerkship, Nominee One stayed in D.C. and worked as an associate and then a partner at a top D.C. law firm. Nominee One then served as the deputy attorney general and acting associate attorney general before being appointed to serve as a federal court of appeals judge himself. He served as a federal judge for eleven years before being nominated to join the Supreme Court.

NOMINEE TWO grew up in an upper-middle-class household. His father ran his own advertising agency and his mother was the director of volunteer services at a religious organization. He grew up in a nice suburb and graduated as valedictorian of a public high school. He went on to attend Harvard on a scholarship and graduated *summa cum laude*. He went straight on to Harvard Law School and graduated *magna cum laude* three years later. Nominee Two then clerked for a prestigious judge on the Second Circuit before gaining a Supreme Court clerkship the next year. Over the course of his legal career Nominee Two worked in the Department of Justice for four years, including a stretch as deputy associate attorney general, as an associate and partner in a prestigious D.C. law firm, and as an assistant U.S. attorney in Washington, D.C. Nominee Two was then appointed to the D.C. Circuit as a Judge. He served as a judge for nineteen years before his nomination to the Supreme Court.

NOMINEE THREE grew up upper-middle class, the child of two lawyers. He attended an exclusive suburban private high school, where he excelled in his classes. He attended Yale undergraduate and went straight on to Yale Law School. He then clerked for two different prestigious federal court of appeals judges and spent a year as a lawyer in the Solicitor General's Office before gaining his own Supreme Court clerkship. Over the course of his legal career he worked in an independent counsel's office, the White House Counsel's Office, briefly in a large law firm, and as the White House Staff Secretary. He was then appointed to the D.C. Circuit as a Judge, where he served for twelve years before his nomination.

If you guessed Gorsuch (1), Garland (2), and Kavanaugh (3), then you know *a lot* of granular trivia about those three individuals, because the differences in their life experiences and resumes are so few. In fact, the radical similarity of these three men tells us volumes about the current model of Supreme Court Justice and just how much that model has changed over the years.

It was not always thus. This book is a study of the backgrounds of America's Supreme Court Justices, starting with the first, John Jay, and continuing through Amy Coney Barrett. I studied and quantified the pre-Court life experiences of all 115 Supreme Court Justices. I use this study to answer a series of related empirical questions and then to draw some conclusions about the state of the Supreme Court and the country as a whole. I also tell a series of anecdotes about the lives of these Justices before they joined the Court to show what we're missing on today's Supreme Court.

What backgrounds predominate among modern Justices? Here Garland, Gorsuch, and Kavanaugh's backgrounds are typical. It turns out that their commonalities reach to the entire Court.

To begin, let's start with the most common elements. The last four nominees (Garland, Gorsuch, Kavanaugh, and Barrett) all grew up in the suburbs of major American cities in relatively prosperous, professional homes. This is of a piece with the other current Justices. Only John Roberts (Long Beach, Indiana), and Clarence Thomas (Savannah, Georgia) grew up outside a major metropolitan area. Five of the Justices went to high school inside the Acela corridor between D.C. and New York City (Alito, Kavanaugh, and Gorsuch join the New Yorkers Kagan and Sotomayor). The majority of today's Justices also come from upper-middle-class families in which at least one of their parents were professionals, including five Justices who had a lawyer parent (Breyer, Kagan, Gorsuch, Kavanaugh, and Barrett).

Every Justice except for Clarence Thomas and Amy Coney Barrett attended an Ivy League institution or Stanford for his or her undergraduate degree. This means that each of these seven Justices was not just a decent student in high school; each was exceptional enough to gain admittance to the most competitive universities in the country. In 2018 *Education Week* published a roundup of the high school achievements of the current Justices— it reads as one might expect: valedictorians, class presidents, elite public or private schools, etc.[4]

Ironically, Justice Thomas may actually have achieved the most before college.[5] Thomas was born in 1948, in Pin Point, Georgia, to sharecroppers. Pin Point is a tiny and exceptionally poor town outside of Savannah, Georgia, founded in 1896 by freed slaves on the grounds of a former plantation. Thomas's home had no electricity, heat, or running water. He was raised in a family that spoke Gullah, an African Creole language of former slaves, as its first language. The Supreme Court, like other American institutions, has its share of rags-to-riches stories, but it would be hard to imagine a tougher and more impoverished early childhood than Thomas's. His family scraped out a living as sharecroppers in a manner that had more in common with 1850 than 1950. Thomas's father left when he was two. His home burned down when he was six, and when he was seven his mother sent him to live with his grandparents in Savannah.

Thomas's grandparents enrolled him in Catholic schools. He attended the all-black St. Pius X for ninth and tenth grade. In the mid-1960s there were no desegregated schools in Savannah, public or private. Thomas decided he wanted to be a Catholic priest and knew that he'd have a better chance of graduating and attending seminary if he transferred to the all-white Saint

John Vianney School. Thomas applied and was admitted as the first black student in an all-white Catholic school in Savannah, Georgia, in 1964. Thomas repeated tenth grade so he could study Latin (which was not offered at his previous school) and did well enough to graduate and continue on to Seminary. Like Sonia Sotomayor, whether you admire Justice Thomas as a jurist or not, his biography is a gripping story of triumph over hardship, especially in comparison to the easier paths of his colleagues on the Court.

But the achievements hardly ended in high school. Each of today's Justices excelled in college as well. How do we know? Because almost every recent Justice then enrolled in either Harvard or Yale Law Schools. From the appointment of John Paul Stevens in 1975 (a Northwestern Law grad) until Amy Coney Barret in 2020, *every* Justice attended Yale, Harvard, or Stanford for law school. Then and now these schools were among the most selective institutions of higher education in the world, and each of these Justices did well enough as undergraduates to earn admission into those august institutions. Moreover, Thomas, Sotomayor, and Ginsburg all arrived as relative oddities and trailblazers, facing the added pressure of being visibly dissimilar to their mostly white, male classmates.

In fact, Justice Ginsburg's responsibilities as a young, married mother help explain the one pre-Barrett anomaly among the recent Justices: she attended Harvard for the first two years, but actually graduated from Columbia Law School, mostly due to Harvard's stupidity and rigidity. Ginsburg's husband, Martin, was a year ahead of her at Harvard. During Martin's third year—and Ruth's second year—he contracted testicular cancer and suffered through two operations and radiation therapy. If you think radiation treatments and cancer surgery are hard today, they were worse in 1957. Much worse. Ruth spent her second year of law school nursing her husband back to good health, attending her own classes, helping Martin with his, and serving as the primary caregiver to their two-year-old daughter Jane. Remarkably, she finished the year with exceptional grades.

Martin survived and graduated in 1958 with a plum job at Weil, Gotshal, and Manges, one of the premier New York law firms that hired Jewish lawyers in the 1950s. Most "white shoe" New York firms remained restricted, so a job at Weil was great news. Neither cancer treatments nor Harvard Law School were free, so Martin's new salary would be most welcome. But the good news came with a dilemma. Ruth had to decide whether to divide her family so she could finish up law school at Harvard or to complete her degree in New York where she and young Jane could live with Martin. She decided to take her third year at Columbia. When she asked Harvard Law if she could still have a Harvard diploma if she spent her third year at Columbia they, in their infinite wisdom, declined, costing them one more Justice on the Supreme Court. Harvard's mistake was thus the only impediment to a wholly Yale- and Harvard-educated Supreme Court for the decade before Barrett was appointed.

The current Justices' triumphs continued in law school, an especially impressive feat given how competitive and hierarchical the legal profession can be, especially at the elite level. These competitions exist partially because of the nature of America's legal system. From law school forward, American lawyers are taught to understand and work within hierarchies. Lawyers and judges must discern which precedents are controlling, which are persuasive, and which are to be simply disregarded. They must also fit regulations, statutes, and rules of interpretation within this complex machinery, recognizing that federal, state, and even local laws, regulations, and court precedents predominate in different areas. The ability to slot each law, regulation, and governmental body into its proper place is a critical legal skill.

This keen awareness of hierarchy naturally bleeds over into the nature of the profession itself, and thus to competition. In law school the competitions can grow quite granular. GPA is one obvious example (although Yale Law famously abolished number grades in the 1960s). Membership on law review and editorial positions are another. The competition hardly ends at graduation, as the battle over elite post–law school jobs like clerkships or fellowships can be at least as fierce.

The post-graduation careers of the Justices on the Roberts Court tell us a lot about where exceedingly ambitious and academically inclined lawyers with impeccable credentials choose to work. The most obvious first step is attaining a Supreme Court clerkship. Naturally, Harvard Law grads started the trend. In 1882 Justice Horace Gray hired the first Supreme Court clerk. Gray, one of the eight Supreme Court Justices to graduate from both Harvard College and Harvard Law School, selected Thomas Russell, a recent Harvard Law grad for the honor.[6] Justice Gray apparently paid him out of his own pocket. Congress did not authorize funds for paying law clerks until 1886.

From 1882 forward a Supreme Court clerkship has been the most prestigious job a law school graduate can procure. A whopping two thirds of the Justices on the current Court served as Supreme Court clerks (Breyer, Roberts, Kagan, Gorsuch, Kavanaugh, and Barrett). The trend is actually accelerating: each of the last four Justices served as a Supreme Court clerk, as did Merrick Garland. Here, again, only sexism kept Justice Ginsburg from swelling the ranks of former Supreme Court clerks. Ginsburg finished tied for first in her class at Columbia and received a glowing recommendation from the Dean of Harvard, but Justice Frankfurter declined to hire her, thinking a female clerk was a bridge too far in 1960.[7]

After law school and prestigious clerkships, the Justices began their legal careers, again amongst only the very best of the best. Historically this would have meant a lucrative career in the private practice of law. If you add up all of the work experiences of all of the Justices from Jay to Barrett, you find that they spent the most time working as private lawyers, often as solo practitioners or in small firms. The current Justices, however, reflect a very different set of work experiences. In recent decades, Justices have tended to work as either a law professor, an elite government lawyer, or a corporate lawyer before eventually serving as a federal appellate judge, often on the hyper-specialized D.C. Circuit.

Before the death of Justice Scalia and the retirement of Justice Kennedy, time spent as a law professor on the Court was at an all-time high. With Barrett's appointment it remains the most well represented recent career path on the Court. Scalia, Kennedy, Breyer, Ginsburg, Kagan, and Barrett all spent the bulk of their non-judicial careers in academia, and generally at the highest levels of academia. It is hard to overstate how hard these jobs are to procure. It is certainly very challenging to receive a Supreme Court clerkship. Yet typically thirty-six young lawyers reach that milestone every year. By contrast a top-ten law school will likely hire only one or two new tenure-track professors per year. Kagan, Breyer, Scalia, and Ginsburg all achieved this early in their careers. Each was remarkably decorated as an academic. Kagan eventually rose to become Dean of Harvard Law School, just the eleventh Dean in Harvard Law's existence. Given that there have been 115 Supreme Court Justices, Kagan's latest job is arguably less rarified than her former one. Breyer wrote two enormously influential books on risk and the American regulatory state. Scalia taught at Chicago, Virginia, and Stanford. Ginsburg personally changed the face of constitutional and gender discrimination law from Columbia. Barrett was the rare Notre Dame Law graduate to be hired back there to teach, a remarkable result reflecting

her Scalia clerkship and her position among the most decorated
Notre Dame Law grads in recent memory.

Other Justices chose a no-less-prestigious government-
centric path. After a stretch as a district attorney and corporate
counsel in Missouri, Justice Thomas headed to D.C. to work for
Missouri Senator John C. Danforth and then in the Department
of Education and as the head of the Equal Employment Opportunity Commission (EEOC) under Presidents Reagan and Bush.
Alito and Sotomayor (and Garland) worked as prosecutors in
highly regarded offices. Sotomayor spent five years in the New
York County District Attorney's Office under the legendary
Bob Morgenthau. Alito worked as an Assistant U.S. Attorney
in New Jersey straight from his clerkship, a heady leap for any
young lawyer. He then went on to work in the Solicitor General's
Office (one of the most prestigious jobs in government, since
they argue and brief cases in front of the U.S. Supreme Court)
and eventually as Deputy U.S. Attorney General. He returned
to New Jersey in triumph as the appointed head of the United
States Attorney office for the district where his career had started
just ten years earlier.

Kavanaugh may be the best example of this career path, as
he jumped from one prestigious and politically helpful job to
another before joining the D.C. Circuit as a Judge. Kavanaugh
also worked in the Solicitor General's Office and then worked
on the Whitewater investigation under Kenneth Starr for four
years, establishing both his conservative bona fides and his legal
acumen. Regardless of whether one agrees or disagrees with the
investigation itself, the final report (which was allegedly largely
written by Kavanaugh) laid out the most detailed and legally
airtight version of what Starr found. Kavanaugh followed that
up by working in the White House Counsel's office for Bush and
eventually rising to become staff secretary, the all-important job

that controls access to the president and all of the paperwork that crosses the president's desk.

The current Justices also spent some time in private practice, often in specialized and exclusive practices. Justice Sotomayor spent eight years as an associate and eventually a partner at Pavia and Harcourt in New York, focusing on intellectual property issues for high-end clients like Fendi and Ferrari.[8] John Roberts spent thirteen years in private practice (the most on the current Court). Roberts worked in the D.C. office of the international corporate law firm Hogan & Hartson (now known as Hogan Lovells) for three years as an associate, worked four years as the Deputy Solicitor General, and then returned to Hogan as a partner for ten years. Roberts ran the firm's appellate practice and eventually argued thirty-nine cases before the Supreme Court.

The previous paragraphs cover the pre-judicial parts of the Justices' experiences. Every current Justice except for Kagan eventually went on to serve as a federal appellate court judge, including a third who served on the most prestigious appellate court, the D.C. Circuit (Thomas, Roberts, and Kavanaugh). Like becoming a professor at Harvard or Columbia, becoming a court of appeals judge requires an exceptional career plus excellent connections, especially to earn a slot on the D.C. Circuit. Just as every U.S. Senator wakes up in the morning, looks in the mirror, and says "good morning Mr. (Madame) President," the best and the brightest in the legal profession dream of becoming a federal appeals court judge. This is especially so for the D.C. Circuit, which is (accurately) seen as a greased skid onto the Supreme Court. Eight of these Justices achieved this lifetime goal and then did enough on these courts to distinguish themselves as nominees to the Supreme Court itself.

One sure sign that we have settled on a single mold for Supreme Court Justices is the series of shared experiences among the Justices of the Roberts Court. It is a small world at the highest levels of the American legal profession, and today's Court really shows it. The most glaring example is the first two Trump appointees. Justices Gorsuch and Kavanaugh have traveled together since high school.[9] Both Gorsuch and Kavanaugh attended Georgetown Preparatory School in North Bethesda, Maryland, with Kavanaugh graduating two years ahead of Gorsuch. Gorsuch managed to close the age gap, however, joining Kavanaugh as a clerk in the chambers of Justice Kennedy in the 1993–94 term. Gorsuch was clerking for retired Justice Byron White, but was assigned to Kennedy's chambers for active cases, so he and Kavanaugh worked together all year. A Google search for "Gorsuch Kennedy Kavanaugh clerk photo" unearths several pictures of the impossibly young looking co-clerks with their boss.

A decade later Gorsuch served as the principal deputy and acting associate attorney general under George W. Bush during the period when Kavanaugh was serving as staff secretary and was heavily involved in picking and prepping judicial nominees. They were both nominated to the court of appeals the same year (Kavanaugh the D.C. Circuit and Gorsuch the Tenth). They were even co-authors (with other federal appellate judges and Bryan Garner) on a book entitled *The Law of Judicial Precedent*.[10] And these are just the obvious overlaps. Both Kavanaugh and Gorsuch have long been members of, or affiliated with, the Federalist Society and run in the same conservative legal circles.[11]

But elite credentials are not just for Republicans. To the contrary: remove the political leanings from the resumes, and Merrick Garland looks almost identical to Gorsuch and Kavanaugh. Read Justice Alito's resume next to Justice Sotomayor's—they are remarkably similar from orientation at Princeton to the day they each joined the Court.

Those who have paid attention to the increasing divisiveness of American politics in the last decade or so may find this bipartisan accord on elite credentials surprising. We are living in a time of exceptionally strong partisan divisions, especially concerning the Supreme Court. Further, Donald Trump and others have made the role and nature of American elites perhaps the central electoral issue. Trump railed against "media elites," "political elites," and "elites who led us from one financial and foreign policy disaster to another."[12] Trump was elected to "drain the swamp" and break up the dominance of these elites. Yet, when given the chance to make three Supreme Court nominations, Trump selected not only members of the elite, but the most elite nominees he could find.

In filling Justice Kennedy's slot, for example, President Trump released a list of finalists that included the well-respected Sixth Circuit Judge Raymond Kethledge along with Kavanaugh and others. Judge Kethledge fits the thesis of this book nicely: he also clerked for Justice Kennedy on the Supreme Court, taught as an adjunct at a top law school (The University of Michigan), and was an associate and partner at a large corporate law firm. But reportedly Trump found something he did not like on Kethledge's resume. "A graduate of the University of Michigan Law School, Judge Kethledge does not have the Harvard or Yale pedigree that Mr. Trump has told associates he would like to see in the next justice."[13] Yes, you've read that correctly. Poor Judge Kethledge was forced to attend Michigan rather than Harvard or Yale for law school, and despite doing well enough to secure a Supreme Court clerkship and a seat on the Sixth Circuit he lacked the shine of the "better qualified" Brett Kavanaugh.

Nor was Trump satisfied with just the Harvard or Yale pedigree: he (apparently falsely) claimed that both Justice Gorsuch and Justice Kavanaugh finished first in their law school classes.[14] Yale barely has grades, so there is never an official "first" in any Yale

Law School class, and Gorsuch finished *cum laude* at Harvard, so he was definitely below his classmates who graduated *magna* or *summa cum laude* that year.

Barrett was a departure in some ways. As a graduate of Rhodes in Memphis and then Notre Dame Law School, her educational pedigree looks much more like Justices from a century ago than today. But remember that Barrett received a full ride to Notre Dame and chose to study there at least partially due to her powerful Catholic faith. Moreover, she graduated first in her class and then secured a clerkship with Antonin Scalia, who reportedly called her one of his favorite clerks ever. From law school graduation forward, Barrett's career actually looks quite similar to the hyper elite path of other former law professor Justices.

It is also worth noting that the recent Justices who have differed the most from the current model have tended to be female or nominees of color. Clarence Thomas and Amy Coney Barrett attended neither an Ivy League school nor Stanford for college. Neither Sotomayor nor Thomas clerked for a judge (let alone a Supreme Court Justice) after graduation. Kagan was never a federal judge (although she was admittedly kind of busy as Dean of Harvard Law School). Sotomayor started as a district court judge before joining the Second Circuit Court of Appeals.

Why Has the Elite Model Triumphed?

First, as Supreme Court nominations have become more controversial, the pressure to choose a nominee that will survive the Senate Judiciary Committee and public opinion has risen apace. Because the costs of a misstep are so high, presidents are sorely tempted to take the question of a Justice's credentials off the table altogether. Justices who have sailed through the various credential battles that mark the current Court are very likely to receive a coveted "well-qualified" rating (the highest available rating) from the American Bar Association (ABA), but also from the court of public opinion.[15] Two recent nominations show the danger of risking an ABA rating of "qualified." Harriet Miers was nominated by George W. Bush for the Court and faced a flurry of bipartisan concerns about whether she was qualified. She withdrew before the ABA could rate her, but a "qualified" or even a "not qualified" rating were in play.[16] Likewise, Clarence Thomas received a rare (in modern times) "qualified" rating from the ABA, with a minority of votes for "not qualified."[17]

Second, partisans of both parties have become much more worried about ideological "drift" on the Court. In recent decades Republicans have been most concerned, with many on the right arguing that Justices Stevens, Souter, Kennedy, O'Connor, and even Chief Justice Roberts became more liberal during their time on the Court. This has historically been a bipartisan concern, though, with some liberals expressing concern about conservative drift by Justices Byron White and Felix Frankfurter, among others. Appointing Justices from a seat on a federal court of appeals theoretically allays this concern, allowing presidents and congressmen to pick over the judge's long trail of past decisions, looking for evidence of either political drift or rock-solid dependability. Time spent as a tenure-track law professor also generates a lengthy trail of publications that can be mined for signs of undying fealty. The fact that becoming a federal judge or an Ivy League professor also requires triumphs in elite credentialism is a bonus.

Last, the longer the trend continues the more it becomes the "norm" in the mind of Americans. For example, the last Supreme Court Justice with any experience as an elected official was Sandra Day O'Connor, who spent six years as a State Senator (including a year as the Majority Leader) in Arizona. Yet Justice O'Connor had spent the last six years before appointment as a state court judge and was not a nationally known politician. The last well-known politician to be appointed to the Court was Earl Warren in 1954. Warren had been Governor of California for ten years and the Republican candidate for vice president in 1948. Historically former politicians have been a prime source of Supreme Court Justices. But consider the potential hullabaloo if a president nominated Elizabeth Warren or Ted Cruz to the Court. Americans already object to the "politicization" of the Court, nominating a well-known partisan politician is a risk few current presidents would take. Nominating a former judge whose background resembles the existing Justices is itself comforting. Gorsuch and Kavanaugh are perfect examples. The eerie similarities in their experiences (stretching back to high school!) were a feature, not a bug. President Trump figured that if his supporters liked Gorsuch, why not select Kavanaugh, the nominee who most closely resembled him?

Rising and Bipartisan Concern with the New Model

Yet concern over the backgrounds of our Justices is rising. Consider the late Justice Scalia's dissent in *Obergefell v. Hodges*,[18] one of his last published opinions:

> Judges are selected precisely for their skill as lawyers; whether they reflect the policy views of a particular constituency is not (or should not be) relevant. Not surprisingly then, the Federal Judiciary is hardly a cross-section of America. Take, for example, this Court, which consists of only nine men and women, all of them

successful lawyers who studied at Harvard or Yale Law School. Four of the nine are natives of New York City. Eight of them grew up in east- and west-coast States. Only one hails from the vast expanse in-between. Not a single Southwesterner or even, to tell the truth, a genuine Westerner (California does not count). Not a single evangelical Christian (a group that comprises about one quarter of Americans), or even a Protestant of any denomination.

Justice Scalia was never one to hold his tongue. Still, the above quote is strong stuff. Scalia does more than just disagree with his colleagues. He challenges the legitimacy of the current Supreme Court altogether. During the summer of 2016, both Justices Kagan and Sotomayor more diplomatically expressed similar concerns.[19]

Scalia's *Obergefell* dissent was published in June 2015 and took on particular salience eight months later when he died. President Obama was left with the unenviable (impossible?) task of nominating someone a Republican-controlled Senate might confirm to the Court. As if this was not challenge enough, Obama heard echoes of Scalia's dissent from across the political spectrum. *The New York Times*'s Adam Liptak and Emily Bazelon both decried the similarity of Supreme Court Justice backgrounds.[20] Libertarian *USA Today* columnist Glenn Reynolds has repeatedly criticized the sameness of the Justices, suggesting electing Justices, nominating billionaire investor Peter Thiel, and appointing non-lawyers to the Court as possible solutions.[21] Nevertheless, Obama settled on Merrick Garland, a near facsimile of the other current Justices and almost identical in resume to the next two Trump nominees, Gorsuch and Kavanaugh. President Biden's initial list of lower court nominees showed less of an emphasis on elite credentials, but at the time of publishing he had not nominated a new Justice, so time will tell.

Are These Critiques Legitimate?

These critiques actually raise different types of questions. Some are empirical and quantitative; others are more qualitative. For example, the question of whether the backgrounds of today's Supreme Court Justices differ from previous Courts is an empirical one. If these backgrounds are different, the question of whether the trend is good or bad or indifferent is qualitative. This book seeks to answer both of these questions and also to situate these changes within broader American trends.

Are the backgrounds of the Supreme Court Justices different than they used to be? Unquestionably and demonstrably yes. This book presents the results of an empirical study of pre-Court experiences for every Supreme Court Justice from John Jay to Amy Coney Barrett, demonstrating that today's Justices arrive at the Court with significantly different life experiences than past Justices. Moreover, the study demonstrates that the overall diversity of life experiences on the Court is likewise falling, even as racial and gender diversity are at an all-time high.

The modern Supreme Court specializes in what I call cloistered and elite experiences. Today's Justices have spent more time, as a whole, in elite academic settings (both as students and faculty) than any previous Court. They have likewise spent more time as Federal Appellate Court Judges than any previous Court. These two jobs (tenured law professor and appellate judge) share two critical components: both jobs are basically lifetime appointments that involve little or no contact with the public at large. It is hard to imagine a job that requires less contact with the "outside world" than a federal court of appeals judge. These judges have no real boss and run their own chambers as a small fiefdom. It is largely the same for a tenured law professor.

Measured historically, today's Justices have very limited experiences as practicing lawyers, and even the time they have spent as lawyers is hardly public facing. Elite settings like working in the White House Counsel's or Solicitor General's Office or in a D.C. corporate law firm result in little or no contact with "ordinary" Americans.

Are these changes bad? This book argues yes, with an obvious caveat. Your answer depends upon what exactly you think the Supreme Court does, what you think the Supreme Court should do, and who you think are best suited to meet whatever goals you have for the Court's work. Each of those questions are deeply ideological and it is unlikely that the readers of this book will agree with me or each other on their answers. Further, unlike the empirical portion of the book, we have no clear metric of what a "successful" Supreme Court or Supreme Court Justice looks like. Some studies have used citation references or expert opinion to rank the "best" Supreme Court Justices, and this book will refer to those metrics occasionally, again with the caveat that being ranked as "influential" or "admired" is not necessarily the best measure of success.

That said, this book argues that the hyper elite group of Justices we have now are a poor match for the role we ask the Court to play in our democracy. The current Justices are specialists in what I call technical legal excellence. At every juncture in their lives since at least high school these Justices have faced exceedingly difficult tests meant to sort the best from the rest, focusing especially on a particular type of academic and legal excellence. Think of the life of a current Supreme Court Justice as a series of ever shrinking hoops to jump through, with the final hoop onto the Court as narrower than the proverbial eye of a needle.

Some readers will be cheered by this metaphor. Surely the current Supreme Court is a triumph of meritocracy: these Justices have been the very best of the best in every setting before they reached the Court. What could be bad about wanting the very best for the Court? Shouldn't the Supreme Court represent the very best of the legal profession? Actually, no. Of course, we want the best, but why only measure excellence by one criterion—technical legal excellence as measured by elite competitions? The backgrounds of past Supreme Court Justices suggest that we previously used more and different criteria to find "the best."

In Chapter Twelve, I argue that we should spend less time on political or academic considerations and more on what Aristotle called *phronesis* or "practical wisdom" (or its less highfalutin cousin, "common sense"). Aristotle thought that practical wisdom is the foundation for all just decision-making. He also argued that practical wisdom is not gained by cloistered study. Only a rich experience living a varied and challenging life leads to practical wisdom. *Phronesis* is thus eminently practical and to be distinguished from "mere cleverness."

The cloistered experiences of today's Justices are not the best or most valuable for the actual job of serving as a Justice. If the Supreme Court only handled technical legal issues, maybe it would make sense to choose Justices solely on their abilities in that area. But the Supreme Court has changed, either in nature or perception, or both. The most important and visible work the Court now does is much more political and policy-based. Does it help to have triumphed at every step of elite competition to decide whether the Constitution guarantees gay marriage or whether the Court should or should not overturn Obamacare based on poor legislative drafting?

This book argues no. To the contrary, technical legal excellence and a cloistered, elite existence are actually bad training for this most important and controversial part of the job. In his 2019 book *Range*, David Epstein collects studies and anecdotes showing that generalists fare much better than specialists when presented with open-ended, real-world problems that are not identical to past problems. Specialists tend to shoehorn every problem into their preferred mode of analysis, regardless of the problem. To a hammer, the saying goes, everything looks like a nail. To nine specialists in highly technical legal reasoning, every hard question appears well suited to ninety-page answers with split votes, concurrences in some, but not all, of the decision, and multiple separate dissents. Read any controversial split decision from the last decade or so of the Court's work. I guarantee you it will shine as a work of technical legal excellence. I also guarantee you it will be an overlong thicket, in which each Justice seemingly must separately demonstrate his or her virtuosity.

Note that in civil law jurisdictions these two Supreme Court functions (technical legal reading of statutes and broad constitutional policymaking) are typically split between two different bodies, staffed by different types of judges. In France and Germany, the highest court for ordinary legal decisions (like issues of statutory interpretation) is staffed by career judges who have risen through the ranks. Presumably these judges have sorted themselves out for technical legal excellence. The highest court of constitutional law, by contrast, is staffed differently, often with former politicians or others, including non-lawyers.

Because we have chosen to unite these functions in a single Court, we should at least consider changing the mix of people who do both jobs for us. In essence this book argues that we are selecting Justices who are likely to be very good at job one but less successful at job two. This is especially so if Justices who are excellent at technical legal decision-making approach the job of constitutional interpretation as if it is merely or solely an exercise in legal analysis.

The sameness of the current Justices has two other downsides. The first is the danger of groupthink. There is substantial evidence that diversity of background and experiences on decision-making bodies results in better decisions. This is especially so for small bodies that are tasked with answering multiple different types of questions, like the Court.

There is also the related difficulty of corralling a group of all-stars, each of whom has been the best of the best his entire career. Forgive the sports metaphor, but think of the Supreme Court as a basketball team. The Justices (players) are asked to work together every term (season). The best Supreme Courts (teams) will have players with complimentary skills *and* the ability to sublimate their own statistics for the good of the team. Countless talent-packed teams have failed because the players didn't complement each other's skillsets, or because every player wanted to shoot each time he touched the ball.

On the Supreme Court, as on the basketball court, there is a danger to gathering too much high-ego talent. Historically the Supreme Court has seen this, most notably in the Courts of the late 1930s and 1940s, as described in Noah Feldman's excellent book, *Scorpions*.[22] These Supreme Courts were loaded with sterling reputations and brilliant legal minds. Based upon this all-star team of primarily FDR-appointed Justices, this Court should have operated smoothly and with near unanimity. Yet dissension and rancor ruled, and the Court splintered across multiple issues.

Similarly, modern Courts write longer opinions, with more dissents and concurrences on average, and more splintered decisions than earlier Courts. There is no better example than the 2020 case of *Ramos v. Louisiana*, in which the Court decided a relatively obvious and uncontroversial issue (whether non-unanimous jury convictions for criminal trials are constitutional, an issue that was decided 6-3 on the merits) with a hideously incoherent and splintered series of opinions, mostly because of an ongoing (and largely academic) feud about when the Court may properly overrule existing precedent.[23] These are all signs of the "all-star" mentality. A mix of different skill sets might let Justices find more room to cooperate, or at least work harder on sublimating their interests to the institutional whole.

This book attempts to answer these challenging questions with a blend of approaches. Part One offers a deep dive into some specific historical biographies to show what we're missing on today's Court, including two Justice Marshalls (John and Thurgood), one "Whizzer" (Justice Byron White, easily the greatest athlete to ever serve on the Court), and the first ten Justices appointed by George Washington. The Washington appointees are especially salient insofar as modern Americans care who the founders thought might be best to serve on the Court. Because these are the first Justices ever appointed, the mix of life experiences is particularly illuminating.

Part Two presents the "years study," which amalgamates the backgrounds of every Justice from Jay to Barrett and demonstrates just how different the backgrounds of today's Justices are, and the diversity study, which demonstrates that while the current Court is the most facially diverse in history (with three women and two people of color) it is at a relatively low ebb for diversity of experience writ large. The book concludes that these changes are bad for the Court and the country and argues for some pretty substantial changes. Each chapter also offers a series of anecdotes about the Justices as exemplars of what we're now missing on the Court.

The current Supreme Court is packed with a very specific type of person: Type-A overachievers who have triumphed in a long tournament measuring academic and technical legal excellence. This Court desperately lacks individuals who reflect a very different type of "merit." When you read about the lives of John or Thurgood Marshall or any of the first ten Justices, ask how many, if any, would be nominated and confirmed today.

Last, and most personally, I am (perhaps strangely) offended by our current version of meritocracy. I say "strangely" because I have repeatedly benefitted from this meritocracy, especially during and after law school. And yet, I still believe there is much more to life than academic excellence. It is unhealthy for a society to establish so many high-stakes competitions that create distinct winners and losers, especially so early in life. Healthier societies offer multiple different routes into success and many fewer routes to failure. We should recognize merit across different types of achievements at all stages of life. "Failing" to gain admission to the Ivy League for undergrad, or Harvard or Yale Law School, should not foreclose whole career paths so firmly, especially not a job as important as joining the Supreme Court.

Nevertheless, hopefully the reader will not come away discouraged or frustrated. The book is, at heart, a love letter to this great and uniquely American institution and its Justices, both famous and obscure.

PART ONE

Ᏹ

WHAT WE ARE MISSING

If the current Court is too focused on experiences that build technical legal excellence rather than practical wisdom, is there a prior model that is superior? Yes. We will spend much time unpacking how previous Supreme Court Justices spent their lives before joining the Court, but for now we cover two different groups of Justices in Part One. We start with three Justices who embody a very different model of "merit" than the current Court: Chief Justice John Marshall (1801–35); and two Justices appointed in the 1960s, one a relative liberal and the other a relative conservative, Thurgood Marshall and Byron White. The next two chapters consider our first ten Justices, each appointed by George Washington, as a window into what the founders looked for on the Court.

There are two main takeaways from these brief thumbnail sketches. The first is that a diversity of experience can have powerful and surprising effects on the Court. In particular, John Marshall is often considered the Court's greatest Justice—and yet his background experiences have been completely excised from today's Courts.

Second, these Justices are a joy to cover simply because of their greatness before they ever joined the Court. We used to nominate giants to the Court, individuals who triumphed in a multitude of arenas and who brought those experiences with them to the Court.

CHAPTER TWO

ॐ

TWO MARSHALLS
AND A WHIZZER

Let's start with John Marshall, who is widely considered either the best Justice or among the very best Justices to ever sit on the Court. He is the Babe Ruth, the Serena Williams, the Michael Jordan of Supreme Court Justices—the G.O.A.T. ("Greatest of all time") by unanimous acclamation. Oliver Wendell Holmes said that "if American law were to be represented by a single figure, sceptic and worshipper alike would agree without dispute that the figure could be but one alone, and that one, John Marshall."[1] And as Joseph Story said, "His proudest epitaph may be written in a single line—Here lies the expounder of the Constitution of the United States."[2]

We'll cover Marshall's background in time, but first, a word on a few of his accomplishments. Most importantly, Marshall was the primary architect of the Supreme Court's position in our democracy. Before Marshall joined the Court it was a backwater and its role under our new Constitution was ill defined.

How do we know the Court was a backwater? Consider how hard it was to even find willing Justices pre-Marshall. Two of George Washington's first six appointments flatly refused to leave their state court positions to join the Court.[3] Patrick Henry also declined.[4] Alexander Hamilton likewise declined an offer to become Chief Justice, "being anxious to renew his law practice and political activities in New York."[5] Fans of either *Hamilton the Musical* or Ron Chernow's book *Alexander Hamilton* will recognize Hamilton's wisdom in turning down a post that required temperance, patience, and the ability to build relationships with one's colleagues. Nevertheless, the fact that someone as ambitious as Hamilton declined an offer to become Chief Justice well establishes the Court's initially low profile.

Or consider the almost accidental appointment of Marshall himself. In the fall of 1800, Chief Justice Oliver Ellsworth unexpectedly resigned as Chief Justice, marking the *fourth* transition of Chief Justices in the Court's first eleven years of existence. By now it was clear that President John Adams's party, the Federalists, had lost the presidency and control of the Senate, so Adams was under intense pressure to appoint a new Chief Justice quickly, before the Democratic-Republicans took over.

Adams's first choice was to ask John Jay, the inaugural Chief Justice of the United States from 1789 to 1795, to take the job again after a break spent negotiating a peace treaty with the British and serving as Governor of New York. Jay was a strong choice. He was well respected amongst his contemporaries and would lend some needed heft, politically and intellectually, to a struggling branch of the government. He also knew the job and what it entailed, which is what actually doomed the possibility from the start.

Jay knew the job too well and declined, citing the challenges of riding circuit (where Justices traveled widely to hold court) and his disappointment in the current state of the Court. Jay's blunt description of the many flaws of the Supreme Court pre-Marshall is incredible to modern readers:

> I left the bench perfectly convinced that under a system so defective it would not obtain the energy, weight, and dignity which are essential to its affording due support to the national government; nor acquire the public confidence and respect which, as the last resort of the justice of the nation, it should possess. Hence I am induced to doubt both the propriety and the expediency of my returning to the bench under the present system.[6]

Adams was now in a tight spot. He needed to appoint a new Chief Justice in the remaining six weeks of his presidency, while the Federalists still controlled the Senate. John Marshall was serving as the Secretary of State and appears to have been in the right place at the right time. Marshall describes Adams's decision:

> When I waited on the President with Mr. Jay's letter declining the appointment he said thoughtfully, "Who shall I nominate now?" I replied that I could not tell....After a moment's hesitation he said, "I believe I must nominate you." I had never before heard myself named for the office and had not even thought of it. I was pleased as well as surprised and bowed in silence. Next day I was nominated.[7]

The appointment of Marshall is thus one of the great "what ifs" in American history. What if Jay had accepted? Could or would he have shepherded the Court into existence as Marshall did? Even better, what if Hamilton had agreed to become Chief Justice rather than Ellsworth in 1796? He probably would not have resigned in 1800 and Marshall might have left government service to return to his law practice and land speculation in Virginia.

John Marshall Defined the Modern Supreme Court and Our Constitutional Architecture Almost Single-Handedly—And Did So with Swagger and Style

As it was, Marshall served longer than any other Chief Justice, more than thirty-four years.[8] He used that time to create the modern Supreme Court. When Marshall joined the Court in 1801, it was not yet clear that the Supreme Court would be the final word in the interpretation of the law or the Constitution. It was not yet clear that the Supreme Court would have the power to invalidate federal or state law. It was not even clear that the Supreme Court's rulings would govern matters of state law. Under Marshall the Supreme Court's power extended into each of these areas in a series of unanimous or nearly unanimous decisions that he himself wrote.

Marshall also changed the decision writing process itself. Before Marshall, each Justice tended to write his own opinion in deciding a case. Marshall instituted the tradition of a single majority opinion stating the controlling law, as well as the occasional dissent.

Marshall wrote almost every seminal Supreme Court decision during this formative era for the Court and the nation. There are too many foundational opinions to cover here, but allow me a brief review of two of Marshall's greatest hits. Marshall wrote *Marbury v. Madison*, which was the first case to squarely hold an act of Congress unconstitutional.[9] This is may be the single most famous Supreme Court opinion and is credited with settling once and for all the Supreme Court's power of constitutional review.

Marbury is also a great introduction to Marshall's over-the-top and plain-spoken writing style. Marshall liked to start from first principles and reason to conclusions, often with generous helpings of hyperbole along the way. Marshall wrote with few references to precedent or law. Here is a typical portion of *Marbury*:

> If an act of the legislature, repugnant to the constitution, is void, does it, notwithstanding its invalidity, bind the courts, and oblige them to give it effect? Or, in other words, though it be not law, does it constitute a rule as operative as if it was a law? This would be to overthrow in fact what was established in theory; and would seem, at first view, an absurdity too gross to be insisted on. It shall, however, receive a more attentive consideration.
>
> It is emphatically the province and duty of the Judicial Department to say what the law is. Those who apply the rule to particular cases must, of necessity, expound and interpret that rule. If two laws conflict with each other, the Courts must decide on the operation of each.[10]

In a case where the sitting President of the United States (Thomas Jefferson) and the Secretary of State and one of the principle architects of the Constitution (James Madison) disagreed with him on the role of the Court, Marshall calls their argument "an absurdity too gross to be insisted on" and then answers his own question "emphatically," *all with no citations*. Humorously, this passage is pretty typical for a high-salience Marshall opinion. The higher the stakes, the more heated his rhetorical style and the more unsubtle his reasoning.

McCulloch v. Maryland is another Marshall classic.[11] Here the Court held that it was constitutional for Congress to create the Second Bank of the United States under the Necessary and Proper Clause of the Constitution, even though the power to do so was not explicitly expressed in the Constitution.

Marshall approached the question with his usual logic, leavened with rhetorical flourish: "If any one proposition could command the universal assent of mankind, we might expect it would be this—that the Government of the Union, though limited in its powers, is supreme within its sphere of action."[12] And what of the opposing argument, that Congress was strictly limited to enumerated powers, and that the necessary and proper clause could not support the creation of a federal bank? Marshall hotly retorted that "the inevitable consequence of giving this very restricted sense to the word 'necessary,' would be to annihilate the very powers it professes to create; and as so gross an absurdity cannot be imputed to the framers of the constitution, this interpretation must be rejected."[13]

So, just to summarize, Marshall's version of constitutional interpretation is the single proposition most likely to "command the universal assent of mankind," and the opposing argument (also known as strict constitutional construction, an interpretive strain that still holds considerable sway today) was "so gross an absurdity" that it was rejected out of hand. Marshall followed these *bon mots* by explaining that the power to establish a federal bank was implied by various other enumerated powers and that "[w]e must never forget that it is a constitution we are expounding."[14] Justice Frankfurter considered this Marshall quote the single greatest statement of the Court's purpose in constitutional interpretation.[15]

Please permit me a short aside here. A dear friend and expert constitutional law scholar thinks I have been "a little too hard" on Marshall's opinion in McCulloch here. This is exactly the opposite of my intent. Marshall's opinion is praiseworthy precisely because of its rhetorical flourishes and appeals to logic rather than to a more technical legal approach. One of the reasons I love Marshall's writing and respect him as a jurist is because he knew when to bring the wood. Marshall set the model for the greatest Supreme Court opinions, which start with obvious, well-worn truths and finish with the legalities—not the other way around. Reread *Brown v. Board of Ed.*, *Gideon v. Wainwright*, *Loving v. Virginia*, or the dissents in *Dred Scott*, *Plessy v. Ferguson*, or *Olmstead v. U.S.* with Marshall in mind and you will hear him echoed in style and content.

Marshall Accomplished All of This with Remarkable Unanimity in a Poisonous Political Atmosphere While Working with Justices Appointed by Political Enemies

I remind readers of these cases and Marshall's written style so we can appreciate the full scope of his achievement as Chief Justice. Not only did Marshall write sweeping opinions cementing the Supreme Court's role, these opinions were more often than not unanimous. Lee Epstein's excellent *Supreme Court Compendium* lists twenty-one "major decisions" during the years of Chief Justice Marshall's time on the Court.[16] Marshall was in the majority in nineteen of these cases, a remarkable winning percentage for any era. He wrote the majority opinion in seventeen of these cases. *Fourteen* of them were unanimous. Across thirty-four years, in an era of controversial and formative cases delineating the constitutional balance between federal and state governments and the judicial, executive, and legislative subdivisions therein, John Marshall only dissented *once* in a constitutional case (*Ogden v. Saunders*).[17]

Such unanimity would be remarkable today. Given who Marshall served with on the Court, it is jaw-dropping. Marshall was appointed by John Adams, the first president from the Federalist Party. George Washington was generally sympathetic to the views of the Federalists, but he ran and governed without official party affiliation.[18] Regardless, even if Washington's appointees were politically sympathetic to Marshall (which they likely were), Marshall spent most of his time on the bench with Justices appointed by unfriendly presidential administrations.

When Marshall joined the Court in 1801, there were five Associate Justices.[19] Two had been appointed by John Adams (Bushrod Washington and Alfred Moore) and three by George Washington (Samuel Chase, William Paterson, and William Cushing). By 1812 all of these Associate Justices except for Bushrod Washington (who served until 1829) had retired and been replaced by new Justices nominated by Democratic-Republican presidents who leaned more towards states' rights. From 1812 until 1823, Marshall served with Bushrod Washington, James Madison's two nominees (Joseph Story and Gabriel Duvall), and Jefferson's three nominees (Thomas Todd, Brockholst Livingston, and William Johnson).

How unfriendly were Jefferson and Madison to Marshall's vision of the Court? In a letter responding to *Marbury v. Madison*, Jefferson wrote that "If this opinion be sound, then indeed is our Constitution a complete *felo de se* [suicide]. The Constitution on this hypothesis is a mere thing of wax in the hands of the judiciary, which they may twist and shape into any form they please." Not only was Jefferson hostile to Marshall's judicial philosophy, the two men (who were actually second cousins) hated each other personally. Jefferson described Marshall as a "gloomy malignity."[20] Marshall considered Jefferson a coward for his lack of combat service in the Revolutionary War and called Jefferson "among the most ambitious [and] unforgiving of men."[21]

Madison and Marshall did not share the same enmity, but Madison was hardly friendlier to Marshall's vision of a muscular Supreme Court. As Jefferson's Secretary of State, James Madison was the named defendant in *Marbury v. Madison*. In response to *McCulloch v. Maryland*, Madison wrote that "few if any of the friends of the Constitution"—the founders—anticipated "that a rule of construction would be introduced as broad and as pliant as what has occurred."[22]

And yet, Marshall largely won over fellow Justices who should have been natural enemies to his cause. During Marshall's years on the Court the Justices lived together in a boardinghouse when they were in session, and Marshall's geniality and persuasiveness worked wonders. And of course, it may be easier to convince political opponents to join together on the joint project of expanding your own Court's power than other governance issues. That said, do not underestimate the salience of these Supreme Court opinions. States' rights, the power of the new federal government, and the creation of a national bank were among the most hotly contested political issues of the day and Marshall triumphed in each by working with Justices appointed by presidents largely opposed to his views. The Jefferson and Madison Justices may be the first recorded example of judicial "drift" upon appointment.

Marshall's record speaks for itself. Imagine a Chief Justice appointed by a Democratic president presiding over a Court almost fully staffed by Justices appointed by Republican presidents. Then imagine that Court repeatedly following that Chief Justice's lead, often unanimously, when answering the exact questions of governmental power and policy that were dividing the nation at the time. Marshall achieved this unanimity and recast the Court as a co-equal and critical branch of government. As Marshall biographer Jean Edward Smith puts it: "If George Washington founded the country, John Marshall defined it."[23] During a period in which both the executive and legislative branches were riven by partisan rancor, Marshall oversaw perhaps the most united Supreme Court in history.

So, What Was Marshall's Secret? Can We Learn Anything from His Pre-Court Experiences?

Marshall's background is almost the polar opposite of the current model. Marshall grew up on what was then the frontier of

Virginia, in Fauquier County, in the foothills of the Blue Ridge Mountains.[24] His father, Thomas Marshall, worked as a surveyor and land agent for Lord Fairfax, exploring the western portions of Virginia that eventually became Kentucky and West Virginia. As a surveyor Thomas Marshall was able to purchase particularly promising land, and Marshall's family moved three times in his childhood, always west onto newly surveyed land. For the first fifteen years of his life, Marshall's family lived in two different four-room cabins built by his father. Marshall was the oldest of fifteen children, and while his father eventually accumulated land and means, Marshall remembered a modest childhood: the family made most of their own clothes and grew their own food. Marshall is thus one of the many "frontierspeople" to make it to the Supreme Court. From Marshall through Stephen Field and on to Sandra Day O'Connor there is a rich history of Justices who cut their teeth in the rough and tumble of the relatively unsettled American frontier.

Like other Justices before and after him, Marshall had little formal education of any kind.[25] Partially self-taught, home schooled, and tutored by clergy, Marshall learned what he needed to know largely through his parents and on his own. Marshall's only stint of organized, formal education was "law school" at William and Mary with George Wythe. As historian Herbert Alan Johnson explains:

> Judged by the standards of the present day, or even those of eighteenth-century colonial America, John Marshall was given a paltry foundation in the law. Six weeks of attendance at George Wythe's law lectures at William and Mary were supplemented by some common-placing from Bacon's *Abridgement*.... Marshall for the most part was a lawyer who learned his law while he practiced it.[26]

Self-education has virtually disappeared in modern America, but it is worth noting that Marshall came from a modest educational background even amongst his contemporaries. Marshall replaced Oliver Ellsworth, who had attended Yale and Princeton, and served with William Paterson, a Princeton graduate, and William Cushing, a Harvard graduate. Elite educational backgrounds on the Court are not new, we just used to put less stock in them.

Marshall spent a large chunk of his early adulthood fighting in the Revolutionary War.[27] In the summer of 1775, nineteen-year-old John Marshall was appointed a First Lieutenant in the Fauquier Rifles, a unit of the Culpeper Minutemen. For the next five years Marshall served bravely, fighting in the siege of Norfolk, the Battle of the Brandywine, the Battle of Monmouth, and suffering through the brutal winter of 1777–78 in Valley Forge. No current Justices have spent any time outside of ROTC or the reserves in the military, let alone anything resembling Marshall's formative combat experience.

Justice Marshall then cut his teeth as a lawyer in solo practice, handling trials and appeals alike. Marshall sometimes handled as many as 300 cases a year.[28] He handled criminal and contracts cases. Marshall built one of the most successful law practices in Virginia from virtually nothing. During his first years of practice he had few clients and less money. These early years were rocky enough that some biographers have argued that Marshall was a great statesman, but a poor lawyer. Marshall's eventual success belies this claim, however. By the time Marshall entered full-time government service he was among the very best-known lawyers in Virginia, America's most populous state in the late-eighteenth century. The legal work experiences of current Supreme Court Justices reflect that they were the best of the best coming out of law school and clerkships. Marshall's achievements reflect the success that comes from rising up within the practice by serving regular people on all sorts of legal issues.

Justice Marshall was more than just a lawyer though. He was an entrepreneur, a land speculator, and a hustler.[29] In these activities he followed in the footsteps of his father, who himself built a fortune exploring Virginia and buying up prime acreage for later, profitable resale. Before Marshall joined the Court, he and other family members purchased more than a hundred thousand acres of prime land in Virginia's Northern Neck from Lord Fairfax's heir for a bargain price. But Marshall was actually buying a lawsuit that pitted his property interests against the state of Virginia, which hoped to escheat the land because Lord Fairfax was a foreign national on the losing side of the Revolutionary War. Marshall bet that between the Treaty of Paris (which arguably protected British holdings in America), his skill as a litigator, and his political connections, the land would eventually be his.

The lawsuits over this land lasted for years and eventually ended up in the Supreme Court as the famous 1816 case of *Martin v. Hunter's Lessee*, from which Marshall recused himself. That case finally settled title on the land in Marshall's favor, and he died a wealthy man. But before this victory Marshall faced financial difficulties, which led him to decline appointments as the Attorney General of the United States and as the first U.S. Attorney for the District of Virginia, two posts that were significantly less lucrative than his booming private practice. Some of Marshall's wealth came from being a slave-owner. He owned as many as 150 slaves in his life, but he also considered slavery an evil institution that damaged slaves and slave owners alike. Like many slave-owning founders, he argued that the institution should be abolished.

John Marshall was also politician, and he is generally considered to have been a rather able one.[30] At twenty-seven he was elected to the Virginia House of Delegates for the area around

Fauquier County where he grew up and five years later for the county near Richmond where he then lived as a lawyer. He also served on the Virginia Council of State (an executive super-committee) from 1782 to 1784 along with James Monroe. Marshall's greatest electoral victory was to the United States House of Representatives in 1798. Marshall ran as a Federalist against an incumbent Democratic-Republican in a state dominated by powerful Democratic-Republican politicians (notably Thomas Jefferson and James Madison) and won, a remarkable upset at the time.

Last, and possibly most importantly, John Marshall is a classic example of what Professor Anthony Kronman has called "the lawyer-statesman."[31] After refusing several different Federal appointments under George Washington, Marshall agreed to serve President John Adams as one of three peace envoys to France. The mission was critical, as America and France were teetering on the edge of war and France had been seizing American ships in the West Indies. Marshall's mission to France is now known as the XYZ affair, because three different French emissaries (labeled X, Y, and Z by Marshall to protect their identities) demanded a significant bribe from the Americans before meeting with the French delegation for peace terms. Marshall and the other two envoys refused, and when Marshall's description of the affair became public in the United States, he was hailed as a hero. After a term in Congress Adams appointed him as Secretary of State. In this position he helped negotiate peace with France at the Convention of 1800. Our current Justices have limited non-legal or executive experience. Certainly none have held positions as important as Secretary of State, or done work like negotiating peace treaties.

John Marshall's biography and successes are in some ways a reminder of a different America that was packed with able generalists who were pressed into all sorts of activities by circumstances, from high level diplomacy to front line combat to the solo practice of law and eventually running the Supreme Court. Perhaps it is not possible to find resumes like these today? Two Justices from the 1960s suggest otherwise.

Another Marshall and a Whizzer

If John Marshall seems too ancient a reference point, consider two Justices appointed in the 1960s who brought a similarly varied mix of experiences to the Court: Thurgood Marshall and Byron White. I will note at the outset that these Justices, unlike John Marshall, are not considered among the greatest Justices of all time, measured by impact or influence. One study of the first ninety-nine Justices had Thurgood Marshall ranked forty-sixth and Byron White thirtieth.[32] Nevertheless, they are among the last of their kind in terms of their varied backgrounds and sheer greatness before joining the Court. They also brought a unique set of experiences to the Court, experiences that were reflected in their judicial work and the Court as a whole.

Moreover, just as it is silly to measure pre-Court experiences along a narrow vision of "merit," it is likewise misguided to measure Justices solely based upon "influence" or opinions written. On a nine-person body it is impossible and also self-defeating to try to maximize "influence" or scholarly popularity with every pick. Successful Courts include "glue guys and gals" and coalition members along with coalition builders and leaders. Too many head chefs can spoil the soup.

It is not a coincidence that two of the last Justices to match John Marshall's breadth of experiences come from the 1960s. It is not possible to choose a single period when our new model of Justice began to dominate, but 1968–69 is a definite contender. In those two years the Senate filibustered Lyndon Johnson's nomination of Abe Fortas for Chief Justice and then blocked Nixon's nominations of Clement Haynesworth and Harold Carswell. It was then clear that the Supreme Court had reemerged as a political football and that nominees were going to face a new level of scrutiny. Finding less controversial nominees became the order of the day, and an unimpeachable academic and judicial background became *de rigueur*.

Both Thurgood Marshall and Byron White reflect a radically different and older model of Supreme Court Justice. Like John Marshall they demonstrated greatness pre-Court across a bevy of life experiences and struggles. Texas Law Professor Sanford Levinson is the primary updater of Robert McCloskey's historical masterwork, *The American Supreme Court*, and in his 2016 coda to the book Levinson nicely describes the difference between choosing Justices based upon judicial experience and academic credentials versus demonstrated greatness:

> One of the more striking differences between the Warren and post-Warren Courts concerns the preappointment experiences of the Justices. The 1954 Court that decided *Brown*, for example, was headed by the immensely popular former governor of California...three former senators (Hugo Black, Sherman Minton, and Harold Burton); two of the leading academics of their time (Felix Frankfurter and William O. Douglas), both of whom had been involved at the highest level of the Roosevelt administration during the New Deal; two former Solicitor Generals (Robert Jackson and Stanley Reed); and two former attorneys general (Jackson and Tom Clark)....
>
> Only one of Kennedy and Johnson's four appointees—Thurgood Marshall—had judicial experience, and no one seriously would focus on that aspect of Marshall's pre-Court career when

assessing his fitness for the Court. Far more important was his status as perhaps the leading public lawyer of the age, the central architect of the NAACP attack on segregation. Marshall would have merited a full-scale biography had he been run over by a truck the day before joining the Court, as would have been true of at least half of the justices that heard his argument in *Brown*.[33]

I actually like Levinson's suggested test for any potential Justice—the "hit by a truck before appointment" standard. It nicely captures what this book is looking for on the Court and also neatly explains just how lacking the backgrounds of recent Justices are. Ginsburg would merit such treatment, as the Thurgood Marshall of the gender battles before the Supreme Court. Thomas or Sotomayor might as well, as first-of-their-kind lawyers and judges who overcame immense challenges to reach the pinnacle of the legal profession before joining the Court. Otherwise, it's been a quiet fifty years.

Thurgood Marshall

Like John Marshall, it is hard to overstate Thurgood Marshall's impact upon America and its constitutional structure. Biographer Juan Williams argues that Thurgood Marshall's "lifework…literally defined the movement of race relations through the century."[34] Mark Tushnet called Marshall "the most important lawyer of the twentieth century."[35] He was the driving force behind the NAACP's desegregation campaign. Between 1938 and 1961 Marshall argued thirty-two cases before the Court on behalf of the NAACP, winning twenty-nine of them, both records for his time.[36] Marshall traveled all over the country handling civil rights cases, but also high-profile and racially charged criminal cases. Marshall was thus both the most decorated Supreme Court advocate of his time and among its best known and most successful trial lawyers. In

2015, *The Atlantic* ran an overview of Marshall's legal career aptly entitled "Thurgood Marshall, Badass Lawyer."[37]

Marshall was also a legendary storyteller; Sandra Day O'Connor famously dubbed him a first-class raconteur. He was a life-long rascal, quick with a self-deprecating anecdote or the occasional practical joke. Marshall never wrote an autobiography, but there are multiple outstanding biographies packed with hilarious stories told by Marshall and others who remember a "high-spirited and rambunctious" young man who was often in trouble, followed by stories of the brilliant and influential lawyer that Marshall would become.[38]

Marshall was born in segregated Baltimore, Maryland, on July 2, 1908.[39] For an African-American living in one of the most highly segregated cities in the South, Marshall lived a middle-class life. He grew up in the relatively wealthy Druid Hill neighborhood on a "respectable street" in West Baltimore. His father worked as railroad porter and his mother was a teacher. Thurgood himself started working odd jobs when he was seven, and he worked a variety of jobs, ranging from delivery person for a hat store to waiter at an all-white social club to a porter on the B&O Railroad, before he eventually became a lawyer.

Marshall came from a family that put a high premium on education, but Marshall was hardly an "A" student or model citizen. The stories of Marshall's hijinks before law school run the gamut from pulling pigtails to throwing chalk and sassing back. One schoolmate said Marshall was "full of the devil" and "mischievous."[40] Marshall himself remembered that a school principal would send troublemakers to the basement of the school with a copy of the U.S. Constitution and a requirement to memorize a provision. Marshall noted that "before I left that school I knew the entire Constitution by heart."[41]

Marshall remained a troublemaker as an undergraduate at Lincoln University, then an all-black university in Pennsylvania.

He recalled some pretty aggressive fraternity hazing, including an unfortunate story that includes pickles, bare bottoms, and some very sad freshmen eating the results, but modesty demands I say no more. Marshall and some fellow fraternity members were even suspended during his sophomore year for their hazing and had to petition for reinstatement. Marshall's classmates and friends at Lincoln included the great jazz singer Cab Calloway ("Minnie the Moocher") and the poet Langston Hughes.

Marshall was a good student, but until law school he was far from the top of the class. He was a "B" student in High School and again at Lincoln. By his own description he spent more time in his first years at college playing pinochle, dating, and drinking than he did studying. Things changed when he met and married his first wife, Vivian "Buster" Burey. Marshall's newfound seriousness was reflected in several ways. He and some classmates helped integrate a movie theater in nearby Oxford, Pennsylvania. Marshall also led the charge to integrate the Lincoln University faculty, which had included an all-white professoriate teaching an all-black student body. Marshall also starred on the debate team.

After graduation he and Buster moved into Marshall's parent's house in Baltimore so Marshall could go to law school. The biographies are at odds over whether Marshall bothered to apply to the all-white University of Maryland Law School or not, but everyone agrees that Marshall had no chance to attend the segregated in-state school (a wrong that Marshall would avenge soon enough). Instead, Marshall scrimped and saved and commuted daily to Washington, D.C., to attend Howard University Law School. His mother sold her wedding ring to help pay his first year's tuition.

Marshall arrived at Howard Law at a turning point. Charles Hamilton Houston took over as the Dean of Howard in 1929 as part of an aggressive push to make the law school a first-class institution and to earn ABA accreditation. Marshall started in 1930, the first year Howard eliminated its night program and became a full-time, day-only law school. Houston greeted Marshall's first year class by explicitly stating that he would get "great pleasure" in failing out students who did not make the grade: "Each one of you look at the man to your right and then the man to your left. Realize that two of you won't be here next year."[42] Houston was good to his word. Marshall remembered starting with thirty classmates and graduating with eight or ten. Houston even had a catchphrase for any who complained: "no tea for the feeble, no crepe for the dead."[43]

It was a brutal year for Marshall. He woke up at 5:00 am every morning to catch the commuter train to Washington. He read for class on the ride and then walked to Howard for the day's classes. He returned to Baltimore and worked a night job before falling asleep at midnight and starting the whole thing again. He lost thirty pounds in a year and finished his first year of law school at 6'1" and just 140 pounds. Marshall also finished first in his class and earned a job in the law library that paid for his tuition. The job also allowed Marshall a chance to work directly with Houston and other contemporaries on the NAACP lawsuits and strategies for fighting segregation. Houston was a mentor and a friend to Marshall, and the Howard law library job was the launching point for one of America's great legal partnerships.

Marshall did well enough in law school that he was offered a full scholarship to pursue a further doctorate degree at Harvard Law School under Dean Roscoe Pound. But Marshall turned it down, wanting instead to practice law right away: "Harvard was training people to join big law firms. Howard was teaching lawyers to go to court. The emphasis was not on theory, the emphasis in this school was in practice, on how to get it done."[44] Pause for a minute here and contemplate the choice that Marshall made. He was a brilliant black lawyer in the heart of the Depression and *Harvard Law School* was offering him free tuition and room and board to study in an institution that was elite for white lawyers. If he wanted to return to Howard to teach or to maximize his income this was the obvious choice. But Marshall wanted to *practice* law, not study it. He went to law school to change lives and the law. Time spent at Harvard would have been a detour. This decision alone tells you everything you need to know about the difference between Marshall and our current crop of Justices.

Nevertheless, it was the heart of the Great Depression and Marshall could hardly have chosen a worse time to start a solo practice as a young black man in Baltimore. He took whatever business came in the door: wills, contracts, divorces, criminal cases from rape to murder, and (characteristically) a great deal of unpaid pro bono work. Marshall recalled a particular client who came to his office with no money but a serious legal issue. She had been referred by a white judge who said Marshall would help because "he's a freebie lawyer." Marshall thought "I've got to stop that crap right now."[45] Marshall lost $3500 his first year in practice, but his hard work paid off, and over time he built a strong practice while still pursuing a mix of NAACP matters. Marshall became a full-time employee of the NAACP in 1936.

Marshall's first desegregation case was close to his heart—he brought suit against the University of Maryland Law School for refusing to admit black students. The case was heard in 1935 and Marshall and Charles Hamilton Houston argued it together. They won at trial and again on appeal before the Maryland Supreme Court. H. L. Mencken, the famous *Baltimore Sun* columnist and gadfly, summed the ruling up: "There will be an Ethiop among the Aryans when the larval Blackstones [next] assemble."[46]

Marshall's career from this point forward is better known, and also too exceptional to try to thumbnail. Mark Tushnet's two-part biography of Marshall is a detailed and excellent account of this history and I highly recommend it. Hopefully you have already read enough to know why a tale of two Marshalls makes sense for this book. These two great legal minds lived lives of action and achievement much more than lives of academic splendor.

Thurgood Marshall could not match John Marshall's legacy of unanimous and foundational opinions (no later Justice has), but he created his own legacy on the Court. The legacy includes a string of powerful dissents in race and poverty opinions that were directly informed by his own experiences. He was also a powerful influence on the other Justices. Consider Sandra Day O'Connor's reflections: "It was rare during our conference deliberations that [Marshall] would not share an anecdote, a joke or a story.... In my early months as a junior Justice, I looked forward to these tales as welcome diversions.... But over time, as I heard more clearly what Justice Marshall was saying, I realized that behind most of the anecdotes there was a relevant legal point."[47] As an example, O'Connor remembered Marshall telling harrowing stories of the unfairness of the death penalty for black defendants in the Jim Crow South. Here Marshall's own experiences well elucidated "the impact of legal rules on human lives."[48]

Byron White—The Only Justice Who Was More Famous at Twenty than When He Joined the Court?

A lot of famous people have joined the Court. William Howard Taft was a former President of the United States when he joined the Court in 1921. The Court has seen a parade of former Senators, major party candidates for president like Charles Evan Hughes, and vice president (Earl Warren), and national legal celebrities like Louis Brandeis and Oliver Wendell Holmes. Nevertheless, White's extraordinarily successful college and professional career as a two-sport star easily makes him the most famous at the earliest age.

White was born in Fort Collins, Colorado, in 1917 and came of age in the teeth of the Great Depression. He worked in the sugar beet fields from the age of eight and attended tiny Wellington High School. White himself explained that he was no world-class athlete as a young man: "As a high school freshman, I weighed only a little over 100 pounds, so I was too small for football.... By the time I was a junior or senior in High School I broke my shoulder and couldn't play or practice football for the entire season."[49] White was an excellent student in high school. The valedictorian of every public school in Colorado got an academic scholarship to the University of Colorado, so White worked his way to first in his class to earn that scholarship.[50]

When White arrived at Colorado he was hardly a decorated football recruit. He did not even start on the freshman team. White then blew out his knee in the first game of his sophomore season, so his football career was off to an inauspicious start. Moreover, it was not as if White was joining a football powerhouse. Colorado started playing football in 1890 and had competed in the underwhelming Rocky Mountain Conference ("RMC") since 1910. The RMC included football programs like the Western State Mountaineers and the Colorado School of Mines Orediggers. Colorado had never been invited to a bowl game and had never been nationally ranked when White arrived.

White broke into the starting lineup as a junior and earned all-conference honors. He scored four touchdowns and kicked an extra point in Colorado's win over Utah, setting a Colorado record for points in a game. But it was only in 1937, White's senior year, that the legend of the "Whizzer" really took off. White led the Colorado Buffaloes to an undefeated regular season and a berth in the Cotton Bowl in Dallas. He was the tailback in a single wing offense, so he ran, passed, and occasionally kicked the ball, and even played on the other side of the field as a defensive back. White had one of the greatest statistical seasons in NCAA history, leading the nation in both scoring and total yards. He again saved his best for Utah, in one of his greatest games ever. He returned a punt ninety-five yards for a touchdown, scored again on a fifty-seven-yard sprint, kicked a fifteen-yard field goal, and kicked both extra points. He scored all of Colorado's points. The school retired White's jersey number (24) that Thanksgiving while he was still a student.

Colorado earned an invitation to play Rice in the Cotton Bowl in Dallas, a first for the school and a huge honor. The game started well for White. He threw a touchdown pass for an early 7-0 lead, and then intercepted Rice and ran it back for a 47-yard touchdown, and then kicked the extra point afterwards. Sadly, Rice rallied and scored twenty-eight unanswered points on an exhausted Colorado defense. White capped off the year as an All-American in football and finished second in the voting for the Heisman Trophy. I highly recommend googling the 2007 Rocky Mountain Fox Sports Net special on White and watching it on YouTube if you're at all interested. The special focuses mostly on White's athletic career and has amazing grainy black and white video of White cutting through defenses like a hot knife through butter.

After the football season, White played basketball for a Colorado team that went 10-2 and won their conference and was one of four teams invited to the inaugural NIT tournament in Madison Square Garden. This was before the creation of the NCAA tournament; the NIT served as an unofficial national championship tourney. White led the team to the final game against eventual winner and national champion Temple. Colorado essentially was runner up for the national championship in basketball and football in White's senior year, establishing the school as a national sports powerhouse and White as a star.

All the while, White was an exceptional student. He gained membership to Phi Beta Kappa and earned a Rhodes Scholarship his senior year. When Colorado's football coach saw White reading a textbook the coach ordered White to read the playbook instead. White replied: "You take care of the football. I'll take care of the books." Oxford would have to wait, however, as the Pittsburgh Pirates (later the Steelers) selected White first in the NFL Draft and offered him the highest salary in the league, $15,800 for the season.[51] This was an exceptionally large sum of money, apparently *three times* what Arthur Rooney had paid for the team, and more than twice as much as what other NFL stars were earning.[52]

The dons at Oxford allowed White to wait until winter to begin, allowing him to play his first season in the NFL. He led the league in rushing attempts, rushing yards, and touchdowns in 1938 while playing on a Pittsburgh team with a losing record.[53] He arrived in Oxford in January of 1939 and studied through September, when the outbreak of war with Germany meant the Americans were all sent home. White immediately enrolled in Yale Law School and finished his first year between 1939–40.

In the Fall of 1940 White returned to the NFL, playing for the Detroit Lions and again leading the league in rushing attempts and yards on a losing team, all while squeezing in Yale Law School around NFL games and practices. White's last year in the NFL was 1941, because he joined the Navy that December to fight in World War II.

White served as a lieutenant-commander in naval intelligence. He was deployed to the Solomon Islands and handled naval intelligence in the South Pacific, including writing the report on the sinking of PT Boat 109, made famous by its commanding officer John F. Kennedy. White was awarded two Bronze Stars for his service. It was an earlier time and a different country, but note that White left behind an extremely lucrative athletic career and Yale Law School to join the Navy.

Returning home and finishing up at Yale Law School, White graduated *magna cum laude* and first in his class in 1946. He was then selected to clerk for Chief Justice Vinson on the Supreme Court. After clerking White headed home to Colorado rather than stay in D.C. or join a large firm in New York City. White worked in Denver as a lawyer in relative anonymity for fourteen years. When Kennedy was elected president, White joined that administration as Deputy Attorney General and then a Supreme Court appointee.

The sources of White's fame—and his greatest pre-Court achievements—were largely non-legal activities. Few athletes of any generation have been as decorated and multi-talented as White. His athletic and collegiate career read like a combination of Bo Jackson's multi-sport successes with Bill Bradley's Rhodes Scholarship, but with a more successful professional career (in its peak if not its totality). Bo Jackson did not lead teams in two different sports to the verge of national championships and Bill Bradley, while great, was never arguably the best basketball player in the country, as White was for several years of football. Admittedly, neither the NFL nor the Colorado football or basketball teams were desegregated when White played, so he never faced the same level of competition that Bill Bradley or Bo Jackson did, but still.

White is thus a throwback to an earlier time, when Justices joined the Court after demonstrated excellence in a variety and wide range of endeavors. He is also one of the last Justices to join the Court straight from practice with no judicial experience at all. He is also a modern Justice in some notable ways. White earned a Rhodes Scholarship, graduated from Yale Law School and clerked on the Supreme Court, all of which have become regular features on the modern Courts.

He is also one of the Justices who "drifted" over time, eventually voting more often with conservative Justices despite being appointed by John F. Kennedy. White is thus also partially responsible for why we see so few Justices like him (with a wide range of experiences and limited partisan or judicial experience) on the Court. Modern presidents now seek to hedge against the possibility of drift.

❧

CHAPTER THREE

WASHINGTON'S FIRST SIX

Founders, Politicians, Entrepreneurs,
and One Cushing

In the following two chapters we will examine the first ten Justices of the Supreme Court, George Washington's initial appointees, as a comparison point to the present. You will not be surprised to find that Washington had a quite different view on "merit" than recent presidents. This is not to say that Washington didn't in some way presage the modern criteria for choosing justices. He appointed a few sitting judges as well as lawyers from elite educational backgrounds. But he did not choose *only* those sorts of Justices. He chose entrepreneurs and prominent lawyers. He chose politicians and diplomats. He chose former governors and senators and elected officials of all stripes. Above all he chose giants of the legal profession from all over the new United States. The single uniting factor among these Justices was their reputation as lawyers and their work in drafting or ratifying the new Constitution.

Article III itself is notably thin on the makeup of the Supreme Court. It is largely silent on the qualifications for Justices or even how many there would be. It does not even require that the Justices be lawyers! Washington was truly working from a blank slate when he appointed his Justices. Originalists should pay special attention to Washington's selections, since they are our best information on the founders' vision for the Court and who should serve on it.

Washington took his responsibility to select the Justices very seriously. He knew that the Court would be on the front lines of the ever-controversial issues of federalism and the division of powers, and understood that the survival of the new country depended upon finding consensus when possible, so he endeavored to choose wisely. Of course, this meant appointing brilliant Justices who would bring honor and excellence to the new Court. But more importantly, Washington wanted Justices who had wrestled with the separation of powers issues that dominated the day and jurists who could unite the Country around the new Constitution. Washington had no idea how the Court would handle the knotty issues of separation of powers and state's rights. Nor did he choose only partisans who had pledged a particular approach to those problems. Instead Washington tried to appoint a particular kind of patriot to the Court, individuals who had worked hard to draft or ratify the Constitution, rather than trying to find a particular judicial approach or philosophy. Washington was famously against factionalism, so he would likely be particularly horrified to find that today's Justices must pass a series of political litmus tests before nomination.

Washington's Justices share some common characteristics. All of them except for Samuel Chase were either involved in the drafting of the Constitution or strong advocates for its ratification, and often both. Most of them were also heavily involved in drafting their own state constitutions.

All of them (with the possible exception of William Cushing) were exceptional lawyers, and among the very best lawyers in their state. Lawyers of this era handled every flavor of case and controversy, so these Justices cut their teeth in courtrooms and contract drafting.

Almost all of these Justices spent at least some time reading the law as apprentices in the offices of prominent lawyers. Reading these biographies makes you appreciate just how much the "right" apprenticeship mattered. Many of these Justices rose to the top of the legal profession partially because they apprenticed for an earlier leading light. Some of these apprenticeships seem to be clearly the result of family connections, but several other Justices were young men of little wealth and no family name who gained great apprenticeships through hustle, ability, and guile.

Every one of these Justices was a giant in the public life and governance of his home state. Only Iredell and Cushing were not elected politicians during their careers, and they were deeply involved in state governance as judges and advocates. Each of the other eight Justices were well-known and highly successful politicians.

Many of these Justices were entrepreneurs and risk-takers (sometimes to their personal detriment), a marked difference from the more cautious, resume-driven Justices we have today. It is worth remembering that the winners in the Revolutionary War were the rebels, so the prominent lawyers of the new Republic were all gamblers. Still, it is remarkable to see that three of Washington's Justices faced serious financial troubles from failed investments and that six of them were heavily involved in outside business interests like land speculation or running an ironworks.

Washington also placed a heavy emphasis upon geographic diversity. Nine of his first ten Justices came from different states in the Union (in order—New York, South Carolina, Massachusetts, Pennsylvania, Virginia, North Carolina, Maryland, New Jersey, and Connecticut). This was not accidental. Contemporary sources establish that Washington wanted to make sure that the

Court was balanced geographically so that each state had some stake in the new Court and Constitution.

It will sound odd to contemporary readers, but Supreme Court Justices were among the *most* public facing members of the new federal government in the 1790s because of circuit riding. The original Justices spent much of their time on the road, sitting as district court or appellate judges on a circuit ride all over the country. The original federal court design included no separate circuit courts, so the Justices handled any intermediate appeals as well as Supreme Court appeals. Washington's Justices faced a very light Supreme Court docket, but a very heavy burden traveling to hear cases in every state in the new country. The Justices were on the road for the majority of the year, so Washington wanted to make sure they were familiar with the local laws and cultures.

Many of these names are now long forgotten, but reading their life experiences together, one cannot help but be staggered by the rich lives of our founding jurists.

John Jay

Washington's first appointment to the Court was perhaps his most inspired: the great John Jay. Often overlooked among the Founding Fathers, Jay played a key public and intellectual role in the creation, growth, and survival of the United States. He is also a peculiar hybrid of the new school and old school model of Justice. He went to the finest schools, had a tremendously helpful apprenticeship, and forged over time the resume of an inveterate hoop-jumper. Yet he hardly lived a cloistered life. Few Americans of any era have accomplished more in public life than Jay.

John Jay was born to a well-known New York City family in 1745. His grandfather Augustus Jay was of French Huguenot heritage and arrived in New York in 1686. Augustus began a prosperous business importing, exporting, and selling all types of colonial wares. His son (and John's father) Peter Jay eventually took over the business and, like New York City itself, was a roaring success. Peter earned enough to retire to the family manor in Rye, New York, in 1745 at the age of forty. Jay's mother, Mary Van Cortland, was the daughter of Jacobus Van Cortland, the scion of one of New York's wealthiest and most influential Dutch families. Jay's family was thus French on one side and Dutch on the other, making him the rare founding father who had no English lineage. Jay's mixed French and Dutch heritage is an early sign of New York City's cosmopolitan and mercantile nature. Success in business has long mattered more than lineage. Of course, wealth has its privileges, as Jay reveals.

John Jay was the eighth of ten children. Three of his siblings died before adulthood, and two were struck blind by the smallpox epidemic of 1739. From Jay's childhood forward he had every academic opportunity. His mother taught him English and Latin grammar. At the age of eleven he moved in with the Swiss Reverend Peter Stoope for official tutelage. Jay's instruction was primarily in French, making him multilingual at an early age. In 1760, at the age of fourteen, Jay headed to Kings College in New York City (now Columbia). The Kings College curriculum was based upon those of Cambridge and Oxford, so the young student learned Greek, Latin, and some philosophy and natural law.

Jay decided to pursue a career in law. He graduated in 1764 and was fortunate enough to be hired as a clerk in the law office of Benjamin Kissam, among the most prominent and successful attorneys in New York City. The clerkship was doubly fortuitous, because from 1756 until 1764 attorneys in New York agreed to hire no clerks at all in an effort to limit entry to what they deemed an over-crowded bar in the city.[1] This meant that Jay entered apprenticeship just as the freeze ended, a stroke of excellent luck.

(It is also amusing to note that lawyers as far back as 1756 were working together to restrict access to the profession for economic reasons. As Adam Smith's 1790 masterwork, *The Wealth of Nations*, famously noted: "People of the same trade seldom meet together, even for merriment and diversion, but the conversation ends in a conspiracy against the public, or in some contrivance to raise prices."[2] America's long history of limiting entry into the legal profession out of self-interest thus predates the country itself.)

For the next four years, Jay wrote pleadings and apprenticed for Kissam, while also earning a Master of Arts degree from Kings College in 1767. Here Jay flashed his theoretical and academic muscles. Even wealthy and well-connected Americans were unlikely to have an undergraduate degree in the 1760s. Continuing on for a master's degree showed a true passion for the work. This is especially so since it occurred at the same time as Jay's apprenticeship. Apprenticeship in this era was pretty miserable, as those who have read Herman Melville's classic *Bartleby the Scrivener* know. There was lots of drafting and copying of legal documents by hand. Jay served four years as a clerk and then joined the bar in 1768.

Jay initially formed a partnership with another famous son of New York City, Robert Livingston, Jr. A legal partnership was almost unheard of in pre-Revolution New York. Most lawyers ran their own office in a manner quite like today's solo practitioners. But times were tight for lawyers and Livingston and Jay successfully leveraged their joint family connections into a successful shared practice. The partnership ended in 1771 when Jay's practice grew large enough to support itself. By the eve of the Revolution he was one of the best-known and most successful lawyers in New York City.

Historian Herbert A. Johnson's excellent book, *John Jay: Colonial Lawyer*, focuses solely on Jay's life as a lawyer. It combs through billing records, correspondence, and even court dockets from pre-Revolution New York to paint a detailed portrait of Jay's practice. In the Mayor's Court of New York City, for example, Jay handled everything from collection matters to criminal charges of Assault and Battery. Johnson goes out of his way to establish Jay's bona fides as a successful and brilliant lawyer, but he does not skip over the occasional failure. In one particularly ill-fated case Jay brought suit seeking £15 in damages. After a year's delay Jay lost a nonsuit and *Jay's* client was charged £5. The book dryly notes that this "was not the most successful case that Jay tried."[3] Even the best lawyers lose sometimes.

By 1774 New York was already the commercial and legal heart of the Colonies, and Jay had established himself as one of its finest lawyers. Here his long and distinguished career in public service began. Jay was selected as a New York delegate to the Continental Congress in 1774 and served through 1779. Jay was a moderate from the beginning, avoiding the extremes of either loyalism or the most passionate advocates of revolution. In 1775 Jay helped draft the Olive Branch Petition in a last-ditch effort to avoid war with Britain.

From 1776–77 Jay also served as a delegate to the Convention drafting New York's new constitution. Following its ratification Jay was appointed the first Chief Justice of the newly created New York Supreme Court. Jay served in that role until 1778, when he was appointed President of the Second Continental Congress, the highest executive position in the new American government. Jay took the position in the heat of the Revolutionary War and at a time when its outcome was far from certain. William Howard Taft is the only former president to serve on the Supreme Court, but here Jay likewise rose to the highest office in our nascent country.

In September 1779 Jay began his diplomatic career as the U.S. Minister Plenipotentiary to Spain. Jay was sent to try to gain Spanish support in the Revolutionary War and Spanish recognition of the new American state, a mission that was critical to the survival of the country and winning the war. Jay remained in Spain for three years with limited formal progress, but some critical informal success as Spain secretly provided the Americans with arms and money throughout the war. In 1782 Jay went to Paris to help negotiate the peace treaty that ended the Revolutionary War between America and England. The Continental Congress then appointed him Secretary for Foreign Affairs for the new country in 1784. Jay served in this role until his appointment as Chief Justice of the United States under the new Constitution.

Jay did not participate in the drafting of the new Constitution because of his duties as Secretary for Foreign Affairs. He did, however, play a critical role in its ratification. Jay joined Alexander Hamilton and James Madison in drafting *the Federalist Papers*, which described the benefits of the new Constitution and argued for its ratification. Jay wrote numbers 2 through 5 and then fell ill, returning to draft number 64. Jay's contribution is notable for the work itself but also for the heft and gravitas Jay brought to the argument when the authors eventually became known. Jay also wrote an influential pro-ratification pamphlet entitled "An Address to the People of the State of New York." Jay's efforts came to a head during New York's ratification convention, which lasted forty days and was a squeaker. New York became the critical ninth State to ratify the Constitution by a vote of 30 to 27. Jay was pivotal. John Adams described Jay's role in ratification of the Constitution as "one of more importance than any of the rest, indeed of almost as much weight as all the rest."[4]

When George Washington became the first president under the new Constitution he offered Jay the post of Secretary of State out of respect for Jay's abilities and diplomatic experiences. Jay declined, apparently seeking a break from international travel and negotiation. Washington then offered the position of Chief Justice of the new Supreme Court, which Jay gratefully accepted.

Consider the full breadth of Jay's achievements before joining the Court. He had served as the chief executive officer of the United States. He had been the Chief Justice of New York's highest court. He had been an enormously successful practicing lawyer and a tremendous student at Kings College. He had worked on *the Federalist Papers*, still one of the greatest American writings on our government. He had been America's top diplomat for years, handling the most sensitive and important international tasks, including helping to negotiate the treaty that ended the Revolutionary War. Perhaps it's unfair to compare Jay's resume to those of current Chief Justices: hardly anyone covers as much ground now as Jay did then. Nevertheless, if one considers Jay (and later Ellsworth and Marshall) to be the model for what Chief Justices *should* be, we have been running at a loss since Earl Warren.

Because this is a book about Justice background experiences *before* they joined the Court, we would typically end our discussion of Jay here. And yet Jay's career during and after his tenure on the Supreme Court is a great window into the type of individuals that originally served as Chief Justice. Jay spent his last term as Chief Justice (1794–95) in England negotiating the Jay Treaty of 1795. Britain and France were at war. Opinions in America, and in George Washington's cabinet, were split. Some strongly advocated joining the war on France's side. Others favored neutrality. Fans of the play *Hamilton* will know that this debate was covered in the hilarious rap battle between Hamilton and Jefferson, "Cabinet Battle #2." At the same time, tensions were rising with Britain over trade issues, the continued placement of British troops east of the Mississippi in the Ohio Valley, and seizures of American ships in the French West Indies.

Public opinion on the Jay Treaty was mixed; historical judgments have been mixed as well. On the one hand, America had limited leverage in the negotiations, so, unsurprisingly, the deal was not particularly favorable. On the other hand, further war with England was forestalled until 1812. Either way, consider for a moment that in its hour of greatest diplomatic need America chose to send the sitting Chief Justice to negotiate a critical treaty. Looking at Jay's background and in particular his experience in negotiating the Treaty of Paris a decade earlier, Washington's decision makes perfect sense. It clarifies just how varied and valuable Jay's skills and experiences were to the new country. It also shows how far America has drifted from a more generalist vision of merit in regards to its Supreme Court picks. Imagine Presidents Trump or Biden sending John Roberts to negotiate a treaty with Russia.

While Jay was in England negotiating the second treaty he learned that he had been elected Governor of New York. Jay returned to the United States and resigned from the Supreme Court to serve two three-year terms as Governor. To modern readers the decision to leave the Chief Justiceship to pursue other interests will read quite strangely. For our current Justices their role on the Court is a culmination of their life's work. Why would they ever resign for another job? But Jay's term as Chief Justice was just one of the many achievements in a life filled with service to his country and his state.

Jay shows us the sort of well-rounded and experienced leader that Washington sought for the Supreme Court. A person who had excelled not just in school or as a judge, but in every aspect of public life. Washington himself put it well when he wrote to Jay sending him his commission as Chief Justice, aptly praising

Jay's "talents, knowledge, and integrity" as the qualifications necessary to head "that department which must be considered as the keystone of our political future."[5]

John Rutledge

Washington's second appointment to the Supreme Court, John Rutledge, had one of the strangest careers of any Justice while on the Court. Washington actually considered three people for the inaugural Chief Justice: Jay, Rutledge, and James Wilson. When Washington settled on Jay he then made Rutledge the Court's second Justice. But Rutledge never actually sat with the whole Court during his first stint, leaving the Court after a year and a half to become the Chief Justice of the South Carolina Court of Common Pleas (the highest judicial office in the state). When John Jay resigned as Chief Justice in 1795, Rutledge wrote Washington and asked for the job. Washington recess appointed Rutledge as Chief Justice, and Rutledge actually sat as Chief Justice and heard cases for six months before political headwinds and rumors of mental illness led the Senate to reject his nomination, the first time a presidential appointment to a major office had not been confirmed by the Senate.

John Rutledge was born to a wealthy and politically connected family in Charleston, South Carolina, in 1739. Rutledge's family, and eventually Rutledge himself, generated much of their considerable income from plantation property and slaves. As a teenager Rutledge read law and apprenticed in the law office of his uncle Andrew Rutledge. Andrew Rutledge was Speaker of the South Carolina Commons House of Assembly and also a prominent lawyer. John followed up his apprenticeship with three years of legal study at the Middle Temple in London. In the pre-revolutionary period there was no more prestigious start to a lawyer's career than a trip to the Middle Temple in England. This was partially because of the perceived excellence of legal training in London, then arguably the greatest city in the world, but also due to the sheer expense of the education. To put the expense into perspective, when it looked like apprenticeships were going to be barred in New York City, John Jay's quite wealthy family looked into sending Jay to London and the Middle Temple, but decided the cost was too prohibitive.

John Rutledge joined the bar in England in 1760 and headed back to Charleston in 1761. At the age of twenty-one he immediately established himself as a successful lawyer and politician. In 1763, just two years later, his correspondence reflects that he took no legal work without a retainer of £100 sterling, a small fortune at the time. Like his contemporaries, he worked in a solo practice that focused on business and land issues, but also included a mix of criminal defense and whatever else came in the door.

Rutledge served in a series of high-profile elected and appointed political offices, often while maintaining his law practice. He was elected to the South Carolina House of Commons three months after returning in 1761 and served in that body continuously until 1778. The Crown appointed him Attorney General for the colony from 1764 to 1765. Rutledge represented South Carolina in the First and Second Continental Congresses. As the Revolution began Rutledge returned to South Carolina to help draft the state's first constitution. He was also named President of the South Carolina General Assembly from 1776 to 1778, serving as the lead executive in the state during the height of the war. Rutledge's order to protect Fort Sumter at all costs led to the first American victory in the Revolutionary War. Rutledge remained the chief executive throughout the war, suffering through the British siege and capture of Charleston and leading the eventual American liberation of the city in 1782.

After the war, Rutledge served as Governor and as a Judge in the Chancery Court for South Carolina. In 1787 he served as a delegate to the Constitutional Convention and was an active participant, advocating, among other things, against the direct election of representatives. Rutledge also served on the influential Committee on Detail (along with his future fellow Justice James Wilson) that helped draft the compromises that resulted in the final version of the Constitution. When Rutledge returned to South Carolina he was instrumental in ratification efforts.

If John Jay had taken Washington up on his offer to become Secretary of State, Rutledge might well have been the nation's first Chief Justice. Instead Rutledge had to settle for becoming the first Associate Justice.

William Cushing

Washington's third Justice, William Cushing, is less impressive than Jay or Rutledge, both of whom were supremely talented lawyers and statesmen. William Cushing was less so, and thus he's the first (and hardly the last) relative mediocrity to reach the Court.

Like Jay and Rutledge, Cushing came from a wealthy family. His father and grandfather were judges and members of the Governor's Council in Massachusetts. Like Jay and Rutledge, Cushing had a first-class education as the first "Harvard man" to join the Court. Cushing graduated with an A.B. in 1751, then followed in his family's footsteps and read the law in the office of a prominent Boston attorney, Jeremiah Gridley. Cushing joined the bar in 1755 and opened a solo practice in his home town of Scituate, Massachusetts.

Thus far Cushing's biography sounds quite similar to Jay and

Rutledge's: wealthy family, excellent education, strong foundation in apprenticeship. Cushing's experiences in the practice of law, however, were quite distinct, mostly because contemporary sources suggest that Cushing was not a very good lawyer. First, Cushing could not garner enough business to make it as a lawyer in Scituate, where his father and grandfather had been prominent lawyers and judges. A bad sign for future prospects, surely. Family connections alone should have floated Cushing in Scituate. Instead, he decamped to the northern frontier in Lincoln County, near modern-day Dresden, Maine. Cushing gained an appointment as the justice of the peace for the county and also went north with a number of logging interests as clients. Given that logging was the main commercial activity that far north, and that Cushing was simultaneously serving in the main judicial office, he should have been well positioned for success.

Nevertheless, Cushing's practice failed to thrive. Herbert Alan Johnson's short biography of the future Justice presents a brutally unfavorable assessment:

> Despite [Cushing's] professional advantages, he achieved more success in business ventures than in practice.... Eventually Cushing lost his corporate clients to other attorneys.... Among Cushing's private papers there is ample evidence that the suspicions of his clients were not without adequate foundation.... Throughout his life Cushing was unsure of the law. [W]ithout powerful family connections and a winning personality, such an attorney would never have survived in the highly educated and articulate bar that produced a practitioner of the caliber of John Adams.[6]

Cushing was saved by his father, who pushed for his appointment as a Judge on the Superior Court of Massachusetts. Cushing served in that role, first under the loyalist government and then under the new commonwealth, from 1772 to 1789, serving as Chief Judge (the highest judicial office in Massachusetts) from 1777 on. In this role Cushing's primary success seems to have been keeping his job despite the shifting political winds. One reason why there were few former judges with lengthy careers for Washington to choose from was that most royal courts were, unsurprisingly, not super friendly to non-loyalists, so many of them lost their jobs (or even their lives) during or after the war. Cushing somehow managed to serve as a loyal judge in the royal courts and then shifted into roughly the same office post-war, even gaining a promotion.

Part of Cushing's success was his perceived fairness as a judge of the royal courts. Another part was family connections. But perhaps the single biggest factor was Cushing's willingness to keep riding circuit and hearing cases throughout the Revolutionary War, while his colleagues avoided combat areas. Avoiding combat meant avoiding most of the state. Nor was the danger limited to official combat forces. In 1779 Cushing arrived in Berkshire County, Massachusetts, to hear cases in the middle of the riots of the Berkshire Constitutionalists. Cushing cancelled court and was fortunate to escape unharmed, but for Cushing to retreat at all was an exceptional occurrence. Typically, he just held court as per usual. Cushing's willingness to ride circuit during wartime, riots, bad weather, and any number of other obstacles paid off in the post-Revolutionary period. As Woody Allen has noted, "80 percent of success is just showing up"—Cushing embodied that attitude unfailingly.

Cushing was selected as a member of the drafting convention for the new Massachusetts Constitution in 1779–80, but he seems to have made a limited impact. There is nary a mention of Cushing in the recorded proceedings and Cushing's own contemporary notes are filled with doodles and passing the time. For example,

Cushing's boredom with the discussions "led him to jot down a list of materials he would need to make a new suit of clothes."[7] In 1788 Cushing served as vice president of the successful Massachusetts ratifying convention for the new federal Constitution, again with no record that he contributed very much.

Washington appointed Cushing to the Court in 1789 as America's third Justice, and he served until his death in 1810, sitting under four different Chief Justices and offering critical support to John Marshall. Nevertheless, Cushing was not an ambitious man; despite his years on the Court he left a limited jurisprudential legacy. Again, Johnson's biography of Cushing presents a portrait of a relatively silly person:

> [W]hen Cushing arrived for the first sitting of the Court in New York City he wore his old-fashioned full-bottomed judicial wig. About one hundred little boys followed him down the street, watching him with curiosity and awe. The crowd grew and gradually it dawned upon the Justice that he was the object of unusual attention, although he did not know the reason why. Finally a sailor was astonished into exclaiming, "My eyes! What a wig!" The new Associate Justice of the Supreme Court returned to his hotel room, ordered a peruke maker to prepare a more fashionable headpiece for him, and was never seen again in his judge's wig.[8]

Other evidence of Cushing's relative lack of ambition was his decision to decline an appointment as Chief Justice. When Jay resigned and Rutledge was rejected by the Senate (more on this in Chapter Four), Washington turned to Cushing. Given that Cushing was already on the Court, Rutledge had been rejected by the Senate, and Washington had subsequently had several others decline the position, Cushing must have seemed a safe and easy choice. He actually initially said yes to Washington's request, and his one semi-official act was to sit at Washington's side at a dinner party in the seat of honor as the new Chief Justice of the Supreme Court. Apparently this experience was too much for Cushing. Later that week he declined the appointment for reasons of health but stayed on as an Associate Justice and served another fifteen years in that role.

Cushing is now a barely remembered Supreme Court Justice who wrote a small number of relatively straightforward opinions. In fact he's probably best known for declining to become the Chief Justice. He is surely among the least noteworthy Justices to ever serve on the Court: though he served for over twenty years, he wrote only nineteen opinions, each of limited scope. Nor were these cases of particular note. Here's the CQ Press's summary of Cushing's Court service: "Cushing delivered only nineteen brief opinions during his twenty-one years on the bench, and his decisions were direct, noncomplex, or as some have said, 'simple.' If succinctness is a blessing, then Cushing was a saint."[9]

Readers may think this thumbnail biography is an indictment of Washington's decision to appoint him, and I'll actually make that case in Chapter Seven. As devil's advocate here I'll argue the opposite. The Supreme Court has a long tradition of mediocre Justices, and on a nine-member decision making body (or six- or seven-member during Cushing's tenure) having some individuals who are happy to "go along to get along" is quite important. Cushing knew his limitations and did his job to the best of his relatively limited abilities. I say that as praise! Successful organizations have a mix of personalities, experiences, and followers to go along with leaders. John Marshall's successes came at least partially due to Cushing and his brethren being willing to let Marshall shine.

James Wilson

James Wilson is surely among the most bizarre Supreme Court stories. His tale begins with a rapid ascent from relative destitution in Scotland to a classic American immigrant success story. He was a brilliant political philosopher, a lawyer without peer, a leading light at the Constitutional Convention, one of America's first law professors, and a land speculator. Unfortunately, the last role led to Wilson's downfall. He borrowed heavily to build his empire and his debt issues eventually grew so unwieldy that he was thrown into debtor's prison while he was a sitting Supreme Court Justice, and he died in relative ignominy while still on the lam.

Wilson, Rutledge, and Jay were Washington's finalists for the position of Chief Justice. Each of them had a remarkable career before, during, and after the Revolution, and each experienced exceptional success as a lawyer. Yet Wilson and Rutledge's fates sadly diverged substantially from Jay's later in life.

The first three appointees to the Supreme Court all shared the advantages of being born into wealthy and influential colonial families, and all were given several legs up in their rise to prominence. Wilson had no such advantages. Born in 1742 in Fifeshire, Scotland, Wilson was the eldest of seven children of a hard-working but relatively poor farmer. Wilson's family was Calvinist, and his parents desperately wanted him to become a "minister of the Kirk." Ministers needed to be educated, so when Wilson turned fourteen he earned a bursary scholarship to St Andrews, and his parents scraped together the remainder of the support from their meager earnings on the farm. He studied mathematics, Latin, Greek, and philosophy for five years in Scottish universities before Wilson's father died.

At this point Wilson was forced to quit his studies and help support his widowed mother and siblings. He left the university, abandoned the ministry, and worked for a period as a private tutor. Once his brothers and the farm became more self-supporting, Wilson moved to Edinburgh to briefly study accounting before deciding that Scotland severely limited the prospects of an ambitious and brilliant young man. He set sail for America in 1765.

Wilson headed to Philadelphia and became a tutor at the College of Philadelphia (now the University of Pennsylvania), an academic home that he would return to later in life. But Wilson did not move to America to reprise his role as a lowly tutor, so in 1766 he found a position as an apprentice to read the law with John Dickinson, a prominent Philadelphia attorney. Dickinson was one of the leading lawyers in Philadelphia and had himself studied at the London Inns of Court. Wilson served in this role for just two years and was a member of the bar of Pennsylvania by 1767.

Here we see the first signs of Wilson's spectacular abilities as a legal mind, but also as a self-promoter. As the stories of Jay, Rutledge, and Cushing well establish, a good apprenticeship was the eighteenth-century version of a Harvard Law degree—it launched young lawyers into their careers. They were thus almost as difficult to obtain as a modern Harvard Law degree, especially for a brash Scotsman with no particular family connections or wealth. Wilson's ability to garner this apprenticeship alone shows a remarkable talent. Terms as an apprentice were also expensive, so Wilson borrowed the fees from his cousin Robert Annan. Debt is sadly to become a theme of Wilson's later life. Note also the differences in the period of study. Jay and Cushing each read the law for four years and Rutledge spent three years at Middle Temple after a few years of reading the law with his uncle. Wilson was done in under two.

Wilson began his legal career in Reading, Pennsylvania, before heading west again to Carlisle. Like Cushing, Wilson sought his fortune on the expanding American frontier, but unlike Cushing, Wilson was a smashing success. He was by all accounts an exceptional lawyer, focusing on litigation and land speculation, both of which were in great supply on the western frontier of Pennsylvania. He also married into a wealthy family and for a time lived the American immigrant's dream—wealth and prominence from sheer force of will and ability.

Wilson's background in political philosophy and his time studying at St Andrews during the period known as the Scottish Enlightenment led him naturally to involving himself with the intellectual movements underpinning the bubbling American Revolution. In 1774, two years before the Declaration of Independence, Wilson wrote the highly influential pamphlet "Considerations on the Nature and Extent of the Legislative Authority of the British Parliament." Wilson was one of the first and most prominent American voices arguing that the British Parliament had *no* authority over the colonies because the colonists had no role in selecting representatives. This was a radical argument at the time, and Wilson was well ahead of the curve in making it forcefully and explicitly. This too was a theme of Wilson's life.

In 1774 Wilson's prominence led to his selection to represent Pennsylvania in the Continental Congress. He signed the Declaration of Independence and served in the Continental Congress off and on until becoming a Pennsylvania delegate to the Constitutional Convention in 1787. While less celebrated than Hamilton or Madison, Wilson is widely seen as one of the prime architects of our Constitution. He was the primary drafter in the all-important Committee of Detail, which hammered out many critical compromises.

Wilson held a unique assortment of different political positions at the Convention. He argued for a powerful central government, so he aligned with the Federalists in some ways, but also for more direct democratic control, so sometimes in line with the Anti-federalists. He argued for direct election of the President and the Senate, views well ahead of his time on those structural issues. Moreover, Wilson is one of the earliest proponents of the general principal of "one man one vote." Of all the founders, Wilson may be the one whose views most closely track with the country we eventually became. Wilson then helped persuade Pennsylvania to ratify the new Constitution and helped draft the Pennsylvania Constitution of 1790.

Meanwhile, Wilson's legal career continued to prosper. Wilson moved to Philadelphia in 1777 and was prominent enough to serve as the Avocat Général in maritime and commercial causes for the French government from 1779 to 1783. This was a lucrative and high-profile representation involving the highest levels of the governments of America and France. Wilson also earned large fees defending prominent and wealthy Philadelphians accused of being Tory sympathizers. This proved lucrative, if controversial, work, and it shows the breadth of Wilson's practice: from criminal defense to international relations and maritime law, to land speculation and contract and property law.

Wilson also became the first Professor of Law at the College of Philadelphia and promptly began working on a magnum opus explaining the role of the common law in the new American constitutional scheme. Wilson sought to draw an explicit distinction between Sir William Blackstone's vision of law as a rule prescribed by a superior and the new American conception of law's legitimacy arising from "the consent of those whose obedience the law requires."[10] This was an extremely controversial position at the time, but one in line with Wilson's long-held belief that the power of the government came from the consent of the people, not from a higher authority.

Wilson was never satisfied to be just a professor or a politician or a successful lawyer; he also continuously sought great wealth. In the eighteenth century, as today, it is possible to make a very good living as a lawyer working for fees, but it is much harder to gain generational wealth. In that pursuit he engaged in land and business speculation from his earliest days, sometimes at a breakneck and reckless speed. He bought and sold lots of land. He operated an ironworks. He borrowed heavily in all of these endeavors.

Wilson proposed himself to Washington as the first Chief Justice but had to settle for a position as an Associate Justice. He served until 1798, and his work on the Court shows little of his visionary legal mind. During his tenure the Court was still a rather minor force in national affairs, and Wilson decided relatively few weighty cases.

Wilson's rapidly deteriorating finances also likely distracted him from his judicial duties. Before and immediately after the Revolution, American land speculators assumed that a continuing flood of European immigration would make frontier land ever more valuable, so there was a wild rush to purchase as much as possible. Remember that John Marshall bought his large holdings in the Northern Neck of Virginia in this same period. When the flood of immigration slowed to a trickle and the post-war economy slumped, the party came to an abrupt and unfortunate end, and Wilson struggled to stay ahead of his creditors.

It seems unbelievable today, but Wilson was pursued by creditors while riding circuit as a Supreme Court Justice for months, one step ahead of debtor's prison at each stop until they finally caught up with him and threw him into debtor's prison in Burlington, New Jersey. Wilson's eldest son bailed him out and Wilson fled to Edenton, North Carolina, the hometown of his fellow Justice, James Iredell. Here yet another creditor, the former South Carolina Senator Pierce Butler (and his fellow member of the Constitutional Convention) chased Wilson down and jailed him again. Wilson's son bailed him out again, and Wilson died soon thereafter of malaria, sweltering in the North Carolina summer heat. At the time of his death Wilson owed Butler $197,000, an unimaginably large sum in 1798. And Butler was hardly Wilson's only creditor.

Wilson is thus a quintessential modern American character. Like Alexander Hamilton, he was a first-generation immigrant who made it big in America solely due to his intellect and work ethic. He was also a political philosopher of remarkable prescience, forcefully arguing for a democratic vision of America that would triumph long after his death. He is also one of those founders that makes you wonder how it was possible to be engaged in so many different undertakings, as a leading voice in drafting the Constitution, a brilliant professor of law, a decorated politician, a world class lawyer, and an active (if ultimately unsuccessful) businessman. Robert McCloskey's write-up on Wilson in *The Justices of the United States Supreme Court* wraps up a uniquely American life quite nicely:

> [Wilson] had many of the qualities we might look for in a great constitutional statesman-judge: learning, industry, insight, all far beyond the common measure. If he lacked some of the others that a man like Marshall had, those deficiencies might have been overcome, in the right time and place, by the sheer force of his abilities. But he wanted too many things, and he seemed congenitally unable to choose between them. He wanted to be, not a freebooting financier, or a politician, or a revered constitutional statesman, but all three. This may be too much for any man to ask at any time. It was certainly too much for a man like Wilson.[11]

Wilson went from having a key role in the drafting of our Constitution and an inaugural seat on the Supreme Court to a *Death of a Salesman*-esque final chapter, dying penniless in North

Carolina. He was buried on James Iredell's plantation because his family could not afford to have the body returned to Philadelphia. He now survives as a footnote in American History.

John Blair, Jr.

I quoted the mixed review of Wilson and the acerbic biography of Cushing from the excellent compendium *The Justices of United States Supreme Court* above. The authors sometimes express their disdain for a Justice less directly, through brevity. Fred Israel's history of John Blair, Jr., is in that vein. Blair garners a rather grim-looking portrait and seven brief pages of text, one of the shortest treatments in all five volumes. It is not that Blair did not have a distinguished pre-Court career. It is just that his story pales in comparison to those of Jay, Wilson, and Rutledge.

Blair was born into one of the leading political families in Virginia in 1732. His father, John Blair, Senior, served colonial Virginia in the House of Burgesses, as a member of the Governor's Council, and as acting Governor in 1758. Blair's great uncle, James Blair, founded William and Mary College in 1693 and served as "President for Life" of the institution for fifty years until 1743.

Blair came from a family of wealthy land and slave owners and was thus afforded an exceptional education. He graduated from William and Mary with Honors in 1754 and studied law at the Middle Temple in London from 1755 to 1756. (Again, note how wealthy plantation owners were in the pre-Revolution Southern colonies. John Jay's New York City merchant father could not afford to send him to London, but Rutledge and Blair's slave plantation–supported families could.)

After completing his studies abroad, Blair returned to Williamsburg and became a well-known and well-compensated member of the bar. Blair is unusual among early Supreme Court Justices in that he joined the bar immediately upon returning from the Middle Temple rather than serving in an American apprenticeship. This likely reflects the extraordinary credit given to a Middle Temple education.

Blair entered public service in 1765 as a member of the elected House of Burgesses. He was originally a relatively conservative politician: in 1765 he opposed Patrick Henry's strident attacks on the royal Stamp Act and pushed for a peaceful resolution to the disputes. In 1770 he became the Clerk to the powerful Governor's Council. But as revolution grew more likely Blair came to side with his countrymen, and he was a leading member of the 1776 Virginia convention that drafted a new state constitution. The constitution reorganized the judiciary, and Blair began his career as a judge. He became a General Court Judge in 1777 and then the Chief Judge of that Court in 1779. In 1780 he was elevated to the three-judge Court of Chancery, and in 1789 he joined the newly created Supreme Court of Appeals of Virginia.

Blair was also a member of the illustrious Virginia Delegation to the Constitutional Convention of 1787 along with George Washington, Edmund Randolph, James Madison, and George Mason. Madison and Robert Yates's notes on the convention suggest that Blair never gave a speech at the Convention; it would be hard not to be overshadowed by his fellow Virginians. In this way Blair resembles Cushing—he was a (relatively speaking) B-list lawyer from a state filled with true legal giants. He was also primarily a former judge by the time he was appointed. Like Cushing it is harsh to condemn Blair as a mediocrity. He was chosen to represent Virginia, the wealthiest and most populous state in the union and the home to many of the most decorated lawyers and leaders in the country, at the Constitutional Convention, so he surely was respected by his peers.

Blair signed the Constitution on behalf of Virginia and likewise advocated for Virginia's adoption of the Constitution in 1788. Blair was the fifth Washington nominee to the Court, and he joined Jay and his fellow Justices in New York City (then the U.S. Capital) in February 1790 for the Court's first sitting. He served until his resignation for health reasons in 1796.

James Iredell

James Iredell was born October 5, 1751, in Lewes, England. His father was a prosperous merchant in Bristol until he fell ill at some point during the 1760s. The illness debilitated his father's health and business. The situation grew dire enough that in 1768, at seventeen years old, James Iredell sailed for Edenton, North Carolina, to become Comptroller of His Majesty's Customs. The position was purchased by a cousin, and the £30 salary was to be paid directly to Iredell's father. Iredell was to earn roughly £100 a year on "fees."

The job did not turn out to be the easy sinecure that Iredell's family expected. The bulk of Iredell's income was to come from customs fees, which had recently proven extremely controversial. The Stamp Act was a particular flashpoint. In January, 1766, the North Carolina Sons of Liberty burned the customs agent in Cape Fear, NC, in effigy and by February over 1,000 armed and rowdy dissidents forced the reopening of the port and ended Stamp Act collections.[12] The Stamp Act was repealed later that year, but the atmosphere was hardly conducive to friendly relations between the Crown's customs agents (like Iredell) and the people of North Carolina.

Iredell was an ambitious young man, and soon after arriving in Edenton he began an apprenticeship with a leading local lawyer, Samuel Johnston. Johnston would later serve as North Carolina's

Governor and U.S. Senator and was among the leading lights of North Carolina's bar. Iredell studied hard under Johnston, hard enough that in his contemporary diary he reprimands himself for the "indolence" of taking a break from studying Lyttleton's *Tenures on Rents* to lose "three or four games at billiards."[13] Contemporary law students will surely recognize this struggle.

Iredell was a quick study and he joined the Bar of North Carolina in 1770 and began to build a successful legal practice. Like his contemporaries he took all sorts of legal work, including admiralty suits, land disputes, will drafting, and much more. He was successful enough that he described himself as "beset with clients" and at one point stopped taking new business.[14]

As the Revolution dawned, Iredell's relatives in England were concerned about young James's fading loyalty to the Crown. In 1775 his uncle wrote, "I am concerned to find you so full of politics … they can be of no use to you as a King's officer.… The people of America are certainly mad."[15] Notwithstanding these exhortations, Iredell chose his new home over the old and became an influential political writer in North Carolina in support of the Revolutionary cause.

After North Carolina became independent in 1776, Iredell took a leading role in drafting and revising the existing statutes to reflect the new state constitution. He then served a year as one of three Superior Court Judges in the state, holding one of North Carolina's highest judicial offices at the age of twenty-seven. Circuit riding in North Carolina proved too taxing, and Iredell returned to practice and then to serve as Attorney General for North Carolina from 1779 to 1781. As the state's primary prosecutor, he tried criminal cases all over the state. In 1781 he again returned to his profitable law practice.

In 1788 Iredell turned to advocating for the ratification of the new U.S. Constitution. He gave a leading speech during the 1788 convention.[16] The initial vote for ratification was unsuccessful (North Carolina did not ratify until 1789), but Iredell's efforts were sufficient to draw national attention. In 1790, when Robert Harrison of Maryland declined to join the Court for health reasons, Washington appointed Iredell. Iredell was thus one of the first six Justices on the Court, but not among the first six nominees. In his diary Washington praised Iredell's "abilities, legal knowledge, and respectability of character," and noted that "he is of a State of some importance in the Union that has given no character to a federal office."

The Original Supreme Court

We now have the original Supreme Court. In February 1790 the Court met for the first time with just five confirmed Justices: Jay, Rutledge, Cushing, Wilson, and Blair. The Court's second sitting, in August 1790, included Iredell, so every seat was finally filled. Rutledge was absent from both of the first two sittings, and both times the Court convened and then almost immediately adjourned for lack of business. For the first few years the bulk of their actual work was done while riding circuit.

Washington's first Justices were a diverse and accomplished group of lawyers. They reflected the best from the colonies. Each had fought hard for independence and again in support of the new Constitution. Washington probably hoped he was finished dealing with the Court in 1790, but he had no such luck.

∾

CHAPTER FOUR

WASHINGTON'S LAST FOUR
Bankruptcies, Mental Illness, and a Bacon Face

Washington struggled to keep the six seats on the Supreme Court filled. This was partially due to circumstance (it was a new government, after all), but also to mixed opinions of the institution itself.

Evidence abounds for the latter proposition. Washington's initial choice for Iredell's sixth seat on the Court, Robert Hanson Harrison, was actually confirmed by the Senate and officially given the job before he opted to remain Chief Justice of the General Court in Maryland instead. Harrison demurred due to poor health and, frankly, skepticism about the new U.S. Supreme Court, especially the circuit riding duties. Harrison had loyally served as Washington's aide-de-camp through most of the Revolutionary War, so it hurt him dearly to decline this request from his commander-in-chief.

John Rutledge accepted the second seat on the Court but only lasted a year and a half. Rutledge did ride circuit as a Justice, but he never actually sat with the entire Court before resigning to return to the South Carolina judiciary. It seems that between pique over being passed over for the initial appointment as Chief

Justice, a dislike of circuit riding, and concerns over the profile of the new Court, Rutledge preferred to return home over remaining a Justice.

Another sign of the Court's relative standing was Washington's next step upon Rutledge's resignation. Washington wrote a *joint* letter to two leading South Carolina lawyers, Edward Rutledge and C. C. Pinckney, asking if either of them would be willing to take the nomination, and if so, which. Both declined, again in a joint letter. Pause for a minute and imagine a modern President writing two potential Justices a joint letter asking whether they wanted to join the Court, and if so, which one. Then remember that they *both* declined.

Last, consider the relatively small and modest docket of the early Supreme Court. Before John Marshall the Court had a much lower profile. The Justices actually spent more time and energy circuit riding (which they generally despised) than deciding cases as a Court. All of these factors surely contributed to Washington's struggles in filling the first six seats. Perhaps Washington breathed a sigh of relief upon Iredell joining the Court. Six Justices in place, we're done! Sadly, no.

Thomas Johnson Replaces Rutledge in 1791

Unlike Fred Israel's brutally short treatment of John Blair, Herbert Alan Johnson's biography of Thomas Johnson in *The Justices* is respectfully substantial—but it's still pointed. He begins: "Few men have so conducted their lives to escape historical study better than Thomas Johnson of Maryland."[1] Later in the chapter: "One wonders whether Thomas Johnson consciously avoided fame or whether it continuously slipped from his grasp."[2]

The rest of the chapter continues in this vein, detailing all of the things that Thomas Johnson did not do, despite his very close proximity to important people and events. Thomas Johnson did not sign the Declaration of Independence, despite serving in the Second Continental Congress and being close friends with many of the signatories. Johnson had already left Philadelphia to raise a militia in Maryland in advance of the war. Johnson also missed the constitutional convention of 1787. He was semi-retired in Fredrick County, Maryland running his iron works.

Here I lodge a rare disagreement with *The Justices*. A full accounting of Johnson's life suggests an exceedingly effective man of diverse interests and talents. It is fair to consider him an underwhelming Justice, but it is unfair to consider him a cypher who avoided fame.

Thomas Johnson was born in November 1732 in Calvert County, Maryland, the fifth of twelve children. His family were landowners and farmers. Historical records establish that Thomas Johnson himself was a slave owner later in life, but it is unclear whether his family was wealthy enough to have slaves on the family farm. We do know that the family was not wealthy enough to pay for any formal education for Johnson: his first education outside the home came as a law clerk and apprentice in Annapolis.

Johnson began his career as a clerk of the Provincial Court. Over time he signed on to read the law and apprentice with Stephen Bordley, a well-known Maryland lawyer and politician. The exact dates of this period are fuzzy, but we do know that Johnson did not join the bar until 1760, when he was a comparatively older twenty-seven. This suggests that Johnson worked for a few years as a clerk and then again as an apprentice before becoming a lawyer. Likewise, it suggests that Johnson must have been a hard-working and very able young man to earn a spot studying under Bordley from his position in the clerk's office. Johnson is thus the second Supreme Court Justice (after James Wilson) to have risen to the heights of the legal profession without significant family connections or wealth as steppingstones.

As a new lawyer Thomas quickly launched a successful political career. In 1762 he was elected to the Provincial Assembly and served in that role for twelve years. From 1774–77 Johnson served in the First and Second Continental Congresses. His role in the Second Continental Congress was especially significant. He served on the highly sensitive Secret Committee on Correspondence, which was tasked with reaching out to France, Spain, and other foreign powers to see if they would support independence for the colonies. Johnson also had the honor of nominating his friend George Washington to become the Commander-in-Chief of the American forces.

Johnson had gotten to know Washington earlier. Starting in 1761 Johnson bought up land along the Potomac River on the Maryland side and became enamored with the idea of making the river navigable. Navigability would increase trade and commerce along the banks, and consequently increase the value of his own extensive landholdings. Washington owned land on the Virginia side of the Potomac, and sometime around 1770 the two men began a correspondence. They discussed plans for a canal or other improvements to allow for boats to travel farther upstream. Johnson wrote to Washington, for instance, about the river's "obstructions" that "might easily be removed at very small expense" by "an Englishman in whom I have very great confidence and a German who has been long employed in blowing [up] rocks."[3]

Johnson, like many of the other first Justices, was a remarkably successful lawyer, but he was also, like some of them, an active businessman and investor. Along with his land and farms, Johnson owned a profitable iron works in Fredrick. Records suggest the forge was operated with slave labor, which was likely an especially grim life, even for American slaves.

The friendship with Washington bore fruit for both men. Johnson was one of Washington's biggest supporters during the war. He raised a militia of 1,800 men and commanded them as a Brigadier General. In 1777 he was chosen as the first Governor of Maryland and served for three consecutive one-year terms in the teeth of the war effort. Johnson also continuously raised supplies and arms and was considered one of the most effective Governors in supporting the war effort.

After the war, Johnson continued apace. He served in the Maryland House of Delegates for two different terms, and, like the original members of Washington's Supreme Court, he argued fiercely for Maryland to ratify the new U.S. Constitution. Washington and Johnson also created the Potomack Company, a corporation established under Virginia and Maryland law, aimed at achieving their long-held dream of improving the Potomac via a canal. Washington served as the first president of the company. When he became the President of the United States, Johnson took over. The company's plans for a canal along the Potomac did not come to fruition in Johnson or Washington's lifetimes, although the Chesapeake and Ohio Canal eventually opened in 1831.

In 1790 Johnson became the Chief Judge of the Maryland General Court, replacing the deceased Robert Hanson Harrison. This was followed quickly by two new federal appointments by George Washington. The first, in January 1791, was as the head of the Board of Commissioners of the Federal City, tasked with establishing the new American Capital (not coincidentally) along the Potomac. In the Summer of 1791 Washington invited Johnson to join the U.S. Supreme Court to take the barely warm seat of John Rutledge.

Johnson was suspicious of the rigors of riding circuit, especially as he would be assigned to the Southern Circuit, which covered a massive amount of geography by poor roads and through difficult weather. The contemporary reports from Rutledge, Johnson, and

Iredell (the first Justices to ride the Southern Circuit) are packed with bitter complaints: impassable roads, primitive lodgings, long horseback rides, canoe trips along rivers through otherwise inaccessible country, and more. Washington badly wanted Johnson to take the job—partially to have a Justice from Maryland, but also to get a functioning group of Justices on the Court after the almost immediate loss of Rutledge. Johnson was skeptical but took the job out of deference to Washington.

Like Rutledge, Johnson lasted only a year and a half, as bad health and the rigors of travel proved too onerous. He resigned from the Court in 1793 but remained as the head of the Board of Commissioners, an apparently easier and more satisfying project. That same year he presided over the laying of the Capitol building's cornerstone, signaling the end of the planning and land acquisition phase and the beginning of the building phase. Regardless of Johnson's limited impact on the Court, he played a pivotal role in the creation of Washington, D.C., and the nation's new capital buildings.

In 1795 Washington asked Johnson to consider becoming Secretary of State, but this time Johnson refused Washington's request and retired fully from public life. He lived until 1819, tending to his business interests and dying a wealthy man at the old age of eighty-seven.

William Paterson Follows Thomas Johnson in 1793

William Paterson is our third immigrant Justice. He was born December 24, 1745, in County Antrim, Ireland, and he arrived in America as a two-year-old. In conducting the empirical study discussed in Part II, I tried to calculate the number of years each Justice had lived in any state (or foreign country) before joining the Supreme Court. Some Justices were easy. Johnson or Cushing, for example, basically lived in one state their whole lives before joining the Court.

Other Justices were harder, especially Justices like Paterson that came from modest circumstances. Justices from wealthy families like Jay or Rutledge are easy to locate because they owned massive properties and were public figures. Recent immigrants like Paterson are much harder to find. The Patersons apparently landed in Newcastle, Delaware, in 1747 and then lived in New York and Connecticut for indeterminate stretches of time before settling in Princeton, New Jersey, for good in 1750.

Paterson's father made and sold tin plate and did well enough that an Irish immigrant and craftsman sent his son to the College of New Jersey (now Princeton University). Here Paterson made lifelong friends, including with the future Chief Justice (and his future political ally at the Constitutional Convention of 1787 and in the Senate) Oliver Ellsworth.

Paterson graduated in 1763 and, like John Jay, pursued further education, gaining a Master of Arts degree from Princeton in 1766 while simultaneously reading the law under Richard Stockton, a local lawyer. Paterson's decision to earn a Master's was an unusual choice in the 1760s, even more so for a rising young man of limited means, which suggests that that he truly delighted in the academic environment and the pursuit of knowledge.

Paterson joined the Bar in 1769. It should be apparent by now that the vast majority of eighteenth-century American lawyers spent at least some time "reading the law" before joining the bar. It is interesting to note the wide variation in how long these apprenticeships lasted, and how that seems to track with class and wealth, but probably also variations amongst the colonies. Paterson and Thomas, both men from less wealthy backgrounds, took six years or more, while others Justices studied for less than two years.

Paterson began his practice in New Bromley, New Jersey, for three years before returning to Princeton. He struggled to find business in New Bromley but eventually built a successful practice in Princeton. As the Revolution loomed in 1775, Paterson began a long career in public service. He served in the Provincial Congress of New Jersey as the Secretary and in 1776 he helped draw up the first New Jersey Constitution. During the Revolutionary War he served five years as New Jersey's Attorney General and as a Minuteman in Somerset County. He was also a member of the New Jersey Council of Safety and the Legislative Council.

Following the war Paterson returned to his successful private practice until public service called again. Paterson was selected as a New Jersey representative to the Constitutional Convention of 1787. Paterson proved an influential member, advocating the "New Jersey" or "Paterson" plan, in which a single legislative body represented the states, not individuals, and in which each state had an equal vote regardless of population or wealth. This was obviously a favorable design for smaller states like New Jersey. The convention proved lengthy and contentious, especially on the issue of how to structure the legislative branch. Paterson joined in on the "great compromise" of a bicameral legislature, with the Senate basically following the Paterson plan and the House more directly representative of the nation's overall population. Paterson signed the Constitution and promptly became one of its staunchest defenders. James Madison called him "a federalist of federalists."[4]

Paterson was then selected as one of New Jersey's first U.S. Senators in 1789. Here Paterson teamed up with his old college classmate Oliver Ellsworth to help draft the seminal and critically important Judiciary Act of 1789. Article III of the Constitution offered limited guidance on court design, so the Act created the federal judiciary virtually from scratch. The first nine sections of the Act were reportedly written in Paterson's hand and the balance in Ellsworth's.

In 1790, Paterson succeeded William Livingston as the Governor of New Jersey, and he was reelected annually until his appointment to the Supreme Court by George Washington in 1793 as a replacement for Thomas Johnson. Paterson thus filled the problematic "seat two" of the Court (which was like the rotating series of drummers in the movie *Spinal Tap* for a while). Paterson served for thirteen years in the seat that Rutledge and Johnson had only filled for roughly three years combined.

John Rutledge Redux—1795

John Jay retired as Chief Justice on June 29, 1795, after being elected Governor of New York (while in England!). John Rutledge saw another chance to become Chief Justice and wrote to Washington expressing an interest in returning to the Court. Rutledge had spent the intervening years as a judge in South Carolina and had apparently come to regret his decision to leave the Court. He had also, not coincidentally, run into financial problems from a bad investment in merchant ships that he had to sell at a significant loss. Like several other original Justices, Rutledge may have left town ahead of bad news from his creditors.

Washington jumped on Rutledge's offer. Rutledge was a well-respected lawyer and judge who had already been confirmed by the Senate just six years earlier. He had also been on the original short list for Chief Justice along with Jay (who just resigned) and James Wilson (who was already an Associate Justice and was starting to suffer financial woes). Rutledge seemed like a relatively safe and easy choice. On July 1, 1795, Washington granted Rutledge a recess appointment as Chief Justice pending Senate confirmation and asked Rutledge to preside over the Court's August term.

As it turned out, Rutledge was less of a sure bet than expected. Soon after being appointed and before heading north to preside over the Court in Philadelphia, Rutledge made an incendiary public speech decrying the Jay Treaty with Britain. Rutledge called it "a prostitution of the dearest rights of free men" and filled with "the grossest absurdities."[5] This was a brash stance for any Federalist, but especially for the man replacing Jay on the Supreme Court. When news of the speech spread, Senate Federalists were hardly pleased, and there was immediate rumbling about denying him confirmation.

Further, accusations of insanity arose against Rutledge. Whether or not Rutledge was actually mentally ill is, of course, impossible to know. Contemporary sources were mixed, and it's imaginable that political enemies spread the idea of his insanity falsely. Alexander Hamilton's correspondences signaling opposition to the appointment of Rutledge indulge in this rumor and others (he called Rutledge "sottish" and said he was involved in "improper conduct in pecuniary transactions").[6] Supporters claimed the opposite.

The combination of these factors led to the Senate to reject Rutledge by a vote of 14-10 on December 15, 1795. This was the first significant executive appointment to be turned back by a Senate vote. Rutledge did, in fact, preside over the Court until December, and he ruled on two cases during that period. After hearing of the Senate's negative vote Rutledge apparently attempted to drown himself off of a pier in Charleston, supporting at least the idea that he was severely depressed. He ultimately lived until 1800 as a recluse.

Samuel Chase Replaces John Blair

Soon we will return to the Chief Justice appointment, but first, Washington needed to replace John Blair, who resigned in 1796 due to health concerns. Washington now faced two vacancies on the Court and was freshly stung by the Rutledge debacle. Democratic-Republican politicians were livid about Rutledge's treatment and considered it evidence of rising factionalism. They clearly believed that Federalist Senators would not allow a Democratic-Republican or Antifederalist on the Court. Jefferson wrote that Rutledge's rejection was proof that "none but Tories" could serve in the government. One anonymous Antifederalist wrote more forcefully: Rutledge's rejection evinced "the violence of party spirit, the force of stock-jobbing influence and the prejudice of [Anglo-men]."[7] Washington hated factionalism, but by choosing only supporters of the new Constitution for his first group of nominations to the Court he was *de facto* privileging Federalists over Antifederalists in a key branch of the government. As these positions hardened into political factions and formal parties, the Antifederalists began to object forcefully.

Washington badly wanted to avoid the impression that he was factionalist, so these accusations smarted. This may explain why Washington turned to Samuel Chase to fill Blair's seat. Heretofore, Washington's picks followed a mostly clear pattern. He valued geographic diversity: all of his original appointees came from different states. He also favored Justices who had helped draft the Constitution and those who had advocated for its ratification.

Samuel Chase fit none of these patterns. He is the first Justice to come from a repeated state (Maryland). The other Maryland Justice, Thomas Johnson, had already retired, but it is notable that Washington went to Maryland again rather than choosing a lawyer from Georgia or Delaware. Two of the original thirteen states have *never* had a Supreme Court Justice (Delaware and Rhode Island), so Washington's decision not to run through the states in some order had lasting consequences.

The choice is further puzzling because Chase was not a supporter of the Constitution and was also an intemperate firebrand,

and, even worse, possibly a war profiteer. Back in Maryland he earned the nickname "bacon face" for his habit of bellowing himself red during political arguments. Washington may have hoped that a seat on the Court would mellow Chase, but sadly he remained intemperate. In 1804 the House impeached Chase for a characteristically over-the-top grand jury address. The Senate declined to remove him and he did eventually settle down for the remaining seven years he served on the Court. He was also a strong supporter of John Marshall, so perhaps it all worked out in the end.

But Chase's appointment makes more sense in context. Analysis of the whole history of Supreme Court appointments reveals that presidents like Washington who were forced to make multiple Supreme Court appointments begin eventually to suffer from what might be considered "selection fatigue." These presidents had already tapped the lawyers and judges they personally knew and trusted; then they ran through a second tier of candidates who were promising acquaintances. After the first three or four selections, one finds a strange randomness in presidential picks, suggesting that the head executive simply lost patience with the process and chose whomever was suggested to them by advisors. Some of the late FDR and Nixon appointments, for example, fit this pattern. Chase surely does.

Samuel Chase was born on April 17, 1741, in Princess Anne, Maryland. His father was an Episcopal Priest. Like Iredell and Johnson, he had no formal education. He was tutored at home by his father and then apprenticed at the law office of Hammond and Hall in Annapolis in 1759. He was a quick study, reading the law for just two years before joining the bar in 1761.

His rise in public life was meteoric. He began serving in the Maryland Assembly in 1764 at the impossibly young age of twenty-three. He was a firebrand, immediately opposing the royal governor and the Crown. He also opposed the Stamp Act of 1765 and was a founding member of the Annapolis Sons of Liberty. As a junior member of the General Assembly, Chase led a Sons of Liberty raid on the government offices in Annapolis, where they destroyed the tax stamps and burned the tax agent in effigy.[8] Chase was so unpopular with the Annapolis officials that the Mayor and Board of Aldermen officially condemned him as a "busy, restless incendiary, a ringleader of mobs, a foul-mouthed and inflaming son of discord."[9]

When the Continental Congress was convened in 1774, Chase was one of five Maryland delegates. He served in the Continental Congress until 1778 and was involved in almost everything that body did. He, Benjamin Franklin, and Charles Carroll led an unsuccessful delegation to Quebec in an effort to convince Canada to join the American colonies in declaring independence. Chase was also partially responsible for convincing the Maryland Assembly to declare independence, and he signed the Declaration of Independence on behalf of Maryland.

Wartime proved turbulent for Chase on multiple fronts. Irving Dilliard describes it thusly:

> Taking advantage of official information available to the Continental Congress, he joined with a few others in an effort to corner the flour market. The scheme became known and Chase was attacked in the *New York Journal* as having "the particular privilege of being universally despised." The excoriation, which bore the signature of "Publius," was plainly the work of Alexander Hamilton who was outraged by such conduct in the midst of the Revolutionary War. Maryland showed its disapproval by dropping Chase from its delegation to the Continental Congress for two years.[10]

Chase's flour gambit was not his only disastrous decision during the war. He invested extensively in coal and iron properties and also in businesses that bought and sold war supplies.

These investments turned out to be so poor that Chase took the humiliating step of officially petitioning his former colleagues in the Maryland legislature for bankruptcy protection in 1789, the year *after* Chase had begun work as a Criminal Court Judge in Baltimore County.

Chase also opposed the new Constitution during this period. Like many Antifederalists, he argued that the new document favored wealthy merchants at the expense of ordinary citizens of states like Maryland. He wrote an anti-Constitution pamphlet under the name of "Caution," and voted against ratifying it in the Maryland Convention. These views were hardly mainstream in Maryland at the time; ratification passed 63-11.

In 1791 Chase also became the Chief Judge for the Maryland General Court, taking over for Thomas Johnson, who had just joined the U.S. Supreme Court. This means that three Chief Justices of the Maryland General Court in a row were nominated to join the Supreme Court: Harrison, Johnson, and then Chase.

Nevertheless, Chase's future remained uncertain. Chase's outsider political views led the Maryland General Assembly to try ousting him from his judicial offices. The vote passed with a majority but failed to hit the necessary two-thirds threshold. Chase remained a Maryland Judge until 1796, when George Washington nominated him to the Supreme Court to fill Blair's seat.

The nomination was understandably controversial among Washington's cabinet and in Federalist circles. But Washington decided to heed the counsel of his Secretary of War, James McHenry, who told the president that Chase had moved beyond his "past errors" and would embarrass neither him nor the Federalists.

Ultimately, Chase did become a dedicated Federalist. But his tendency towards zealotry remained, and Chase's passionate ardor of the recently converted landed him in trouble. Given his new allegiances, Chase strongly supported John Adams for president in 1800 and reacted poorly to the election of Jefferson. In this era Justices riding circuit would preside over the impaneling of the Grand Jury at the outset of each court sitting. It was traditional for the Justices to make an opening speech to the Grand Jury explaining their duties, and also expounding on broader topics like the value of the rule of law in a democracy. Chase used this format to inveigh against the recent expansion of voting rights in Maryland by Democratic-Republican legislation: "The independence of the national judiciary is already shaken to its foundations and the virtue of the people alone can restore it. . . our republican constitution will sink into mobocracy, the worst of all possible governments...peace and order, freedom and property shall be destroyed."[11]

This jury charge, plus other politicized activities, were enough to launch an impeachment effort in the House of Representatives, accusing Chase of "tending to prostitute the high judicial character with which he was invested, to the low purpose of an electioneering partisan."[12] It was a fair description. Impeachment passed 73-32 in the House. The Senate chose not to convict, with the closest vote favoring his removal at 19-15, but still just below the necessary two thirds to convict. Enough Senators apparently thought electioneering from the bench did not reach the definition of "high Crimes and Misdemeanors."

Chase remained a Justice until his death in 1811, which ended one of the most controversial political lives in American history. After the impeachment trial Chase receded largely from the public spotlight, becoming a more quiescent presence on the Court, and, oddly, a staunch but largely silent supporter of John Marshall's coming revolution. In this regard, Chase, like Cushing, eventually settled into a key role as a supportive, back bench member of the team.

Oliver Ellsworth Becomes Chief Justice

With the failure of the Rutledge appointment as Chief Justice, Washington was back at square one. As discussed above, he turned next to William Cushing, but Cushing ultimately declined. Washington then turned to Oliver Ellsworth, an appointment that followed his earlier criteria for selecting Justices.

Ellsworth was born April 29, 1745, on the family farm in Windsor, Connecticut. The farm must have been profitable, because Ellsworth headed to Yale University in 1762 at the age of seventeen to prepare for the ministry. But Ellsworth left Yale after his sophomore year for the College of New Jersey to complete his degree, so Princeton's gain was Yale's loss. The contemporary sources are mixed, but there is some suggestion that Yale dismissed Ellsworth for behavior "in contempt of the Law of the College."[13] Historian Maeva Marcus notes dryly that "Ellsworth's career at Yale was not what might have been expected from a future minister"—he was dismissed in 1764 "after a number of mischievous incidents brought him before the school's disciplinary board."[14] Ellsworth thus joins Thurgood Marshall as a shining example to future high-spirited young people who are disciplined for "mischievous incidents." Hang in there and you might become a Supreme Court Justice.

Ellsworth seems to have found the College of New Jersey a better fit, and he began a lifelong friendship with future Justice William Paterson. Ellsworth graduated in 1766 and proceeded to read the law before joining the Connecticut Bar in 1771. Michael Krauss reports that he encountered little initial success as a lawyer, earning just three pounds in his first three years of practice.[15] Ellsworth supported himself and his family on profits from clearing and selling woodland timber from family property. His struggles eventually paid off: by 1773 he had been appointed to the Connecticut General Assembly and maintained a lucrative practice in Hartford. By the time of his appointment to the Court in 1796, he was among the wealthiest and most successful lawyers in Connecticut.

Ellsworth also served in public office continuously. He was one of five Connecticut delegates to the Continental Congress from 1778 to 1783. He was the State's Attorney for Hartford County for eight years as well. From 1784 to 1789 he served as a Judge on the Connecticut Superior Court. Ellsworth was one of three Connecticut representatives to the Constitutional Convention in 1787, and he and William Paterson played a key role in advocating for the interests of the smaller states. Like Paterson, when the bicameral compromise was reached, Ellsworth became an advocate of the new Constitution and worked hard to ensure Connecticut's ratification.

When the new government began, Ellsworth was selected as one of Connecticut's two inaugural Senators, serving in that role from 1789 to 1796. Here Ellsworth again teamed up with Paterson to draft the Judiciary Act of 1789. Between Ellsworth's work on Article III at the Constitutional Convention and his role in the Judiciary Act, Ellsworth has aptly been called the founder "of the whole system of federal courts."[16]

Ellsworth was thus a natural choice for Washington, and as a staunch Federalist and well-known Senator and patriot he sailed through the Senate confirmation. In 1799 President Adams asked Ellsworth to serve his country as the Minister Plenipotentiary to France to try to negotiate a treaty. America and France were on the brink of war over French raids on American ships and other issues. Ellsworth spent a year traveling to and from France and negotiating a treaty covering some of the American complaints. The trip proved costly to Ellsworth's own health, and when he returned to the United States in 1800 he retired from the Court, paving the way for another former diplomat to France, John Marshall, to become Chief Justice.

CONCLUSION

⌘

For clues as to the type of individuals Washington and other Founders sought as Chief Justice, consider that Ellsworth and Jay both skipped entire years of Court sittings to serve in critical diplomatic roles. Their tendency to take on extra-judiciary duties demonstrates the relative unimportance of the Court before Marshall, but it also underscores that early Chief Justices brought diverse skills and experiences, as well as high political profiles, to the position. Of course, it is not entirely fair to compare the first ten Justices to our most recent ten. Obviously the lawyers who survived and thrived through the tumult of the American Revolution had access to experiences no later American could—most notably, drafting and advocating for the new Constitution. Further, in that earlier, more generalist era, it was more common for people to be great lawyers, Senators, diplomats, and entrepreneurs all at once. All of American life is more specialized these days, not just the Supreme Court.

That said, it is fair to look back to these individuals as evidence for the benefits of a broader set of experiences and skills on the Supreme Court. It is clear that President Washington sought the "best" for the Court, just as Presidents Trump and Obama did during their tenures. That said, it is also clear that Washington's view of what constitutes the "best" was substantially different from our current conception.

PART TWO

ᖰᖰ

THE STUDIES

These biographies of John Marshall, Thurgood Marshall, Byron White, and the first ten Justices show just how far we have drifted from our original conception of who should become a Supreme Court Justice. There are two obvious objections to this argument. First, cherry-picking these thirteen Justices out of the possible 115 through American history makes the argument anecdotal. Second, everything has changed radically since George Washington's presidency, so why shouldn't the background of Supreme Court Justices? Perhaps the lesson of Washington's Justices is that we should bring back lengthy apprenticeships in which young and aspiring lawyers work as scriveners.

Fair enough. The question of if and when the backgrounds of Supreme Court Justices have changed, and by how much, is an empirical question—thirteen thumbnail biographies cannot begin to answer it comprehensively. A longitudinal study of every Supreme Court Justice and every group of Justices to sit together and decide cases, however, certainly is. Part Two discusses a massive study I undertook in 2012 (and have updated to include newer appointments) on how every Justice spent their time before joining the Supreme Court.[1] My research demonstrates just how much the backgrounds of our Justices have shifted over time and how that has affected the diversity of prior experiences on the Court.

A Brief Word on Methodology

To briefly summarize my methodology, the study collects and analyzes the annual pre-appointment experiences of every Justice, from Jay to Barrett, and every Supreme Court, from John Jay's first Court (1790–91) through John Roberts's eighth (2020–present). The study counts the number of years that each Justice spent doing a particular activity. So, for example, every year of a Justice's professional career is counted (years spent in private practice, or years spent as Secretary of State or a state supreme court justice) as well as every year of post-secondary education. I also measured where the Justices lived, and for how long. The point of the study is to measure the breadth and depth of these experiences.

There were three primary sources for the study: *The Biographical Directory of the Federal Judiciary;*[2] Lee Epstein, Thomas G. Walker, Nancy Staudt, Scott Hendrickson, and Jason Roberts's *Supreme Court Justice Database;*[3] and Friedman and Israel's *The Justices of the United States Supreme Court.*[4] In cases where there were discrepancies between these sources, or none of the sources answered a question (such as which years a Justice spent in which localities as a child) I turned to other sources, most notably and wherever possible a Justice's biography or autobiography.

Despite (or perhaps because of) these multiple sources, some discrepancies were inevitable. Justices, especially those from the eighteenth and nineteenth centuries, frequently held two or more jobs at once. As we've seen, most early Justices practiced law while serving as politicians or even as judges. Two more recent

Justices—Horace Lurton and William Howard Taft—served as law school deans (at Vanderbilt and Cincinnati, respectively) while working as Sixth Circuit Judges. Under these circumstances, the study coded both employments for the full number of years, rather than try to divide the years or assign one job primacy. This option required the least amount of determinative judgment on my part and thus was least likely to result in biased or inconsistent choices. That said, readers should remember that earlier Justices were more likely to work two jobs at once.

After settling these sorts of data conflicts, I boiled each Justice's life down to a short biographical sketch and then counted the years spent in different categories and subcategories. The broad categories studied included years spent as a lawyer, a politician, a judge, a law professor; years spent in a particular geographic location; years spent in various academic settings; and years spent in various other fields, such as journalism or entrepreneurship. These were each then divided into several subcategories.

The study then grouped the Justices into sequential "natural Supreme Courts." Each of these begins or ends as Justices retire or join, and the study refers to them by the Chief Justice's last name and a chronological number. So, Jay 1 is the first Court considered and Roberts 8 is the last. Some of these Courts existed for relatively short periods and others for much longer. The period without a chief justice in 1796 following the Senate's rejection of Justice Rutledge as Chief Justice (coded as "no chief 1796") lasted just under two months, while Rehnquist 6 (Justices Rehnquist, Stevens, O'Connor, Scalia, Kennedy, Souter, Thomas, Ginsburg, Breyer) lasted for over eleven years. There are 109 Courts through Barrett's 2020 appointment. The study then aggregates the years spent on any given experience for each natural Court to create a spreadsheet that allows comparisons across time and between Courts.

CHAPTER FIVE

❧

THE LAWYER'S LAWYERS
DISAPPEAR

Many of those who disagree that John Marshall was the great-est Supreme Court Justice instead prefer Louis Brandeis. Jeffrey Rosen's 2016 book *Louis Brandeis: American Prophet* calls Brandeis "the Jewish Jefferson" and argues that the "curse of bigness" that Brandeis deplored remains among America's central issues. Most scholars heap praise upon Brandeis's time on the Court, crediting him as the primary architect of our current approaches to the constitutional law of privacy, free speech, and freedom from government oppression and surveillance, all of which are exceedingly relevant today.

Brandeis proved influential through his dissents as much as (or even more than) through his majority opinions. His dissent in *Olmstead v. United States*, an early Fourth Amendment wiretapping case, is widely considered to be the foundation for the current approach to the right to privacy. Brandeis argued that if the prosecution wanted to use evidence gained from a wiretap of Olmstead's phone against him at trial, it should have first obtained a warrant. More importantly, however, Brandeis argued that the specific concerns of this new technology were less relevant than the individual's general right to be protected against government surveillance. Brandeis argued that the Founders had "conferred against the government, the right to be let alone—the most comprehensive of rights and the right most favored by civilized men."[1] Like John Marshall before him, Brandeis was not afraid to argue by analogy and logic. The word "privacy" does not appear in either the Constitution or the Bill of Rights. Brandeis read these documents together and as a whole, rather than limiting himself through narrow readings of individual texts.

And yet, again like John Marshall, it is hard to imagine any current president nominating Brandeis, partially because he spent his entire legal career in private practice, but also because he vocally and brilliantly denounced the growth of corporations in early twentieth-century America. In comparison to current Justices, Brandeis would look both under-qualified and over-controversial.

Brandeis was born in 1856 in Louisville, Kentucky, the youngest of Adolph and Frederika Brandeis's four children.[2] Adolph and Frederika were Ashkenazi Jews from Prague, then part of the Austro-Hungarian Empire. Adolph left for America in 1848 in search of religious freedom and a better life. By the next year Frederika and the rest of their families had joined him. The families lived in Cincinnati and Madison, Indiana, before settling in Louisville, Kentucky, where Adolph and Frederika eventually became the owners of a sprawling business empire. In 1861, when Louis was five, his father's company owned a flour mill, a tobacco factory, an eleven-hundred-acre farm, and a river steamboat named the *Fannie Brandeis*.

Brandeis spent his first sixteen years in Louisville, attending the German and English Academy and then the public Louisville Male High School. When he was sixteen his father sold his business interests and the family decamped for a fifteen-month tour of Europe. Louis ended up staying in Austria for three years. He was admitted to the German university Annen-Realschule in Dresden, where he studied for three terms. At this time the German university system was the best, or among the best, in the world, and his schooling made a large impression on Louis, "teaching him the importance of inductive reasoning, of developing new ideas by rigorously mastering facts."[3]

Brandeis returned to the United States in 1875 and enrolled in Harvard Law School. This was a brave and unusual decision in 1875, when the vast majority of lawyers entered the profession by "reading the law." Brandeis's uncle, Lewis Dembitz, was among the wealthiest and best-known lawyers in Kentucky. Reading the law under Dembitz was an obvious choice as a launching pad to a successful career in Louisville. This path would have been cheaper, easier, and likelier to result in success. Yet, Brandeis chose the more difficult and intellectually ambitious path. In 1875, Harvard Law School had not started its discriminatory quota system for Jewish students, but this hardly meant that there were many Jews on campus. To the contrary, contemporary records suggest he was either alone or one of a very few Jewish students. Brandeis was also just nineteen when he started, younger than many of his classmates. Yet he finished first in his class and set a GPA record that stood for decades.

Just as Thurgood Marshall arrived at Howard Law at the perfect time, Brandeis arrived at Harvard Law School just as the school was revolutionizing legal pedagogy. Harvard's new and innovative dean, Christopher Columbus Langdell, began just five years earlier, in 1870. Langdell redesigned Harvard's curriculum and blazed a trail for the future of American legal education. Langdell's Harvard followed the example of the German system, emphasizing a more scientific study of the law. The curriculum was built around original texts—mostly written case law. The students read cases and then attempted to synthesize them into an overarching, rational understanding of the "law." Langdell's Harvard was the perfect setting for an intellectual like Brandeis, and the future Justice championed the new approach throughout his career.

After graduating Brandeis practiced for two years in St. Louis. His family hoped he would return to Louisville, but he decided to chart his own course as a lawyer, and St. Louis was a boomtown. Yet Brandeis found the legal market flooded with competitors, and he did not enjoy the work he was able to procure. Brandeis's Harvard classmate Samuel Warren convinced Brandeis to return to Boston to join him in a partnership. Warren came from a wealthy Boston family; between his connections and Brandeis's brilliance they created a thriving corporate practice. Their firm ultimately became one of the most highly regarded and profitable in America.

The nature of Brandeis's practice was quite different from the modern Justices'. Brandeis is what we call a "lawyer's lawyer." He tried cases. He wrote wills. He advised clients. He solved problems. He helped set the model for the modern law firm by hiring graduates straight from Harvard as associates and offering them an opportunity eventually to join him as a partner.[4]

Brandeis approached each of these endeavors thoughtfully and with a deep and abiding passion for the inherent value in the practice of law. Brandeis loved trying cases—the longer and the more complicated the better: "I really long for the excitement of the contest—that is one covering days or weeks. There is a certain joy in the draining exhaustion and backache of a long trial, which shorter skirmishes cannot afford."[5] He wrote his sister, "I have spent much time of late before juries and am becoming quite enamored of the Common Sense of the people."[6]

Brandeis argued that success as a lawyer requires "knowledge, not only of law, but of affairs, and above all of men and human nature."[7] In a similar vein he thought that "[k]nowledge of the decided cases and the rules of law cannot alone make a great lawyer. He must know, must feel 'in his bones' the facts to which they apply.... The man who does not know intimately human affairs is apt to make the law a bed of Procrustes."[8] Like any good trial lawyer, Brandeis had a healthy respect for facts and context, at times ahead of technical legal knowledge. Brandeis's advice in this vein is timeless: "Know thoroughly each fact. Don't believe client witnesses. Examine documents. Reason; use imagination. Know bookkeeping—the universal language of business; know persons."[9]

Nor did Brandeis back into spending the bulk of his career as a lawyer. If Brandeis had sought a more academic life, he could have had one. In 1881 Brandeis taught Evidence for a semester at Harvard as a fill in for James Bradley Thayer. The semester went well enough that Dean Langdell offered Brandeis a job on the faculty, but Brandeis declined. In 1890 Brandeis and Warren co-wrote a *Harvard Law Review* article entitled "The Right to Privacy" that outlined many of the themes Brandeis would revisit while a Justice.[10] It is a brilliant work of scholarship and among the most influential law review articles ever written. It was the most cited law review article in American legal scholarship until 1947. Brandeis could certainly have worked as a law professor at any point before joining the Court. Yet Brandeis was immensely practical, and he was concerned with facts more than theory. Like Thurgood Marshall, Brandeis wanted to make his mark in the hurly-burly world of private law rather than the staid refuge of academia.

Melvin Urofsky's terrific 2009 biography spends a great deal of time detailing Brandeis's unique style of lawyering. Brandeis was legendary for only taking cases he felt were just, which meant he turned down about as much business as he took. He was not only a litigator, but also a counselor and problem solver. Urofsky tells a long story about Brandeis's legal work in a labor dispute between a shoe manufacturer and his workers. The shoe manufacturer claimed that his employees earned more than most shoe-factory workers. Brandeis investigated the manufacturer's business model and learned factory activity was highly volatile, changing dramatically according to customer demand that fluctuated with the seasons. While the workers earned a decent wage, they were often furloughed. Brandeis's solution? Reformat how the customers ordered shoes so that the work could be smoothed out and the manufacturing could be continuous. This helped the workers, giving them more regular work, as well as the company, because extended lead times made fulfilling orders simpler and cheaper. Urofsky's book is packed with similar anecdotes of Brandeis finding creative, business-centered solutions to legal problems, illustrating his passion for the work and his voracious intellectual curiosity. Good lawyering requires a mastery of much more than the law. It requires an understanding of the context surrounding the law. Brandeis loved learning the ins and outs of his clients' lives and businesses. He was enraptured by the opportunity to study life's rich pageant and her players.

In 1914 Brandeis published an incendiary collection of essays entitled *Other People's Money and How the Bankers Use It*.[11] Each chapter in the book had previously been published in *Harper's Weekly*. The book was a scathing attack on American investment banks (especially J. P. Morgan & Co.) and the ways that these banks contributed to monopolies and oligarchies throughout the economy. Brandeis called it the "curse of bigness." The book and the essays were enormously influential, making Brandeis not only one of America's preeminent lawyers, but also a public intellectual of the first order. Brandeis railed against large corporations and dubbed himself the "people's lawyer."

How did Brandeis square his lucrative legal business with this self-branded populist image? To an outsider, Brandeis seemed to live a double life. On the one hand, he was a multimillionaire corporate lawyer when he joined the Court in 1916. He was one of the richest and most successful lawyers in Boston and probably in the whole country. On the other hand, he was among the most influential critics of monopoly and oligarchy in the United States, so hardly an advocate of business-friendly policy.

But to Brandeis there was no conflict. To the contrary, his work as the people's lawyer was part and parcel of the work he did to bring balance and fairness to the affairs of his many business clients. In 1905 Brandeis gave a famous speech to the Harvard Ethical Society on legal ethics. His description of the problem with modern corporate lawyers explains how the "people's lawyer" can and should also serve business interests:

> It is true that at the present time the lawyer does not hold as high a position with the people as he held seventy-five or indeed fifty years ago; but the reason is not lack of opportunity. It is this: Instead of holding a position of independence, between the wealthy and the people, prepared to curb the excesses of either, able lawyers have, to a large extent, allowed themselves to become adjuncts of great corporations and have neglected the obligation to use their powers for the protection of the people. We hear much of the "corporation lawyer," and far too little of the "people's lawyer." The great opportunity of the American Bar is and will be to stand again as it did in the past, ready to protect also the interests of the people.[12]

Brandeis did not see himself as an opponent to capitalism or business. Instead, the people's lawyers worked as a bridge between regular folks and corporations, not as an adjunct to corporations. Thus, while his battle against monopoly and bigness made him an enemy of J. P. Morgan, he felt perfectly comfortable representing businesses that were less harmful, in Brandeis's view, to the public interest and more willing to take his guidance. Brandeis remains a model lawyer for study by ethicists. For example, Fordham law professor Russell Pearce argues that Brandeis is a perfect role model for modern lawyers seeking to balance a robust professional identity along with a religious and moral one.[13]

Brandeis's life and career encompass much more than this brief overview could capture. But consider how a career like Brandeis's can lead to the pragmatism and attention to detail that he displayed as a Justice. Brandeis brought an unusual understanding of the granular details and lives that make up American law to the Court from a lifetime of studying and working on them. Brandeis is a sterling example of how a varied life in the law can lead to practical wisdom.

Yet, it is hard to imagine that Brandeis would ever be nominated or confirmed today (and he was almost not confirmed in 1916). Brandeis spent a full thirty-nine years in the private practice of law before joining the Supreme Court, the most of *any* Justice in the history of the Court. By comparison, Justice Roberts leads his eighth Court with just thirteen years of practice experience.

The last potential nominee who had spent her career as a lawyer first and foremost was Harriet Miers, George W. Bush's White House Counsel, and there was a bipartisan uproar over her qualifications. She withdrew before confirmation hearings. Likewise, a current-day Brandeis would appear thinly qualified based upon "just" practicing law, rather than teaching full time or serving as a judge. But Brandeis would also be dinged for his life as a public intellectual. It is hard to imagine a current president having the fortitude to put forward such a famously vocal critic of American business practices. This is surely a grievous loss to the Court.

The Private Practice of Law Wanes

We now turn to an empirical examination of the historical prevalence of experience in private practice on the Court. Every Supreme Court Justice (and nominee) has been a licensed lawyer and, unsurprisingly, a member of the profession's elite. From the nomination of John Jay to that of Amy Coney Barrett, presidents have endeavored to choose truly exceptional lawyers and judges for the Court. One fringe benefit of this study is to see just how the definition of "elite" has evolved. It is perhaps most obvious in today's uninterest in the actual practice of law.

Given that today's Justices have not spent that much time in private practice, one of the most surprising findings of the study is the complete and total dominance, across the entirety of the Supreme Court's history, of the private practice of law as a pre-Court professional activity. Every Supreme Court Justice save two has had at least some experience in the private practice of law. The only two Justices with none? Breyer and Alito. Every other Justice spent at least two years in private practice before joining the Court.

The total time spent by our nation's Justices in private practice is 1,913 years. The next most prevalent experience? Serving as a judge, with a combined total of 698 years. American Supreme Court Justices spent roughly 250 percent more of their time in private practice than in judging before being appointed to the highest Court. On average the Justices spent more than sixteen years apiece in private practice.

Figure 5.1 shows the per-Justice measure of years spent in private practice. The solid black line shows the precipitous and historically anomalous collapse in time spent in the private practice of law. The dashed line is the average for the life of the Court:

FIGURE 5.1 YEARS OF PRIVATE PRACTICE PER JUSTICE

- -Average ━━Years of Private Practice per Justice

Roberts 8 (2020–present) reflects a new nadir for private practice experience, with just 4.4 years per Justice. This is the lowest amount ever, and well below the average or other historical low points. You can see a tiny uptick with the addition of Gorsuch to Roberts 6 (2017–18), but the trend away from the private practice of law is quite clear. Before 1994, *every* Supreme Court averaged at least 9.5 years of private practice experience per Justice. Waite 2 (1877–1881) was the all-time high, with twenty-five years per Justice. But as late as Burger 4 and Burger 5 (1975–1986) the Court averaged more than twenty years of private practice experience per Justice.

The cumulative numbers are revealing as well. The nine-member Roberts 8 has just forty years of cumulative experience in the private practice of law, less than any other Court, including the five- and six-member Jay, Ellsworth, and Marshall Courts. Louis Brandeis alone spent thirty-nine years in the private practice of law. The downward trend started forty years ago, but even so the Roberts Court is a significant outlier in terms of both cumulative experience and per capita time in private practice.

The Private Practice of Law Changes

The Roberts Justices' limited experience as lawyers is even more narrow than this empirical study suggests, however, because of the nature of the current Justices' law practices. The earliest Justices worked as solo practitioners. That job is remarkably unchanged from the time of John Jay to now. Like solo practitioners today, the early Justices were mostly generalists, taking whatever case walked through the door. They worked on criminal defense, civil suits, contracts, wills, or real estate transactions for individual clients for hourly wages or a fixed fee. The fact that John Jay's business was relatively similar to that of John Marshall, Brandeis, and Thurgood Marshall is a testament to the "small-c" conservatism of American lawyers, who have long resisted any departure from the relatively simple business model of fixed or hourly fees for individualized services.

None of the current Justices have any experience as solo practitioners or generalists. The great bulk of the private practice experience on today's Court comes from highly specialized work in large corporate law firms. The Justice with the most private practice on the current Court is John Roberts, who spent thirteen years in the D.C. office of Hogan & Hartson (now Hogan Lovells) focused largely on appellate work in the Supreme Court for corporate clients.[14] Roberts ran the firm's appellate practice, and between his law firm work and his stretch in the Solicitor General's Office he argued thirty-nine cases before the Supreme Court. In 2005, *The Washington Post* described the highly specialized nature of Roberts's career:

> John G. Roberts Jr. built a golden reputation as a "lawyer's lawyer" without doing most of the things that lawyers do. He never filed a lawsuit, addressed a jury, cross-examined a witness, took

a deposition or negotiated a deal. He never advised a client on a tax return, a plea bargain, a restraining order, a will or a divorce. If he ever got into a confrontation with opposing counsel, no one seems to remember it. That is because Roberts has spent most of his career as a star—by all accounts, a superstar—in the most rarified constellation of the legal galaxy, the exclusive club of Supreme Court appellate specialists.[15]

The other Roberts Justices who have private practice experience also worked in large New York or Washington law firms. This practice experience is narrower than the past in two important ways: the type of work and the type of clients. Big firm lawyers mostly represent organizations or corporations rather than individuals. They are also much less familiar with the ins and outs of courtroom litigation. Big firm lawyers handle large-scale litigations that rarely end in actual jury trials. They likewise spend little time on criminal defense. By contrast, solo practitioners and small firm lawyers have historically (and still) regularly practice in civil and criminal courts, acquiring a well-developed sense of what law looks like in the trenches. This does not mean that there is not much to be learned from a thriving big firm practice, it is just that the lessons favor depth over breadth and a particularly (highly remunerative) corporate sliver of the law. The quality of the experience also matches the seniority. Amy Coney Barrett spent two years as a junior litigation associate at a D.C. law firm, and at her confirmation hearings she could only remember three cases she had actually worked on in practice.

The shift on the Court towards large firm work came over time, as the elite of the bar shifted from solo practice into small firms and then from small firms into the progenitors of today's massive corporate firms. The vast majority of the early Justices worked as solo practitioners. For example, John Jay spent three years in a two-person partnership before striking out into a solo practice. The next twenty Justices only worked as solo practitioners. Over time small firms and partnerships gained ground, then large firms dominated as a result of the Industrial Revolution. During the transition, the line between a small firm and a large one was blurry. For example, when Brandeis joined the Court in 1916 his law firm, one of the largest and most successful in Boston, had just six partners and seven junior associates.[16] In 1872 there were only fourteen law firms in the country that had more than three lawyers. By 1914 there were still only 216 such firms.[17]

The first Justice I code as a "large firm" lawyer is Justice Samuel Blatchford, who practiced with the firm Blatchford, Seward & Griswald from 1854 to 1867. This firm eventually became Cravath, Swain & Moore, which is considered the prototype for future American corporate law firms.[18] Still, the firm was tiny by current standards, with only three partners and a few law clerks for most of Blatchford's tenure. The firm handled the equivalent of corporate law for their time, including cases for railroads, banks, and insurance companies. But they also handled divorces and trusts and estates, as there was limited specialization even in a "large firm" like Blatchford's in the mid-nineteenth century.

By the 1930s the great bulk of the Justices had practiced in a large firm before joining the Court, so Thurgood Marshall and Sandra Day O'Connor are the exceptions that prove the rule. They were pushed into solo practice by discriminatory hiring practices in the larger firms, the vast majority of which hired only white males. They both had to hustle for work. Sandra Day O'Connor took special pride in her humble beginnings in running a "storefront legal practice" while also raising her young children. Like solo practitioners from Jay forward she took a broad mix of work:

> We did everything we could get....If there were local merchants who needed a lease prepared or some advice concerning a contract or commercial matter, we would handle that; if people in the area had a marriage or divorce problem or had a landlord-tenant problem we were available to handle that. And we also took criminal appointments.[19]

Compare O'Connor's experience to that of a large firm attorney, both in terms of the breadth of her practice and the nature of her contacts with regular people and the nuts and bolts of American justice.

Figure 5.2 shows years per Justice in three different practice settings: solo, small partnership, and large law firm. I love this chart because it shows where elite American lawyers practiced for the last 240 years:

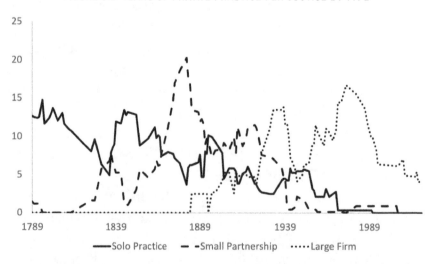

FIGURE 5.2 YEARS OF PRIVATE PRACTICE PER JUSTICE BY TYPE

Note three broad periods of dominance: solo practice from 1789 until 1866; work in small partnerships from 1866 until the 1920s; and work for large firms basically dominating from then to now.

There is one other kind of private practice that has been very rare over the years: working as a corporate or non-profit organizational counsel. Roger Taney was the first Justice with this experience: he served as a Director for the State Bank of Maryland from 1810 to 1815. Pierce Butler worked for six years as corporate counsel for the Chicago, St. Paul, Minneapolis, and Omaha Railroad in the early twentieth century.[20] More recently, three prominent Justices, Thurgood Marshall, Ruth Bader Ginsburg, and Clarence Thomas, had corporate counsel experience. I coded Marshall's twenty-five years with the NAACP, Ginsburg's years with the ACLU Women's Rights Project, and Thomas's two years working for Monsanto in the 1970s under corporate counsel. Obviously all of these are distinct experiences, but they are definitely *not* the same as private practice work for a variety of clients, so it was necessary to code it separately.

Government Lawyer

Given that the Roberts Courts have had limited experience in private practice, perhaps government work serves as a replacement? Unfortunately, not really. While the Roberts Justices do have a decent amount of experience as government lawyers, it does not match the marked decline in private practice. When you aggregate private and government lawyering into a single measure of years in practice, the Roberts Courts are still at a historical low for practice experience.

Working as a lawyer for the government, either federal or state, has historically been less common than doing so in private practice, as measured in total years spent doing either. (Note that service as a government lawyer or prosecutor is counted separately from government jobs that do not require a law license like working as an elected official or as the head of a Cabinet

Department. Those jobs are certainly valuable, but they are not a proxy for the practice of law.)

The 1940s and 1950s were the high-water mark for time spent as a government lawyer, with the first Warren Court, serving from 1953 to 1955, topping the list with seventy-eight total years and almost nine years per Justice. Figure 5.3 shows the Justices' per capita years spent as a government lawyer:[21]

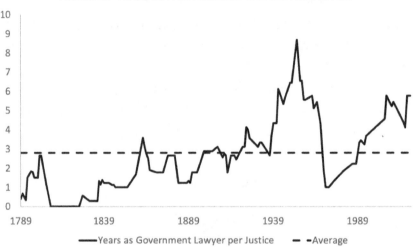

FIGURE 5.3 YEARS AS A GOVERNMENT LAWYER PER JUSTICE

——Years as Government Lawyer per Justice   – –Average

The large spike in 1953 reflects the addition of Earl Warren, who spent most of his pre-Court career working as a lawyer for state and local governments in California. Warren started as the Deputy City Attorney in Oakland and eventually rose to become the Attorney General of the State (and then the Governor). The second rise in the 2000s reflects the addition of Roberts, Alito, Sotomayor, and Kavanaugh, all of whom spent significant time working as government lawyers.

The historical low in this category came when no Justice had any service as a government lawyer from 1807 to 1826 (Marshall 3 through Marshall 7). The streak ended with the appointment of Robert Trimble, who had run Kentucky's district attorney's office for four years. The disappearance of experience as a government lawyer during this period is partially due to historical circumstance: many fewer lawyers worked for state and federal governments in the early United States. These governments were smaller and required little or no legal work.

The Roberts Courts show how experience as a government lawyer has gained prevalence, especially at the expense of private practice. Figure 5.4 is one of my favorite charts in the entire book. It shows the years spent in private practice and in government practice on the same chart. The solid line is private practice and the dashed line is government practice:

FIGURE 5.4 YEARS IN PRIVATE PRACTICE AND GOVERNMENT PRACTICE PER JUSTICE

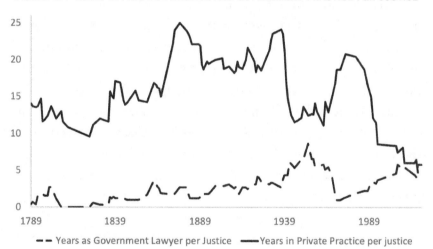

- - Years as Government Lawyer per Justice ——Years in Private Practice per justice

Roberts 7 and 8 are the first Supreme Courts *ever* in which the Justices have more experience working as government lawyers than in private practice, collectively or per capita. This occurred when Brett Kavanaugh, who spent the bulk of his pre-judicial career working in the government, replaced Anthony Kennedy, who practiced in a Sacramento law firm for twelve years.

Moreover, the Roberts Courts' experience lawyering for the government, like their private practice experience, is also weighted towards particularly elite and Supreme Court–related work. For example, the Roberts 8 Court includes four Justices who worked in the U.S. Solicitor General's Office: Roberts, Alito, Kavanaugh, and Kagan, who was herself Solicitor General. These Justices would have spent that time working exclusively on appellate matters. The Roberts 8 Justices also spent a lot of time working for more political governmental entities like the White House or various Congressional Committees. All told, Thomas, Breyer, Roberts, Kagan, and Kavanaugh all have this sort of high-level political lawyering experience, specializing largely in policy and executive or legislative branch constitutional issues.

The traditional government lawyering experience is serving as a prosecutor, and Roberts 8 does, of course, include two former prosecutors: Alito and Sotomayor. These experiences are helpful because they involve appearing in court, trying cases, and interacting with ordinary people: victims of crimes, the accused, jurors, police officers, etc. Breyer and Kavanaugh also have prosecutor-like experiences that again reflect an especially narrow and elite experience. Breyer served as an assistant special prosecutor on the Watergate Special Prosecution Force, and Kavanaugh worked on the Whitewater Investigation. The fact that ordinary prosecutorial experience is outweighed on Roberts 8 by time spent in special counsel prosecutions and the Solicitor General's Office (two jobs staffed by only the most elite American lawyers) tells you everything you need to know about our current model.

Total Practice

When you add together government and private practice into a "total practice" measure, you see that recent Courts show a marked turn away from prior experience as a lawyer since the late nineteenth century. Figure 5.5 shows total practice years per Justice:

FIGURE 5.5 TOTAL PRACTICE YEARS PER JUSTICE

The Court with the least total practice experience turns out actually to have been Marshall 7 (1824–26). John Marshall, Bushrod Washington, and Joseph Story had significant private practice experience as solo practitioners, but the other four Justices (Smith Thompson, Gabriel Duvall, William Johnson, and Thomas Todd) spent more time as court clerks, judges, and politicians. Yet since the late nineteenth century there is still a remarkable trend downwards, culminating in the Roberts Court, (again a low-end outlier) reflecting a steady recent decline in the importance of practicing law as a qualification.

Why It Matters

It may seem silly to a generation weaned on the current version of the Supreme Court, but there is much to learn laboring in the vineyards of the private practice of law. Please take a moment to remember how Brandeis waxed eloquent about all he learned about life and how to live it while he worked as a lawyer. Loyalty. Wisdom. Problem solving. A dedication to learning and understanding the facts on the ground before considering any legal solution. Every

Supreme Court decision affects millions of litigants and lawyers. Having a ground level view of these cases is enormously helpful and encourages pragmatism and modesty above more abstruse and academic concerns.

Furthermore, even the relatively meager practice experience represented on the Court today is heavily slanted towards an understanding of, wait for it, the U.S. Supreme Court itself. Many readers will see this as a bonus: these Justices are surely better prepared to serve on the Court than others with no Supreme Court experience. On this I feel confident that Brandeis, Holmes, O'Connor, and Marshall (both John and Thurgood) would likely disagree. The Court itself is a hermetically sealed chamber (for good reason), so extra time before joining the Court contemplating that chamber is not good training if you care about experience in, or understanding of, the world outside of that Court. By contrast, the rough and tumble of the practice of law as a solo practitioner or prosecutor, where a lawyer rubs elbows with people who have a wide range of legal problems, is much, much better preparation.

Practicing law engenders a healthy dose of humility on at least four different fronts. First, practicing lawyers interact with citizens from all walks of life and learn a healthy dose of respect for these individuals. Brandeis's biography conveys a man who was genuinely interested in the people he met and the lives they led. Anyone who knows an exceptional lawyer will be familiar with this exact trait. Good legal practice cultivates it.

Second, any litigator (and probably any lawyer) will lose in his career. And if he practices long enough he will lose *a lot*, even if he is a skilled advocate. Sometimes the facts are against you. Sometimes the law is against you. Sometimes both. A life practicing law inevitably overcomes any sense of infallibility.

Third, all lawyers are advocates for clients. The client comes first. Properly done, lawyers suppress their own desires to the betterment of the client. From the earliest Canons of Legal Ethics to the most recent Rules of Professional Conduct, it is made clear that the lawyer is an agent of the client and must behave accordingly. Practicing lawyers, even exceptional practicing lawyers like Brandeis, must learn to put the interests of others first.

Fourth, all lawyers in private practice, from Jay to Roberts, are involved in sales. Their job is to convince clients to exchange their money for legal advice and aid. Those working in large firms may not concern themselves with such matters all the time, but at the heart of any private practice is the drive to win paying clients.

Last, practicing lawyers also learn a lot about how courts work from the ground up. It is painfully obvious to say, but the Supreme Court has a massive effect upon the workings of every Court in America, and on every legal proceeding in the Country. The Court has ruled on areas as diverse as the denial of welfare benefits to Grand Jury criminal proceedings to antitrust trials and beyond. The Court is also at the top of the Federal judiciary, and thus plays a critical role in managing the drafting of the Federal Rules of Civil and Criminal Procedure and the Rules of Evidence. In short, when the Supreme Court rules, ripple effects strike in every court or administrative proceeding in the country, and all of the various citizens (and non-citizens) who appear in those settings. It would be optimal to have someone on the Court know something about each of these settings. But, of course, it is probably not possible to have an expert in immigration hearings, state court criminal trials, and every other possible setting on the same nine-person body. Nevertheless, a broad experience in practicing law allows at least *some* insight into the logistical results of a particular decision. Absolute expertise is infeasible, but that does not mean that almost no expertise is acceptable.

Robert Jackson as an Exemplar

Private practice is a humbling experience and has a powerful effect on the Court. It breeds pragmatic decisions of smaller scope and clearer application. Consider the humility and wisdom of Robert Jackson, who spent twenty-one years in solo practice in upstate New York before joining the Court. Jackson repeatedly brought common sense and a lifetime of broad legal practice to bear on the Court. I particularly admire Jackson's concurrence in *Watts v. Indiana*, a 1949 coerced confession case. Jackson wrote separately to note that none of the suspects who had been subject to extended and continuous interrogation had been granted a lawyer. In a strong foreshadowing of where constitutional criminal procedure would go under the Warren Court, Jackson noted that the absence of a lawyer alone made the questioning suspect. Jackson did not suggest this for academic or theoretical purposes. Indeed, Jackson knew exactly what a wise criminal defense lawyer would do: "any lawyer worth his salt will tell the suspect, in no uncertain terms, to make no statement to the police under any circumstances."[22] Here Jackson reflects the learned wisdom from a lifetime spent serving clients. A lawyer is not always necessary for technical legal work or as a trained observer of investigatory procedures. Often a lawyer is needed to tell his or her client to shut up, and as soon as possible.

Of course, Jackson's concurrence in *Watts* is just one example of how his jurisprudence on the Court was deeply grounded in the lived practice of law and common sense. Consider just a sampling of some of his most famous quotes:

With the law books filled with a great assortment of crimes, a prosecutor stands a fair chance of finding at least a technical violation of some act on the part of almost anyone. In such a case, it is not a question of discovering the commission of a crime and then looking for the man who has committed it, it is a question of picking the man and then searching the law books, or putting investigators to work, to pin some offense on him.[23]

- There is danger that, if the Court does not temper its doctrinaire logic with a little practical wisdom, it will convert the constitutional Bill of Rights into a suicide pact.[24]
- Uncontrolled search and seizure is one of the first and most effective weapons in the arsenal of every arbitrary government. And one need only briefly to have dwelt and worked among a people possessed of many admirable qualities but deprived of these rights to know that the human personality deteriorates and dignity and self-reliance disappear where homes, persons, and possessions are subject at any hour to unheralded search and seizure by the police.... So a search against [defendant's] car must be regarded as a search of the car of Everyman.[25]
- Reversal by a higher court is not proof that justice is thereby better done. There is no doubt that if there were a super-Supreme Court, a substantial proportion of our reversals of state courts would also be reversed. We are not final because we are infallible, but we are infallible only because we are final.[26]
- I see no reason why I should be consciously wrong today because I was unconsciously wrong yesterday.[27]
- Now I realize fully what Mark Twain meant when he said, "The more you explain it, the more I don't understand it."[28]

Justices like Jackson do not appear on the Court as a blank slate. They bring with them a lifetime of experiences, and these experiences help shape the work of the Court. Jackson, Brandeis, and most earlier Justices spent their careers grinding out a living case-by-case in the hurly-burly of private practice. It gave them a critical sense of how things operate "in the real world." The current Court hardly reflects this experience or the common sense that comes with it.

CHAPTER SIX

∾

OUR LOST
LAWYER-STATESMEN

In 1993 the Dean of Yale Law School, Anthony Kronman, published *The Lost Lawyer*, his classic book on the declining state of the American legal profession.[1] If you haven't read it, I highly recommend it. It is a *cri de coeur* in the best possible sense. Admittedly it is true that middle-aged men have thought that things are worse now than they used to be since biblical times. It is also true that for as long as there have been American lawyers there have been complaints that creeping commercialism is replacing the higher ideals of the profession. Remember that in 1905 Brandeis made a similar case to the Harvard Ethical Society. Nevertheless, critiques can be longstanding, predictable, and also right.

Kronman builds his case around the decline of the "lawyer-statesman," mythological lawyers of the eighteenth, nineteenth, and early-twentieth centuries who helped found and lead our country. (Kronman uses the term lawyer-states*man*, and it has become a term of art in this context, so this book will as well, but please read "lawyer-statesperson" in any contemporary context.) These lawyers moved seamlessly between private practice, elected office, and high-level executive appointments. They brought experiences and skills from one setting to another. Kronman points to John Marshall and many others we've already discussed as examples of this model. To a certain extent this book is an empirical demonstration of Kronman's argument.

Kronman's model lawyer is based in the Aristotelian concept of practical wisdom:

> The ideal of the lawyer-statesman stands for the value of public service and the virtue of civic-mindedness associated with it. And it stands, too, for the virtue of prudence, of practical wisdom. But this ideal implies more than that prudence and public-spiritedness are traits of a generally admirable kind. In addition it suggests that they are of special importance to lawyers. It suggests that the experience of lawyers promotes these traits, and their professional duties require them, in some regular and important way. The lawyer-statesman ideal points to a connection between the value of statesmanship, on the one hand, and the ordinary circumstances of law practice, on the other, and implies that this basic human excellence has special meaning for lawyers as a group. In that sense the figure of the lawyer-statesman may be said to embody not merely a generalized conception of political virtue but a distinctive professional ideal, as the hyphenated term *lawyer*-statesman suggests.[2]

We will return to an explicit argument for practical wisdom in Chapter Twelve, but the lawyer-statesman does not need to be defined in such theoretical and philosophical terms. Rather, we can know him for what he does: travel back and forth between practice and government; use his lawyerly skills in public service and his public service skills in practicing law.

With this simpler definition, there has been a multitude of lawyer-statesmen on the Court. In previous generations, Justices often arrived with the highest levels of both governmental and private experience. John Jay, John Marshall, and William Howard Taft all come to mind.

But there are other, more obscure Justices whose lives exemplify the lawyer-statesman model. Lucius Quintavius Cincinnatus Lamar II is one, a Justice whose distinctive name matched his strange life story. Just three years after he died, his son-in-law, Edward Mayes, published a hagiographic biography that covers each part of his fascinating life in exquisite detail.[3] I will note at the outset that Lamar was a slaveholder and ardent defender of the system of slavery and the Confederacy for much of his life. As described below, he softened somewhat down the stretch and his overall life story is pretty amazing, but if a reader cannot abide the idea that anyone who supported slavery could be a lawyer-statesman, feel free to skip ahead to the graphs below.

Born in Eatonville, Georgia, in 1825, Lamar came from a wealthy, slave-holding family from "the elite of the plantation aristocracy."[4] His uncle, Mirabeau Bonaparte Lamar, was a Georgia lawyer and newspaper owner who became the second President of the Republic of Texas, (following Sam Houston), just to give you a flavor for the family tradition of law, politics, and colorful names.

Lucius Lamar had his first taste of grief at nine years old when his father, Lucius Quintavius Cincinnatus Lamar I, a prominent Georgia lawyer and judge, shot himself after several months of "profound melancholia."[5] Lamar himself later suffered from spells of "vertigo or apoplexy," and contemporary sources certainly describe a family tradition of Faulknerian melancholy.

Lamar attended the Georgia-Conference Manual-Labor School, a Methodist school that paired academics with character-building farm labor. As described by Mayes, Lamar didn't excel:

> [Lamar] was not regarded by either pupils or teachers as possessed
> of any remarkable intellectual powers, or as a promising boy in
> any respect. Very frail in appearance, small for his age, and with
> a sallow complexion, he was quite reticent, slow in movement,
> giving the impression of constitutional weakness, of sluggishness
> and indolence....The other boys thought him at times morose
> and made but little effort to get near him.[6]

In 1841, at the age of sixteen, Lamar enrolled in Emory College,
a Methodist college led by the Reverend Augustus Longstreet.
Longstreet is himself a fascinating character and a critical player
in Lamar's life. Longstreet was an 1813 graduate of Yale and then
an 1815 graduate of the Tapping Reeve Law School in Litchfield,
Connecticut. Tapping Reeve was arguably the best law training
in America at the time. Its graduates included Aaron Burr, John
C. Calhoun, and Horace Mann, among many others. Longstreet
then moved back to Georgia and embarked upon a remarkably
successful career as a lawyer, judge, and politician.

In 1824 Longstreet lost two of his children to illness; this
trauma eventually led him to abandon his career as a lawyer and
become a Methodist minister. Longstreet again rose to prominence
in his new field, and in 1844 he found himself on the front lines
of the Methodist schism over slavery between North and South.
Longstreet drafted the "Declaration of the Southern Delegates"
to split the Methodist Church in two. Politically and religiously
he was a staunch supporter of slavery. The pre-history to the Civil
War is filled with southern intellectuals, often educated in the
North, who tried to build the intellectual and moral scaffolding
to support slavery. Longstreet is a perfect example.

As fate would have it, Longstreet became Lamar's mentor,
patron, and father-in-law when the younger man married Virginia
Longstreet shortly after graduating from Emory College in 1845.
The marriage sealed the bond between Longstreet and Lamar, as

Arnold Paul writes: "Longstreet exercised a very strong influence on Lamar, personally, professionally, and politically. The two filled perfectly a mutual emptiness in their lives. Longstreet had lost his only son years earlier, and Lamar had lost his father."[7]

Lamar then spent two years reading the law in the office of a Macon attorney, joining the Georgia bar in 1847. He moved to Covington, Georgia, and opened a successful solo practice. Two years later Longstreet became president of the University of Mississippi. He encouraged Lamar to follow him to Oxford to practice law and teach mathematics at the University. The portion of the state around Oxford had recently been seized from Native Americans, so it was a booming frontier town and thus a promising place to build a practice. Lamar agreed and moved to Mississippi in 1849.

Lamar taught math at Ole Miss and practiced law until returning in 1852 to his former practice in Covington. A year later, and just after returning from Mississippi, Lamar won a seat in the Georgia State Legislature as a Democrat in a Whig-controlled county. Encouraged by his success, he then sought the Democratic nomination to Congress and lost.

Disgusted by the loss, Lamar moved back to Mississippi in 1855 to resume his law practice, teach at Ole Miss, and operate a large plantation (named "Solitude") and its slaveholdings. But just two years later, Lamar again ran for Congress, again as a Democrat, but this time in Mississippi and with a winning result. Lamar arrived in Congress in 1857 on the eve of the Civil War. Over his two terms in Congress Lamar vacillated between working with Jefferson Davis to keep the Democratic Party and the nation united and following Longstreet into support of secession. He'd sign a letter arguing for patience and unification in one setting, then argue for secession in fiery speeches. At one point in 1860, Lamar was so torn that he planned to resign from Congress and take a full-time position as a professor of ethics and metaphysics at the University of Mississippi in an apparent attempt to withdraw from national politics before bloodshed became inevitable.

When Lincoln was elected in 1860, however, Lamar resigned from Congress to another purpose. Lamar was finally and wholly settled on secession and led the drafting of Mississippi's secession ordinance. When the war began he served as a Confederate Lieutenant Colonel, leading his troops into the Battle of Williamsburg in May 1862. Later, Lamar's delicate constitution reared its head again, and on two different occasions he was struck by "apoplexy" on the eve of battle and was unable to lead his troops.

In November 1862 Lamar found more suitable service. He was appointed Special Confederate Commissioner to Russia, tasked with earning Russian recognition of the Confederacy as an independent nation. He returned, unsuccessful, in 1863 and spent the balance of the war serving as a Colonel. He was a Judge Advocate with Lee's forces when the Army of Northern Virginia finally surrendered at Appomattox in 1865.

Defeated, Lamar headed home to a ravaged Northern Mississippi. He was deep in debt, his brothers had died in battle, and as a Confederate veteran he was temporarily barred from public office. Moreover, he was humiliated by the defeat of the Confederacy and felt strongly that the leaders of the Confederacy (himself included) had failed the South miserably. He returned to Oxford and resumed his law practice. He also resumed teaching at the University of Mississippi, finally accepting the appointment as a chair in ethics and metaphysics and then later as a professor of law. At this point Lamar was again resigned to living a quiet life as a professor and lawyer, at least the third time in his biography in which he reached that conclusion.

But by 1872 Lamar was back in the statesman saddle, becoming the first Democrat in Mississippi to be elected to Congress since before the Civil War. Mayes's biography paints a picture of a changed and more moderate man, who had learned hard lessons in the Civil War and Reconstruction and ran to protect southern interests and bind the country together. Historian Arnold Paul disagrees, suspecting instead a lifelong dedication to "southern sectionalism and patrician conservatism."[8] Regardless of his motivations, upon reelection to the House Lamar became "the leading southern statesman of national reconciliation."[9]

Lamar's most famous moment, including his time on the Court, came from his 1874 eulogy for the late Massachusetts Senator Charles Sumner. Sumner was a leading abolitionist and widely despised in the South. Before the Civil War he was infamously caned on the Senate Floor by Representative Preston Brooks of South Carolina, and his standing in the South had hardly improved over the intervening years. Nevertheless, Lamar, a freshman representative from Mississippi, used the eulogy as an opportunity to praise and humanize Sumner and to call for national reconciliation and forgiveness. Paul describes the speech thusly: "By every account, Lamar's eulogy of Sumner was one of the great speeches in the history of the House.... Lamar's speech, said to have brought tears from many congressmen, was widely acclaimed in all sections as a statesmanlike act of national reconciliation."[10] John F. Kennedy spent an entire chapter of *Profiles in Courage* praising the speech and Lamar's bravery and wisdom during this period of his career.

Reception to the speech was mixed in Mississippi, but Lamar was selected to represent Mississippi in the U.S. Senate in 1876. As a Senator, Lamar continued to buck local sentiment. He backed an electoral commission that gave the presidency to Republican Rutherford B. Hayes the same year, enraging Mississippi Democrats. He also voted against a "free silver" bill, which would have been economically helpful to silver mines in Mississippi.

These and other actions earned Lamar the title "the Great Pacificator." Historians are more mixed on his legacy, because while he served as a great proponent of national reconciliation in Washington, D.C., he also helped lead the way in dismantling the government of freed slaves in Mississippi and replacing it with repressive Democratic regimes. Reconciliation came at the cost of most of the gains for freed slaves in the early period of reconstruction.

Lamar was again selected to represent Mississippi in the Senate in 1881. With the election of Grover Cleveland in 1884, he was appointed Secretary of the Interior. Lamar proved adept in his new role. He took on corruption and advocated on behalf of the plight of displaced Indian tribes. Lamar's success came despite "his pensive look, slow gait, and habit of stroking his beard and quoting Horace."[11]

When Justice William B. Woods died in 1887, Cleveland nominated Lamar in his place. The Mississippian faced a Republican-controlled Judiciary Committee, embittered that the first new Supreme Court appointment in six years would be a Southerner. The Committee voted against the nomination along party lines, objecting to Lamar's experience and age (he was sixty-two). But the Committee mainly complained that Lamar had spent more time in politics and teaching than as a lawyer. (Note that the seeds of the shift to a focus upon technical legal acumen over broader experiences were already present in the late-nineteenth century.) Nevertheless, when the nomination reached the Senate floor, several western Republican Senators broke ranks and he was confirmed in 1888. He served five relatively undistinguished years on the Court before his death in 1893.

By any measure, Lamar lived an amazing and somewhat bizarre life before becoming a Supreme Court Justice. He won elections in Georgia and Mississippi, and served in Congress both before and after the Civil War. He lived in Europe for a year as a diplomat for the Confederacy. He became the leading southern voice for reconciliation after the war. He was known as one of the great orators of his time. At different points he also worked as a lawyer and a professor of math, ethics, metaphysics, and law. His career appeared finished on multiple occasions and yet he ended his life as a Justice of the Supreme Court.

Lamar seems like an especially strange choice in light of the modern Justice model, since he displayed limited technical legal excellence in his life. Yet he proved his mettle on many different fronts throughout his life, especially as a politician. Nor is he alone in this regard. The Supreme Court once regularly featured Justices who cut their teeth as politicians first and foremost.

The Lost Lawyer-Statesman

American lawyers have always played an outsized role in our government. In 1830, Tocqueville noted the dominance of lawyers and legal reasoning in *Democracy in America*:

> American aristocracy is found at the bar and on the bench.... Since lawyers form the only enlightened class not distrusted by the people, they are naturally summoned to hold most public offices. They fill the ranks of the legislature and head the administrations; they exercise, therefore, a great influence over the shaping of the law and its execution....
>
> Lawyers in the United States constitute a power which is little feared and hardly noticed; it carries no banner of its own and adapts flexibly to the demands of the time, flowing along unresistingly with all the movements of society. Nevertheless it wraps itself around society as a whole, is felt in all social classes, constantly continues to work in secret upon them without their knowing until it has shaped them to its own desires.[12]

Lawyers were particularly dominant in political life during our country's birth. Almost half of the signers of the Declaration of Independence and two thirds of the framers of the Constitution were lawyers.[13] Three of the first four, six of the first eight, ten of the first thirteen, and twelve of the first sixteen presidents were lawyers.[14] Overall, more than half of our presidents have been lawyers. Three quarters of our vice presidents have been as well, as well as three quarters of our Secretaries of State and Treasury.[15] Lawyers have traditionally predominated in both federal and state legislatures.[16]

Every single Supreme Court Justice has been a lawyer, but many have also cut their teeth as politicians or Cabinet Secretaries. Historically there is a long tradition of lawyer-statesmen on the Court. Here we consider the prevalence of political experience pre-appointment.

Elected Office

When Sandra Day O'Connor retired in 2006, for the first time in its history the Supreme Court included no Justices with elected political experience. In some ways O'Connor may seem an unlikely avatar for the politician-Justice. After all, O'Connor's highest elected office was as a state senator in Arizona, and many other Justices had more highly decorated political careers.

And yet, O'Connor's experience in the Arizona State Senate is actually a perfect example of the powerful effect a stint as a politician can have on the Court. In 1969 O'Connor had been appointed to a vacant State Senate seat in Arizona; she then won reelection twice. She eventually rose to become Arizona's Senate Majority Leader, the first woman in America to reach that position in state government. The role required all of O'Connor's many skills. She worked to forward the Republican legislative agenda with a special focus on women's issues like the ERA. She did all of this with trademark style and grace, but also steel. In one heated exchange with a fellow Republican Senator her opponent grew so heated he told O'Connor "If you were a man, I'd punch you in the mouth." To which O'Connor replied, "If you were a man, you could."[17] O'Connor channeled these skills and experiences as a Supreme Court Justice, and she always reflected a special sensitivity to, and understanding of, the challenges of the legislative process.

As a Justice who had previously held elected office, O'Connor was the last of a decorated bunch. The sheer variety and scope of the political experience on the Court throughout its history is staggering. As discussed earlier, William Howard Taft served as president and John Jay as president of the Continental Congress, so two different Chief Justices have held the top executive position in the nation. There have also been fourteen Justices who were previously U.S. Senators, seventeen who had been members of the U.S. House of Representatives, and five who served in the Continental Congress. Ten Justices had been governors. Five had been mayors of cities ranging in size from Detroit in the 1930s (when it was the fourth largest city in America) to Utica, New York, in 1844, when Census figures suggest a population of under 13,000. Forty different Justices had pre-Court experience as state legislators, roughly 35 percent of all Justices in our country's history.

Aggregating all of these experiences demonstrates that Supreme Court Justices spent a large portion of their careers in elected public service. Collectively through 2020, Supreme Court Justices spent 500 total years as elected officials, more than the 452 years they spent as appellate judges. The only two categories that surpass elected office are time spent in private practice and experience as a judge (district and appellate combined).

Since O'Connor's retirement, the Supreme Court has had no Justices with experience as an elected official. Roberts 7 had collectively spent eighty-one years sitting on the Federal Court of Appeals, the most ever on a Court, and *zero* years in elected office. Figure 6.1 shows the precipitous decline in Justice political experience:

FIGURE 6.1 YEARS IN ELECTED OFFICE PER JUSTICE

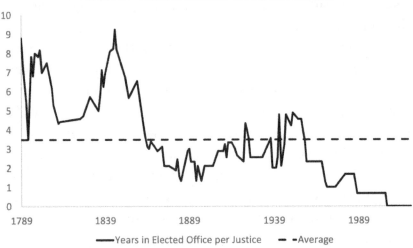

The high point for the Court's electoral experience was Taney 7, in 1845–46. Six of the eight Justices on that Court had been elected to office, including Roger Taney himself (Maryland legislature), John McClain (U.S. House), James Wayne (Mayor of Savannah, U.S. House), John McKinley (Alabama legislature, U.S. Senator), Peter Daniel (Virginia legislature, privy council, and lieutenant governor), and Levi Woodbury (U.S. Senator and Governor of New Hampshire). In addition to these six experienced politicians, a seventh, Samuel Nelson, had unsuccessfully run for the U.S. Senate the year before he was appointed to the Court.

The Court with the second most political experience? The very first Supreme Court, the five-member Jay 1 Court. Four of the first five Justices had experience as elected officials, including John Rutledge's three decades in elected office in South Carolina. Rutledge held almost every elected office in South Carolina except for Senator, servings as a state legislator, the Governor, and a Congressman.

After the Vinson Courts of 1946–1953 and the first three Warren Courts of 1953–56, political experience on the Supreme Court precipitously declined. Is it possible that Warren's extensive experience in elected office, plus that of four other Justices (Reed, Burton, Black, and Minton), was responsible in some way for that Court's ability to reach unanimity on the particularly divisive issue of *Brown v. Board of Education* in 1954?

Of course, Vinson himself was a roadblock to unanimity in *Brown* before he died, and he was himself a decorated congressman from Kentucky. Likewise, Taney 7 included many of the same Justices who decided the disastrous *Dred Scott* decision. Having politicians on the Court doesn't guarantee admirable decisions. It's always important to remember that causation, correlation, and backgrounds can be hard to disentangle on the Court.

Non-Legal, Non-Elected Government Service

Previous Justices also served in high-level, non-judicial appointed positions. For this category I count appointed non-legal service of all stripes, from cabinet level appointments in the federal government to lower-profile appointments to a clerk's office or a schoolboard. I count serving as the Attorney General of the United States in this category because that job is closer to serving as Secretary of the Interior than to a more explicitly legal job like being the U.S. Attorney for a district or Solicitor General.

Here, too, the full scope of pre-Court experiences is breathtaking. Eight different Justices served as the Attorney General of the United States. Five served as Secretary of State. Four were Treasury Secretaries. Three served as Secretary of the Navy and two as Secretary of War.

In a sense, it is not that surprising that these Cabinet members ultimately became Supreme Court Justices. Given their appointments, these figures would have had at least some favor in the eyes of the president. But the last Attorney General to join the Court, for instance, was Tom Clark in 1949, a full seventy years ago. From 1836 to 1949, the vast majority of the Courts had at least one Justice with experience serving as Attorney General. But imagine the political backlash that would ensue today if a president appointed William Barr, Jeff Sessions, Loretta Lynch, or Eric Holder to the Court. Perhaps modern Attorney Generals now accumulate too much baggage for a nomination.

Moreover, compare the breadth of experiences and skillsets of the earlier Justices who held positions as Secretary of State, Secretary of the Navy, or Secretary of the Treasury to the narrower experiences of the current Justices. It is hard to imagine any of these Justices running our military or diplomatic efforts given their lifelong focus on technical legal excellence. Our current Justices are very likely amongst the most book-smart group to ever serve on the Court, but could any of them serve as Secretary of Defense or State?

Justices also served in less ballyhooed governmental roles. The study also coded this work as non-law government service. For example, Lewis Powell served nine years as the appointed Chairman of the Richmond Public School Board.[18] Powell was Chair during the tumultuous post–*Brown v. Board* integration period for public schools, and biographers have long credited that experience with influencing how Powell approached issues of race and the scope of the remedial powers of the Court.[19]

Non-legal, non-elected government service was less common historically than working as a lawyer, judge, or politician. The Roberts Courts have been just above the median, but still in the middle with 14–17 cumulative years and roughly 1.5 years per Justice. Figure 6.2 shows that this experience ran high for the first fifty or so years of the Supreme Court and has remained relatively low since:

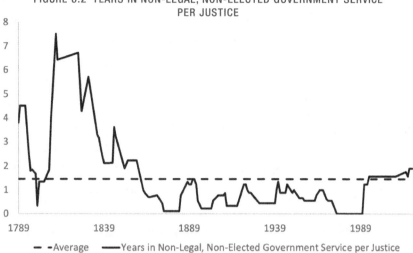

FIGURE 6.2 YEARS IN NON-LEGAL, NON-ELECTED GOVERNMENT SERVICE PER JUSTICE

− −Average ━━Years in Non-Legal, Non-Elected Government Service per Justice

The period between 1975 and 1991, when there was zero non-law service experience on the Court, occurred when William O. Douglas, who had spent five years at the Securities and Exchange Commission, including three as the chairman, left the bench. The streak ended in 1991 with the appointment of Clarence Thomas, who had been the chairman of the Equal Employment Opportunity Commission.

The six-member Marshall 5 Court is the high point for this type of service. Two Justices on that Court had particularly lengthy periods in government service. Thomas Todd spent seventeen years serving as the clerk to various courts and the state house in Kentucky before joining the Court, and Gabriel Duvall spent nine years as Comptroller of the Currency in federal service and another eight years as a court clerk and the Maryland Commissioner to Preserve Confiscated British Property.

The careers of these Justices are particularly strange when compared to those of the modern Court. Justice Gabriel Duvall was appointed while serving as Comptroller of the Currency.

Thomas Todd rose from court clerk for the Kentucky Court of Appeals to serving on that same court, rose again to a seat on the Kentucky Supreme Court, then again to the United States Supreme Court. No other Justice had more experience in a clerk's office than Todd, although other Justices like Duvall, Woodbury, and Matthews also worked as clerks. Under the current model it is hard to imagine a member of the Kentucky Supreme Court joining the Court, let alone a lawyer who had spent the bulk of his career running a clerk's office. Current Supreme Court Justices cut their teeth clerking on the Supreme Court. Older Justices served as the actual clerk of a court. An actual clerk of court spends every day interacting with the public and operating the ground-level mechanics of American justice. Supreme Court clerks focus on research and writing and are almost as cloistered as their bosses.

Why It Matters

The ideal of the lawyer-statesman is at the heart of this book. It may not be the case that every lawyer on the Court should fit this model. That would be historically anomalous and probably unwise. Even the first Jay and Marshall Courts included our friend the non-politician William Cushing. Nevertheless, it is likewise worth considering whether we should have *no* lawyer- statesmen on the bench. By effectively barring politicians we have eliminated one of the main paths to gaining relevant non-law-oriented government experience.

Perhaps this call for more politicians on the Court will sound discordant with the typical view of the Court today. Surely the *problem* with the Court is that it is too political, or at least seen as such. How would appointing politicians possibly help? Many believe that the Court is filled with politicians hiding their biases in the robes, protected by lifetime tenure, dressing up their party-line decision in fancy legalese. Surely adding *actual* politicians to the mix will only make the issue worse.

Here, we run into several different implications of the words "politician" and "political." In modern parlance, "politician" is often an insult, because it insinuates that a person is narrowly partisan and works only for himself or his political party. Yet, despite counting no former "politician" among them, members of the current Court face accusations of political bias that seem more salient than ever. In fact, if we consider the partisanship of a Court to be inversely related to the occurrence of "partisan drift" (Justices drifting away from the positions held by the president who appointed them), then the Court of today is probably more political than that of the mid-twentieth century, when former politicians regularly sat as Justices. Byron White and Felix Frankfurter were Democratic appointees who are often said to have drifted towards a more conservative jurisprudence. A great number of Republican appointees have been accused of drift (including some former politicians and some long-time judges)—Warren, Brennan, Stewart, Blackmun, Stevens, O'Connor, Souter, Kennedy, and Roberts, among others. Fear of drift is actually a driving force behind the current model of Justice. Long experience as judges, professors, and firmly entrenched partisans pre-Court is seen as a way of demonstrating that a particular candidate won't drift after ascending to the bench, regardless of whether these experiences have actually reduced drift in actual practice.

My advocacy for appointing former politicians to the Court is based on their experience of being political in a very general sense: persuading voters to select them for office, and, once elected, persuading both allies and opponents to join them in governance. Being a successful politician in American democracy requires a whole bevy of skills that Supreme Court

Justices need in order find success. O'Connor is a terrific example. Earl Warren is as well. John Marshall is perhaps the greatest example ever.

These former politicians in Supreme Court history have managed to bring disparate coalitions of Justices together to win the majority. Justice biographies are packed with such stories of political persuasion. The most successful Justices work on their colleagues on multiple fronts: They get to know them off the Court. They lobby and cajole them on the Court. They build up good will by voting yes on some cases in the hope of building other coalitions on later cases. They assign opinions strategically to lock in new coalitions featuring junior Justices who aren't necessarily natural allies. They likewise develop long-term alliances with colleagues that they can count on in thick and thin. They rewrite their opinions repeatedly and carefully to keep their majority intact, often answering objections they consider picayune or frankly stupid. They do all of this with an eye towards the long game.

Some will object to the idea of the Justices playing these sorts of games. They should read *Nine Scorpions in a Bottle* or *The Brethren*. It is hard to say whether the current group of Justices has more or less skill in this area than previous ones, as it is hardly a measurable skill. That said, it seems plausible that the current prevalence of 5-4 decisions along hardened partisan lines has at least something to do with the total lack of politicians on the Court. To be sure, Justice Kagan or Roberts, for instance, may well be naturally skilled in this arena (try being Dean of Harvard Law School without learning something about cajolery!), but appointing politicians who have demonstrable expertise in the art of compromise could only help. Paradoxically, eliminating politicians has resulted in a Court that is *more* partisan than before.

Further, remember that the much of the Court's work involves overseeing the activities of the government's other two branches. The Court continuously considers legislative intent, legislative drafting, or the underlying reasoning of executive action. Here experience as an elected politician is, of course, critical. Commentators from *The Federalist* forward have noted that there is something inherently anti-democratic about judicial review of the political branches. This is by design and absolutely appropriate. Nevertheless, given the first waves of Supreme Court appointees, it seems likely that the Framers thought the Court would include former politicians with real knowledge of the legislative process and the messy compromises that legislating or drafting regulations requires. Just as it is easier to interpret and apply contract language if you have actually drafted a contract, knowing how laws are drafted from the inside naturally helps in interpretation.

Would appointing Republican Senator Mike Lee, or former President Barack Obama, really make the Court more functional or less partisan, either in the eyes of Americans or in actuality? In short, yes. Former politicians would bring a different set of skills to the Court and would improve its work. I firmly believe that a broad diversity of experiences is important and that experience as an elected official brings a completely different expertise and approach to problem-solving to the Court. Admittedly, some politicians are more likely to work for pragmatic compromise than others, so Justice Ted Cruz or Elizabeth Warren might be tougher sells. That said, I would prefer the appointment of even a very strong partisan politician to yet another cookie-cutter, hyper-elite judge from the D.C. Circuit.

From its inception in 1789 until Justice O'Connor retired in 2006, the Supreme Court included a Justice with at least some elected political experience. For 217 years this type of experience was a critical element to the Court's makeup. As matter of historical precedent, we have erred in abandoning this tradition. It has made the Court weaker and its work product and decisions worse. We should bring the lawyer-statesperson back to the Court as soon as possible.

CHAPTER SEVEN

❦

THE TRIUMPH OF THE CIRCUIT COURT JUDGE

There is, of course, a strong, intuitive appeal to appointing former appellate judges to the Supreme Court. First, former judges have already succeeded at a job closest to that of serving on the Supreme Court. Demonstrated excellence at being a judge would seem to indicate readiness for being a Justice. Second, presidents want an idea of how a Justice will behave on the Court in order to avoid drift. A demonstrated judicial record gives presidents that evidence.

And yet, experience as a judge has hardly been a guarantor of success or predictability on the Court. The three Justices who joined the Court with the most judicial experience—William Cushing, David Brewer, and Horace Lurton—hardly serve as endorsements for judicial experience. Of course, other Justices with extensive and exceptional judicial experience had stronger records and results. Among these are Oliver Wendell Holmes and Benjamin Cardozo, whom I will discuss at length below.

William Cushing Redux

The Justice with the longest pre-Court experience as a judge is

William Cushing, who, you'll notice, has become something of a punching bag in this book. Cushing worked a full twenty-nine years as a judge before joining the Court, the most time spent in that role pre-appointment in Supreme Court history. Cushing had a full soup-to-nuts experience, handling every level of judicial work available in Colonial and post-Revolution Massachusetts. Cushing served as a Justice of the Peace and Probate Court Judge in rural Lincoln County, then as a Superior Court Judge, and finally as the Chief Judge of the Superior Court in the new Commonwealth of Massachusetts, the highest judicial office in the State.

Given Cushing's long tenure on the bench and track record, Washington probably hoped Cushing would shine on the Court. Not so much. In twenty-one years on the Court he wrote just nineteen opinions, most of which were short and straightforward. Cushing is in the running for the title of least impactful Justice ever.

David Brewer

The Justice with the second most pre-Court experience as a judge, David Brewer, undoubtedly had a much greater impact than Cushing. Whether that impact was a positive one—or what his appointing president, Benjamin Harrison, was hoping for—is much less clear.

Brewer spent twenty-eight years in judicial office before joining the Court. Like Cushing, he served at every level of the judiciary before becoming a Justice, working his way up from an administrative post to the Kansas Supreme Court and a federal judgeship on the Eighth Circuit. Brewer was born in 1837 in Smyrna, a city in the Ottoman Empire (now Izmir, Turkey). His parents were missionaries. He was raised in Connecticut, graduated from Yale in 1856, attended Albany Law School, and read the law with his uncle, David Dudley Field. (He was also related to Justice Stephen Field.) From here Brewer's life took an adventurous turn. He traveled west and briefly (and apparently unsuccessfully) prospected for gold on Pike's Peak in Colorado before settling down in Leavenworth, Kansas.

Brewer practiced law for three years in Leavenworth before beginning his judicial career in 1861 as the commissioner of the federal district court, an administrative position. He was elected to the county court bench as a Probate and Criminal Court Judge in 1862. In 1865 he became a Judge in Kansas's First Judicial District. In 1870 he was elected to the Kansas Supreme Court and then reelected in 1876 and 1882.

In 1884 President Chester A. Arthur appointed Brewer to the U.S. Circuit Court for the Eighth Circuit. Five years later Benjamin Harrison appointed Brewer to the Supreme Court to replace the recently deceased Stanley Matthews. Harrison was a one-term Republican president serving from 1889 to 1893 during a tumultuous period in American history. Among his signature achievements were the passage of the Sherman Antitrust Act and the appointment of four Supreme Court Justices. It can be difficult to map today's ideological denominations on political figures of the past, but between the Sherman Antitrust Act and a large increase in federal spending under Harrison, it is fair to say that the president was not a limited federal government, "small-c" conservative.

It appears he was looking to shape a Court that would sign off on this legislative economic agenda. With Brewer's lengthy history as a judge, Harrison presumably thought he had a good read on what kind of Justice he would be on the Court. Harrison's Attorney General, William Miller, described Brewer as a judge who had "not only the courage to decide against wealth and power and corporations, but what is a much more severe test to decide in their favor when the law and justice of a case demand it."[1]

As it turned out, Brewer proved much more adept at Miller's "severe test" of ruling in favor of freedom of contract and against government economic regulations than in ruling against wealth, power, and corporations. Historian Henry Abraham describes Harrison's legacy:

> Together with Justice Peckham, [Brewer] became the leader of the ultraconservative economic *laissez-faire* advocates on the Court, not only smoothly fitting into the Fuller Court's approach to public policy but going well beyond it in terms of judicial activism on behalf of vested property rights based on the "freedom of contract" doctrine.[2]

Nor did Brewer take much time to "drift." He argued these points publicly and while Harrison was still president, including at an 1891 Yale Law School address entitled "Protection to Private Property from Public Attack," in which Brewer pilloried governmental efforts to rein in private property rights, including at least by implication many of Harrison's own policies.[3]

Brewer lived up to these words when he joined the majority in *U.S. v. E.C. Knight Company*, an 1895 case that severely limited the reach of the Sherman Antitrust Act by limiting it solely to interstate, rather than intrastate, activities.[4] Thus, Benjamin Harrison's nominee helped cripple one of his main legislative achievements just six years after his appointment. Brewer's vote was not determinative (it was an 8-1 decision), but, regardless, Harrison could not have been pleased. Brewer's lengthy record as a Judge hardly offered Harrison much protection against unfavorable votes in critical cases.

Horace Lurton

Horace Lurton is the Justice with the third most experience as a judge, at twenty-six years on the bench before appointment to the Court. Like Brewer and Cushing, he worked at every level of the judiciary. But before we cover Lurton's judicial career, a word on his more swashbuckling youth.

Lurton was born in Kentucky but spent the bulk of his life in Clarksville, Tennessee, a medium-sized town on the Cumberland River, roughly forty miles north of Nashville. It is unclear from the historical record whether Lurton's family owned slaves (his name does not appear on several lists of former slave owners on the Court), but there is no doubt that Lurton was a supporter of the Confederacy and of southern interests, especially as a young man. Lurton left Tennessee to attend Douglas University (now defunct) in Chicago at the age of sixteen.

In 1861, when the Civil War began, Lurton dropped out of school and joined the Fifth Tennessee Infantry Regiment. By February 1862 he was a battle-hardened sergeant major. Here he developed a serious lung ailment, and Lurton was ordered to rest and recuperate. He returned home but only rested for three weeks before re-enlisting. (He had heard that General Grant and Union troops were advancing on Fort Henry, on the Cumberland River, and Fort Donelson, on the Tennessee, and rushed to join the Second Kentucky Infantry.) The battles went poorly for the Confederates: Lurton and twelve thousand other Rebels were captured at Fort Donelson.

Lurton was marched to the military prison at Camp Chase in Columbus, Ohio. A few weeks later he and some compatriots escaped, "taking advantage of Camp Chase's notoriously lax security."[5] Here Lurton signed on with General John Hunt Morgan, the "Thunderbolt of the Confederacy." Morgan commanded an irregular cavalry that waged a guerilla war against the Union forces behind enemy lines, attacking supply routes, burning bridges, and dynamiting railroad tracks. Lurton joined Morgan as the cavalry group robbed, stole, and killed its way through Union-occupied Tennessee, Indiana, Kentucky, and Ohio. Over time, defeating these guerillas became a priority for the Union, and Morgan grew a little too bold. Lurton and the bulk of Morgan's forces were defeated and captured in 1863 in Salineville, Ohio, after wandering perhaps too far behind enemy lines.

Lurton was again sent to a prison camp, this time for eighteen months on Johnson's Island in Lake Erie, a less porous jail than Camp Chase. Here Lurton's lung ailment returned and worsened into tuberculosis—close to a death sentence in 1865, especially in a military prison on an island in Lake Erie. Lurton's mother visited him in the prison and became so alarmed at his health that she traveled to Washington, D.C., to personally petition Abraham Lincoln for Lurton's release into her care. Through a series of extremely fortuitous events, Sarah Lurton met with Lincoln on February 23, 1865. Justice Lurton reportedly told the story thusly:

> "Mr. President my boy is doomed to death unless I can get him back to Tennessee. I want to take him home," said Sarah Lurton.
>
> Lincoln replied, "I will parole him in sick leave."
>
> "But," she said, "then it will be too late. I want to take him home with me." President Lincoln then wrote a note "Let the boy go home with his mother."[6]

Lurton repeated this story with gusto and apparent admiration of Lincoln for the rest of his life. The young soldier did, in fact, leave prison with his mother to recuperate in Clarksville, marking the begin of a new, and much calmer, life. Thereafter he graduated from Tennessee's Cumberland Law School and then spent the balance of his career in private practice and on the bench, living in Clarksville, Tennessee, until he joined the Supreme Court in 1909. Lurton was a classic small-town lawyer, practicing in small partnerships, serving part-time as the President of the Farmers and Merchants Bank, and as a vestryman in the Trinity Episcopal Church.

Lurton's judicial career began with his appointment to the Chancery Court in 1875. After three years he left the bench to return to his more lucrative work in the private sector. In 1886 he was elected to the Tennessee Supreme Court and served as an Associate Justice until 1893, when Grover Cleveland appointed him to the Sixth Circuit Court of Appeals.

The Sixth Circuit was a powerhouse during Lurton's sixteen years serving on it. Lurton replaced his fellow Tennessean, Howell Jackson, who just been appointed to the Supreme Court. William Howard Taft, at the young age of thirty-six, was the presiding judge when Lurton joined the court. Also on the Sixth Circuit was future-Justice William Rufus Day.

Lurton came quite close to being appointed to the Supreme Court by Theodore Roosevelt in 1906, but the president chose to appoint a fellow Republican, William Moody, despite strong recommendations from Lurton's former colleagues on the Sixth Circuit, Taft and Day. Lurton finally had his chance when Taft became president in 1909. At sixty-five Lurton was the oldest person ever appointed to the Court, and he only served for a little over four years before he died.

Given that his appointment was basically a lifetime achievement award given by a dear friend and former colleague, it would be somewhat unfair to say that Lurton's performance on the Court was a disappointment. There were multiple excellent political and practical reasons for Taft to appoint a younger Republican from a state that hadn't seceded. Lurton was no decorated Justice, nor was he a key part of Taft's legacy. Henry Abraham described his tenure as too short "to establish a record, let alone leave an imprint; what little there was pointed to a cautious, competent jurist steeped in judicial self-restraint."[7]

Counterpoint? Oliver Wendell Holmes and Benjamin Cardozo

As we've seen, long experience as a judge hardly guarantees an exceptional career on the Court, nor does it eliminate the possibility of partisan drift. That is not to say that all former judges have been disappointments. Any list of the greatest jurists to sit on the Court would include Oliver Wendell Holmes and Benjamin Cardozo, both of whom were appointed after lengthy, distinguished careers as judges. President Hoover selected Cardozo to replace Holmes on the Court, seeking to replace one intellectual giant with another. And yet the example of these two Justices doesn't quite require us to endorse pre-Court judicial experience.

It is true that Cardozo joined the Court after an exceptionally distinguished eighteen years serving as a justice or judge on the highest court in New York State. It is also true that Cardozo is among the most influential American legal thinkers and judges, an easy selection for a "Mount Rushmore" of jurists. But it is also true that Cardozo built his reputation, not on the Supreme Court, but as America's greatest common law judge. Any first-year student of Torts or Contracts can reel off some of Cardozo's greatest hits on the New York Court of Appeals: *MacPherson v. Buick* (eliminating the privity bar in torts), *Murphy v. Steeplechase* (the "Flopper" case establishing acceptance of risk as a defense to negligence), *Palsgraf v. LIRR* (the seminal explanation of proximate cause in negligence), or *Jacobs & Young v. Kent* (constructive conditions in contracts).

Perhaps it is unfair to compare Cardozo's work during his six years as a junior Justice on the Court to eighteen years of absolute mastery on New York's highest court. Cardozo may well be the greatest American judge, but he definitely did not match that performance in his relatively short stint on the Court. Some of this is circumstance. Junior Justices rarely get to write the juiciest cases. Some of it is bad luck. Cardozo fell ill and died at just sixty-eight, while Holmes served thirty years on the Supreme Court. Some of it was disposition. The Supreme Court did not actually play to Cardozo's strengths. As Cardozo himself stated, "[The New York Court of Appeals] is a great common law court; its problems are lawyer's problems. But the Supreme Court is occupied chiefly with statutory construction—which no man can make interesting—and with politics."[8] Cardozo's common law opinions are packed with these sorts of common sense bon mots delivered to devastating effect. These skills seemingly went to waste on the nation's highest Court.

Holmes, of course, is a different story. Those who disagree with my earlier suggestion that either Marshall or Brandeis was our greatest Justice might instead endorse Holmes for the title. It is absolutely a valid stance to take: Holmes was one of the very best Justices we've had as a nation. He also had a lengthy pre-Court judicial career. It is fair to consider Holmes a counterpoint to the Justices discussed above.

Yet, unlike these other Justices, the pre-Court Holmes was not only a judge, but also a famous public intellectual and legal scholar. This is not to denigrate Holmes as a state court judge. Though he didn't write a dozen exceptionally excellent state court opinions, as did Cardozo, Holmes was still a very fine Massachusetts justice, by all accounts. It is rather to argue that his pre-Court career was more notable for his work as a legal thinker. He served as the editor to the *American Law Review*, revised the highly influential Kent's *Commentaries*, and most importantly, wrote *The Common Law* and *The Path of the Law*, still among the finest and most trenchant commentaries on American law. *The Common Law* is a short, crisp argument for legal realism and remains a terrific and very translatable read today. Professor Lisi Schoenbach situates Holmes as a "pragmatic modernist," and that perhaps explains why his writings remain powerful today: we are still living through a Holmesian intellectual moment.[9] Holmes's academic work was excellent enough that Brandeis funded a chair for him at Harvard Law in 1881 (though he taught at Harvard for less than a year before joining the Massachusetts Supreme Court).

Holmes did have a distinguished career on that court, so it is certainly fair to consider him as evidence for the benefits of appointing longstanding judges to the Supreme Court. But prior experience as a judge is hardly a guarantee of triumph on the Court, as we've seen with some other historical examples.

Total Judicial Experience

Nevertheless, judicial experience, and particularly experience as a federal court of appeals judge (preferably from the D.C. Circuit), has become the dominant pre-Court experience. Every Supreme Court in our history, from Jay 1 to the current Court, has had at least one Justice with some prior judicial experience, and most have had multiple former judges. Figure 7.1 on the next page shows the years per Justice spent as a judge before appointment, including experience as any sort of judge—state or federal, appellate or trial.

Figure 7.1 shows three distinct periods when prior judicial experience was dominant on the Court: the first Jay Courts, the Fuller Courts of 1893–1910, and the Roberts Courts. The Supreme Court with the most judicial experience is actually the very first Court, the five-Justice Jay 1 Court that sat from 1789 to

FIGURE 7.1 YEARS OF JUDICIAL EXPERIENCE PER JUSTICE

1790. Cushing, Blair, Jay, and Rutledge all served on state courts before joining the Supreme Court, and Cushing's twenty-nine years alone pushed the per-Justice average significantly higher. The 1790 addition of a sixth Justice with just a year of judicial experience, James Iredell, caused the per-Justice average to dive from over ten to under eight, and the general downward trend in judicial experience continued on through the Marshall Court.

There are also three eras of generally below-average judicial experience, culminating in the nadir of Hughes 6 and 7, when only *one* Justice had prior judicial experience: Hugo Black, who served for two years as a Police Court Judge in Birmingham, Alabama. Judicial experience remained limited from the 1940s until as late as the Warren Courts of the mid-1960s. For example, Potter Stewart's paltry four years as a Federal Judge on the Sixth Circuit led the Warren 8 Court (1965–67) in judicial experience.

Things have certainly drifted the other way since, as judicial experience has climbed from 1.7 years per Justice on Warren 8 to 9.8 per Justice on Roberts 6, the highest since Fuller 5 topped out at over 10 years per Justice (1893–94). Eight of the nine Justices on Roberts 6 had prior judicial experience (Kagan did not). Sotomayor and Alito led the charge with 18 and 16 years, respectively. The late decline reflects Justice Barrett's relatively short three years on the bench, in comparison to Ginsburg's thirteen.

Federal Appellate Court Experience Comes to Dominate

Looking at Figure 7.1 tells us that the Roberts Courts have had a relatively high degree of judicial experience but are not without precedent. It is the precise nature of the more modern Justices' judicial experience, however, that really sets the Roberts Courts apart. Figure 7.2 shows that Roberts 6 is a high point for prior experience on a federal court of appeals (9 years per Justice), and that recent Courts are true outliers:

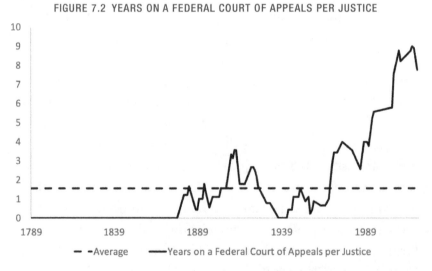

FIGURE 7.2 YEARS ON A FEDERAL COURT OF APPEALS PER JUSTICE

Of course, there was not a separate federal court of appeals before the Judiciary Act of 1869, so naturally there were no Justices with federal appellate court experience before then. Nevertheless, we've had 150 years since Circuit Courts were created, and from 1937 to 1942 the Supreme Court included no Justice who had served on those courts, so the growth has hardly been linear. Federal appellate experience remained relatively low through the 1960s. It has grown almost exponentially since.

The rise of the federal appellate court experience has meant the virtual disappearance of two other kinds of judging: trial court and state court. Looking at Figure 7.3, which shows both trial court experience and appellate court experience (including both state and federal) per Justice, it becomes clear that the rise of appellate court experience has come at the loss of time on a trial court:

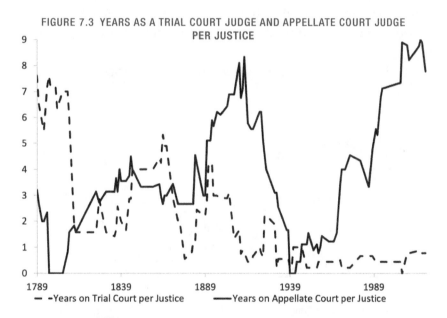

FIGURE 7.3 YEARS AS A TRIAL COURT JUDGE AND APPELLATE COURT JUDGE PER JUSTICE

For the first thirty years or so, trial judging was more common than appellate judging, which is notable because presidents had their pick of state supreme court justices if they valued appellate experience. Instead, they chose appointees with extensive trial court experience.

From 1866 to the present, appellate court judging has been the more common experience, except for the brief period of 1939–46 when appellate judging hit a modern nadir. Since 1946, appellate judging triumphed and experience as a trial judge has been negligible.

The all-time low for trial judging was 2006–2009, when the Roberts 2 Court had no Justice with any trial court experience whatsoever. Samuel Alito replaced Sandra Day O'Connor in 2006 and we lost all experience as a trial judge on the Court. In 2009 Justice Sotomayor brought seven years of experience as a federal district court judge to the Supreme Court, but trial court judging experience nevertheless remains woefully underrepresented.

Even more starkly, Figure 7.4 establishes that state court experience has entirely disappeared, after being for the majority of our nation's existence more common than federal court experience:

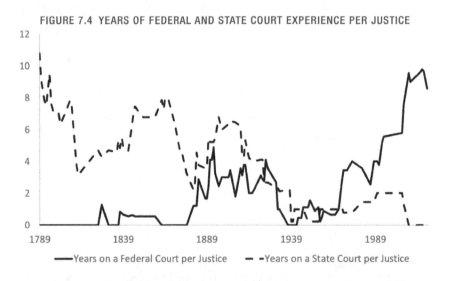

FIGURE 7.4 YEARS OF FEDERAL AND STATE COURT EXPERIENCE PER JUSTICE

——Years on a Federal Court per Justice ‒ ‒Years on a State Court per Justice

From 1789 to 1923, state court experience ran higher than federal court experience every year. It was not until 1969, when Warren Burger (who spent thirteen years on the D.C. Circuit) joined the Court, that federal court experience overtook state court for good.

The D.C. Circuit is the single most prevalent judicial experience on the modern Supreme Court. Four Justices on Roberts 7 came from that Circuit: Thomas, Ginsburg, Roberts, and Kavanaugh, making the D.C. Circuit more concentrated on that Supreme Court than any previous iterations. Wiley Rutledge was the first Justice appointed from the D.C. Circuit by President Franklin Delano Roosevelt in 1943. Since then D.C. Circuit experience has gained steam and is now the dominant judicial experience on the Court.

Another turning point came with the retirement of Justice Souter in 2009, which marked the end of any state court experience on the Court at all. This was the first time in the history of the Supreme Court that the Court lacked state court experience altogether.

Why It Matters

There is nothing wrong with having a some or even a good amount of prior judicial experience on the Court. Historically, there has always been at least one Justice with such experience. Much of the Court's work does, of course, affect and involve the daily operations of the courts. Having some former judges makes sense. That said, do we need to have *only* former judges?

There is hardly any American job, legal or otherwise, that has less contact with "ordinary people" than a federal appellate judge. Federal judges have lifetime tenure. Appellate judges are kept far from litigants and even lawyers, dealing with their cases only on lengthy paper records and monthly oral arguments. There are important institutional reasons for cloistering federal appellate judges. Wherever possible, the founders wanted to keep judges protected from bias or governmental interference. Appellate judges are supposed to stick to the record in their cases and should *not* leave their chambers to do separate investigation or interviews—all to mitigate the possibility of outside influence. That said, years spent avoiding the public hardly broaden a future Justice's horizons.

D.C. Circuit Judges are an even more rarified group, because that Circuit carries a special mix of cases focusing especially on America's administrative state.[10] Because the D.C. Circuit has direct oversight over so many federal agencies, it is often called the "second most powerful court in the country." Because of its location, its subject matter, and now its enhanced position as a stepping stone to the Supreme Court, the D.C. Circuit has become the most prestigious in the country. It draws the most competitive clerks and judges in an American legal profession obsessed with hierarchy. But why should a Circuit dominated by issues of administrative law be considered the optimal training for Supreme Court Justices? Every Circuit deals with some amount of administrative law, and they also have a much richer diversity of cases covering more aspects of American life, especially criminal and civil law.

Like much else in America, we have confused prestige with useful experience. Administrative law is complicated and important, but so are other areas of law that have a much more direct effect on Americans, such as constitutional law or criminal law. Likewise, what exactly has been the benefit of appointing these "experts" in administrative law from the D.C. Circuit? Has administrative law gotten clearer and easier to apply now that we've put the experts in charge? Hardly. Ask anyone familiar with this abstruse area: I promise you it has not improved despite the current experiences of our Justices. If we really cared so much about administrative law, we should return to appointing the heads of federal agencies like Defense or Interior to the Supreme Court. These Cabinet Secretaries surely have a better understanding of administrative law as applied in the trenches than D.C. Circuit Judges.

The loss of state and trial court experience likewise strips the Court of necessary institutional knowledge. The state court system is much bigger and more important than the federal one. The sheer caseload of state courts dwarfs that of federal courts. Gathering exact numbers for state caseloads is a challenge because of the different ways that the fifty states gather (or do not gather) their data, but in 2006 there were an estimated 102.4 million cases filed in state courts of all kinds.[11] Excluding bankruptcy, there were roughly 312,000 cases filed in federal civil and criminal courts that year.[12]

Moreover, state courts handle the great bulk of the cases that ordinary Americans encounter, including most criminal prosecutions, divorces, child custody cases, debt collection, and many others. These state courts are less fancy than their federal counterparts—they're more crowded and are typically less well funded. They are on the front line of America's access to justice and pro se litigant crises. The Supreme Court has an outsized effect on the work of these courts. Every year the Supreme Court creates case law that effects state courts in constitutional areas, criminal procedure, antitrust, etc. Our current Justices have a much more limited idea than their predecessors of how their rulings might affect the bulk of the courts in America. They also have less awareness of the popular dissatisfaction with the speed and nature of American courts, and of how additional procedural hurdles can be both a blessing and a curse.

State courts tend to be much closer to their constituents. In thirty-nine states, some or all of the judges face some type of election; state supreme courts are elected (or retained by election) in thirty-eight.[13] These elections tend to be less prominent than those for other political offices, and they're often non-partisan. Nevertheless, having a Supreme Court with state court experience could have the added benefit of adding experience in electoral politics to the highest bench.

Many would argue that a stretch as a life-tenured appellate court judge is great training for the Supreme Court. After all, the sooner Justices can get the hang of deciding cases on the merits without worrying about political blowback the better. Not all Americans agree, I promise, and a stretch on a state supreme court, or any elected court, can create a helpful counterbalance to lifetime tenure.

The lack of district court experience is likewise concerning. Sotomayor is the only current Justice with any experience as a trial court judge. District court judges have a radically different job than appellate judges or state supreme court justices. They come in contact with members of the public and many kinds of lawyers almost every day. They are typically tasked with managing a diverse range of cases, stretching from criminal trials to civil suits to rarer cases like constitutional or antitrust matters. They are also managers of a caseload that requires constant attention: deciding motions, awarding sanctions, and holding trials (although trials are less frequent today than in the past).

District courts are also tasked with working with juries, a vivid reminder of the importance that our system places on the judgment of ordinary Americans. In most civil law countries, judges of all kinds decide issues without input from juries. In America, the Sixth and Seventh Amendments guarantee a jury trial in both civil and criminal trials (with exceptions of course), and district courts have a natural dose of humility as they watch juries make the actual call as to guilt or innocence or civil liability. If you've noticed the collapse of the American jury trial and wondered what happened, the Supreme Court has chipped away at the right to a jury over the years (one example is that criminal defendants have a broader right to appointed counsel than to a jury trial). It would be fair to argue that the Court's opinions on punitive damages or civil procedure are also hostile in nature to juries. Correlation is, of course, not the same as causation, but the prevalence of trial court judging experience on the Supreme Court has collapsed during the same period in which the Court has come to treat juries as a hassle to be carefully managed, rather than a preeminent part of the system. This is, of course, the exact opposite of the constitutional design. The Framers considered the jury co-equal to judges, if not more important, not despite their lack of specialized legal knowledge, but precisely because of it!

In sum, the judicial experience of the current Supreme Court is evidence for how we have let our perception of Justice "merit" dominate our interest in having a wide range of experiences on the Court. Appellate court judging is seen as higher-level or more prestigious than trial judging, so we elevate candidates with those experiences to the Court. Likewise, because federal judges are considered higher-profile than their state judge counterparts, state court experience has been eliminated from the Court. As a result, we have a less diverse Court with less experience operating outside of the hermetically sealed world of the federal appellate courts.

CHAPTER EIGHT

❧

CHANGING CASE CONFERENCES TO FACULTY MEETINGS

The Rise of Law Professors

Whenever I hear a friend complain that the Supreme Court has never been more politicized, or that attacks on the Court have reached an all-time low, I point out that things have definitely been worse. Say, for example, when the Supreme Court was widely blamed for a decision that caused (or at least contributed to the creation of) a civil war that killed roughly 620,000 Americans (*Dred Scott*). Or when a Republican-led Congress got so sideways with a Democratic president's agenda that it shrank the size of the court from ten seats to seven, just to deny that president a chance to appoint any Justices at all (Andrew Johnson). Or, just three years later, after a Republican president was elected, when Congress boosted the Court back from seven to nine, immediately giving the new president two appointees (Grant). Or when those two new appointees arrived just in time for the Court to reverse itself on the constitutionality of paper money, despite the original precedent being set just two years before (the Legal Tender Cases).

Or consider the last time that Congress and the president came close to changing the size of the Court for political purposes: President Franklin Delano Roosevelt's court packing plan. FDR defeated incumbent Herbert Hoover in a landslide in 1932, pledging an activist response to the Great Depression. As soon as FDR was sworn in he hit the ground running. FDR was not the first leader to tout his achievements in the first 100 days in office (that honor has been attributed to Napoleon Bonaparte's first 100 days after escaping Elba), but he certainly popularized it in America. FDR's first 100 days included fifteen major pieces of "New Deal" legislation and over seventy-five laws in total, still a record for initial productivity.

Yet much of FDR's agenda was soon stymied by the Supreme Court. In a series of cases dominated by the so-called "four horsemen" (Pierce Butler, James McReynolds, George Sutherland, and Willis Van Devanter), the Court declared big chunks of the New Deal unconstitutional, including the National Industrial Recovery Act, the Agricultural Adjustment Act, railway pension legislation, farm debt relief, and state minimum wage legislation.

Roosevelt did not take these defeats lying down. In 1935 he publicly excoriated the Court for denying "the Federal Government the powers which exist in the National Governments of every other nation in the world. We have been relegated to the horse-and-buggy definition of interstate commerce."[1] The Court created a "no-man's land where no Government—State or Federal—can function."[2] These decisions had not come out of the blue. The period from 1890 to 1937 is called the "Lochner era" of the Supreme Court, after the 1905 case of *Lochner v. New York*. In this era the Court that emphasized freedom of contract and evinced a deep skepticism to any legislation regulating private enterprise. This skepticism crashed head on into the New Deal, or vice versa, depending on one's perspective. During Roosevelt's first term it looked like the Court might declare most or all of the New Deal unconstitutional.

Following a landslide reelection in 1936, FDR reached the end of his patience with the Court. In early 1937 FDR introduced the "Judicial Procedures Reform Bill of 1937," which has since become known as his court-packing plan. The proposed law allowed the president to nominate one new Justice to the Court for every sitting Justice who stayed on the Court past his seventieth birthday. The Hughes 3 Court (which sat 1932–37) was among the oldest in history. FDR could have appointed as many as six new Justices to the court. The longevity of the Hughes 3 Court was likely another motivation for Court packing. FDR had terrible luck with the Court in his first term. He faced a hostile five-man majority of Justices who refused to retire (or die) and thus had no opportunity to alter the Court's makeup to his liking.

Roosevelt hoped to leverage his popularity into quick passage of the plan, and he lobbied hard. Consider the following from a March 9, 1937, fireside chat:

> The Courts, however, have cast doubts on the ability of the elected Congress to protect us against catastrophe by meeting squarely our modern social and economic conditions.... The Court has been acting not as a judicial body, but as a policy-making body.... We have, therefore, reached the point as a nation where we must take action to save the Constitution from the Court and the Court from itself.

Again, while the verbiage is a little calmer, FDR sounds quite Trumpian in his attack on the Court and especially on the Justices who were standing in the way of the New Deal. Calling the Supreme Court a policy-making body has always been the cruelest cut.

Just three weeks after this speech and before the Court packing plan had made much progress in Congress, the Supreme Court (perhaps not coincidentally) upheld a Washington State minimum wage statute in *West Coast Hotel Co. v. Parrish*, 5-4 with Justice Owen Roberts abandoning the four horsemen to side with the Justices that were more open to the constitutionality of economic regulation. This was the so-called "switch in time that saved nine," and Roosevelt's plan never made it out of committee in the House or Senate. From *Parish* forward, New Deal legislation found a much more welcoming Court.

The need for Court packing was further eroded by a sudden change in FDR's appointment luck. In his first term he appointed no new Justices. Over his next six years FDR would appoint *eight* new Justices to the Court, completely remaking it. No one but Washington has appointed more Justices, before or since.

In selecting his Justices, Roosevelt applied several hard-earned lessons from his early battles with the Court. He remained livid at the legal establishment that had lined up to support the Court's application of *stare decisis* to delay and in some spots cripple the New Deal. Roosevelt decided that neither bar association support, nor prior judicial experience, nor long practice as a corporate lawyer was necessary, or even to be preferred. Instead, a commitment to fighting for the New Deal became the key criteria for Justices. Roosevelt's Attorney General, future Justice Frank Murphy, suggested that one way to find suitable Justices was to look to law school faculties rather than on the bench. "Murphy argued [to Roosevelt] that legal interpretation should be entrusted to men who have a philosophy based on history and on a theory of public welfare rather than to those who looked only at the text of a law."[3]

This helps explain the prevalence of former law professors amongst the Roosevelt appointments. Five of Roosevelt's eight appointments had some experience teaching law. Roosevelt's second appointment, Felix Frankfurter, led the way with twenty-two years teaching administrative law at Harvard. Roosevelt's choice as Chief Justice, Harlan Fiske Stone, was both the Dean of Columbia Law School and a professor there for a total of twenty-one years. Wiley Rutledge taught at three law schools (Colorado, Washington University, and Iowa) and served as Dean at Washington University and Iowa. William O. Douglas taught at Columbia and Yale for ten years. Even Frank Murphy, who had spent other chunks of his career as the Mayor of Detroit and the Attorney General of the United States, taught law for five years at the University of Detroit, which may explain his support for time in academia as a qualification.

These five Justices joined the lone non-Roosevelt holdover—Owen Roberts, who had taught for twenty-one years at the University of Pennsylvania Law School—to form the Supreme Court with second most experience ever teaching law. Stone 2 (which sat 1943–45) had a collective ninety-four years in law teaching under its belt, more than ten years per Justice. Stone 2 is only surpassed by the ninety-five collective years in teaching law represented on Roberts 4 (discussed below).

Too Many Chefs

As one might imagine, hopes were high for a Supreme Court utterly dominated by FDR appointees and led by his hand-picked Chief Justice, Harlan Stone. After all, the Court had not been so dominated by appointees of the same political party since nominees from Republican presidents dominated in the late-nineteenth century (partially due to Congress barring Andrew Johnson from selecting any Justices by shrinking the Court). Surely a welcome era of Supreme Court harmony and efficacy was to follow the bitterness and acrimony that marked the end of the *Lochner* era.

Sadly, no. Chief Justice Stone presided over a divided Court that greatly disappointed Democratic hopes. Robert Harrison summarizes:

> There were more than *twice* as many nonunanimous judgments handed down during practically every term from 1941–1949 than there had been even in 1935–36 and 1936–37 when the Old Court had been divided into rather sharply defined liberal and conservative voting blocs. Not only the percentage of nonunanimous opinions, but the total number of dissenting votes cast per case doubled, and then tripled, during the tenure of the Roosevelt Court, and there were, for example, thirty 5-4 decisions in the 1944 term compared to the Old Court's worst year, 1936–1937, when thirteen decisions were [5-4].[4]

Peter Renstrom notes that the Stone Court was "the most frequently divided, the most openly quarrelsome in history. The conflict included personal sniping and bickering, as well as substantive differences on issues."[5] The Stone Court "indulged in a stridency…which diminished the prestige of the tribunal, as did an excess of dissents and concurrences.… In consequence, the Court often failed to speak with a clear, or even a calm, voice on the great issues of that time."[6]

In one particularly sad episode, the Justices had traditionally sent a joint letter of appreciation upon the retirement of a colleague. The Court was apparently so divided it could not agree on what to write to Owen Roberts upon his retirement, so no letter was sent.[7] You know you work in a dysfunctional office when the joint drafting of a *tribute* letter fails over personal and professional acrimony. In another episode, Hugo Black and William Douglas apparently lobbied President Truman against the elevation of Robert Jackson to Chief Justice in 1946, threatening to quit if Jackson got the job. When Jackson learned of the betrayal he publicly pledged: "If war is to be declared on me, I propose to wage it with the weapons of the open warrior, not those of the stealthy assassin."[8]

Many blamed Stone himself for the failure of his Court. According to Peter Renstrom, Stone "proved ineffective in the post. He disliked administrative work and lacked the skills necessary to unify his Court and keep differences under control."[9] To make an unfair comparison, John Marshall presided over a Court with Justices that were almost all appointed by hostile presidents, and he still managed to unify the Court and produce a series of groundbreaking and unanimous opinions. Stone had a Court filled with Justices who should have been allies, and he produced one of the least successful Chief Justiceships in the Court's history.

But what if Stone has gotten a bad rap? What if there was something about the mix of Justices that made his Court unmanageable? The Stone Courts were remarkable for more than just discord and dissents: they were dominated by law professors. Again, correlation does not prove causation, but those readers who have ever attended a law school faculty meeting will be especially unsurprised to find out that a Supreme Court dominated by teachers of the law had a hard time getting along.

Consider how badly the relationship between Frankfurter and Douglas, who had previously been lifelong friends and allies, deteriorated on the Court. It seems as if the Court was too small for these great intellects (and massive egos). Again, anyone who knows a superstar law faculty will find these disputes, even among intellectual and political allies, unsurprising to the point of inevitability.

Law Professors on the Court

As noted above the Stone Court has only been outdone once for professorial experience. Roberts 4 had an even more professorial bent, as Figure 8.1 demonstrates:

FIGURE 8.1 YEARS AS A LAW PROFESSOR PER JUSTICE

For the first 100 years of the Court's existence the Justices had almost no experience teaching law. The tiny bump from 1789 to 1798 reflects James Wilson's short career as a lecturer in law at the College of Philadelphia (now the University of Pennsylvania) the year before he was seated on the Court. After Wilson, it was not until the appointment of Henry Billings Brown in 1890 that another Justice was appointed with any law-teaching experience. Brown was a Lecturer in Law at the University of Michigan from 1860 to 1875 and a Professor of Medical Jurisprudence at the Detroit Medical College from 1868 to 1871. (Yes, you read that correctly: Brown taught law *and* medicine at the same time for three years. Justice Brown was thus an early pioneer in the study of law and medicine.)

Students of the Court may wonder why Joseph Story, who

famously taught as the Dane Professor of Law at Harvard from 1829 to 1845, and wrote the 1833 masterpiece, *Commentaries on the Constitution of the United States*, is not reflected above. Story is certainly among the most famous and accomplished of the many Justices who were also law professors. The problem is that Story began teaching in 1829, seventeen years *after* he joined the Court, so I did not count his teaching as part of his pre-Court background.

Looking at Figure 8.1, it is clear that experience as a law professor was exceedingly rare before the 1880s. On the one hand, it makes sense that early Courts would lack prior experience as a law professor. After all, the great bulk of lawyers in this era entered the profession by "reading the law" rather than attending law school. On the other hand, Yale, Harvard, University of Pennsylvania, the University of Maryland, and William and Mary (among others) all had law faculties of some size during this period, staffed by foremost experts in jurisprudence, including giants like William and Mary's George Wythe. Wythe actually taught both President Jefferson and Monroe, so they were exceedingly familiar with him. The fact that neither Wythe nor any of the other first American law professors made it onto the Court suggests that earlier presidents preferred politicians and sitting judges over more academic appointments.

Note that when law schools became more formalized in the twentieth century I stop counting teaching part-time as an adjunct as a separate background experience. This is because adjuncts are rarely a part of the larger faculty and only work part-time in their role. This is true of even the most famous of adjuncts like then–Tenth Circuit Judge Neil Gorsuch at Colorado Law School or then–D.C. Circuit Judge Brett Kavanaugh at Harvard. Surely, these experiences were meaningful to Kavanaugh and Gorsuch (and the other twentieth- and twenty-first-century adjuncts who were also Justices), but it would be a stretch to say that adjunct teaching was equal to or more important than their jobs as judges. Further, for better or worse, scholarly productivity is now the dominant law professor activity, and adjuncts are not expected to publish at all.

Legal Academics Dominated the Stone and Roberts Courts

Historically, there have been two periods of Court dominance by law professors. The first we have already discussed—the Stone Courts of the 1940s. The second is the Roberts Courts, marked by the all-time law-professor high point of Roberts 4. Five of the nine Roberts 4 Justices spent a significant portion of their careers at the highest levels of academia. Teaching law was the single most prevalent experience on that Court, ahead of both practicing law and sitting as a judge.

The Roberts 4 Justices taught at the most elite law schools in the country, with four Justices teaching at a top-ten law school before joining the Court. Justice Scalia spent twelve years teaching at the University of Virginia and the University of Chicago, with stops at Georgetown and Stanford along the way. Ginsburg taught for twenty-six years at Rutgers and Columbia. Breyer taught for twenty-six years at Harvard. Kagan taught for nineteen years at Harvard and the University of Chicago, including six years as Dean of Harvard Law School. Kennedy taught law for twenty-two years at the University of the Pacific, McGeorge School of Law—a fine California law school, but not the elite experience of his colleagues.

Replacing Scalia, Kennedy, and Ginsburg with Gorsuch, Kavanaugh, and Barrett marked a decline in the Court's experience in law teaching, despite the fact that Barrett has spent the bulk of her professional career in legal academia (sixteen years). Nevertheless, this is still ten years fewer than Ginsburg, mostly reflecting Barrett's much younger age at the time of her appointment. Barrett arrived on the Court at the age of forty-eight; Ginsburg was appointed at sixty.

Why It Matters

As in other areas, the recent trend is towards a particularly elite type of law teaching. It is an achievement to earn a position on the faculty of any law school in America. Historically law professors have not had an advanced degree beyond a J.D., so over time there were a lot of Americans facially qualified to teach the subject. Law schools and faculties obviously needed to find a way to winnow. One could imagine a world in which law schools used this flexibility to hire applicants who excelled in the practice of law or in its teaching, and possibly even in both! Needless to say, that is *not* what law schools chose to do.

Instead, most law schools sort for academic ability, in the hope of predicting promise as a legal scholar. Teaching and practice experience are more distant considerations. Generally speaking, modern law professors had an outstanding record in law school. They should also have an impressive clerkship. Supreme Court clerkships are particularly prized. Add a strong record of publication, with contributions to top-ranked journals counting extra. In recent decades, law schools have also elevated applicants who have a PhD in another academic area, such as economics or psychology.

Strangely, a lengthy history of excellence as a practicing lawyer is not prioritized and can even count against candidates. After all, why would a true legal scholar "waste" his time practicing law when he could be writing law review articles? Modern legal scholarship, and especially the scholarship at the elite schools, tends to be highly theoretical and divorced from the actual practice of law, so time spent in the salt mines of lawyering does not actually "count" towards building a store of knowledge for future law review articles. It is mostly just seen as time that could have been better spent writing.

The route to becoming a law professor at any school, including a solid but middle-of-the-road law school like that of the University of the Pacific, is quite narrow and requires a high level of technical and theoretical legal excellence. The route to joining a top-ten law school's faculty, as four of the Roberts 4 Justices did, is narrow beyond measure and almost solely focused on publishing. Getting a tenure-track job at Harvard is not as challenging as becoming a Supreme Court Justice, but it's at least in the neighborhood. Being named Dean of Harvard Law School, as Justice Kagan was in 2003, is, in fact, even harder than becoming a Supreme Court Justice, at least by a head count of those who have held the respective positions. It is funny to say that becoming a Supreme Court Justice is the second most rarified job Elena Kagan has obtained, but it is accurate.

These academic achievements are salient because they again evince the extreme obsession with technical legal excellence on the modern Supreme Court. This is not a shot at how hard these Justices worked or how much they have accomplished. To the contrary, Kennedy, Kagan, Breyer, Scalia, Ginsburg, and Barrett's careers as legal academics are exceptionally impressive and rare. It is just a recognition that technical legal excellence should not be the *only* criteria that matters in selecting a Justice. And again, it may well be that there should always be a Justice or two with a professorial bent on the Court. Story, Holmes, and Frankfurter all brought a particularly academic approach to the Court and added much. But Roberts 4 and Stone 2 are examples of too much of a good thing. Diversity suffers and you get too many chefs in the kitchen.

Being a tenured law professor at a top-ten law school is another intensely cloistered job. We don't call it the "ivory tower" for nothing. Like federal judges, a tenured law professor basically cannot be fired from his job. As with the federal judiciary, there are good reasons for this policy—it protects academic freedom and encourages adventurous scholarship and teaching. But like the federal judiciary it places individuals at arms-length from some of the most basic concerns of ordinary people: Will I get fired? Will my salary go down or up? It also means that professors and appellate judges do not really have a boss. Law school deans describe managing a tenured faculty as "herding cats" partially because they have so little direct control over the terms and conditions of a tenured professor's job.

Tenured law professors and federal appellate judges also only have to deal with a very narrow group of people, many of whom are basically supplicants. The bulk of a federal appellate judge's human interactions involve his staff or the lawyers who appear before him. No matter how generous the judge, those are not relationships among equals. The same is true for a professor and his students. Even the best and most teaching-oriented professors sit on the privileged side of a very stringent hierarchy.

Both professors and appellate judges have colleagues, of course, and those interactions are among equals, but, again, lifetime tenure means that these are not traditional workplace relationships. It is, of course, usually preferable to get along, but there are few job-related punishments for not getting along. This explains why some academic or judicial disputes can get so out of hand. Reading the details of the disputes on the Stone Court, it is revealing how petty and academic they seemed. This should not be surprising. Many of the players were law professors.

Law professors are also encouraged to teach and write about law from an elevated and neutral position. Again, this makes sense. A law school classroom should be welcoming to students of all stripes and the best scholarship comes from a place of open-mindedness. But approaching the law neutrally and from ten thousand feet is not necessarily the best route for a Supreme Court Justice. Yes, they should remain neutral on the outcome if they can, but there is something to be said for being in touch with a ground eye view of how the law affects citizens.

Insofar as law professors have direct contact with the law, it is often through appellate opinions. While some classes rely upon statutes or regulations, the "case method" in American law schools means that the primary texts taught (and, to a lesser extent, written about) are appellate and Supreme Court cases. Law schools do this so that students (and readers of scholarship) can understand how these cases weave together to create governing law. The problem with this approach is that appellate court opinions freeze the facts of each case, often presenting a short or slanted version of what happened. This enforces a cloistered view of the law as depending on larger jurisprudential principles or trends, rather than as a reaction to the lived experience of the people involved in the disputes.

In fairness to Chief Justice Stone, John Marshall had the great good luck to preside over a Court with several happy backbenchers, such as Bushrod Washington, Samuel Chase (especially after his failed impeachment), and our mascot William Cushing. If Stone had faced a similarly constituted Court, perhaps he would be remembered as a great and unifying leader. Alas, a spicy mix of former law professors with outsized egos spoiled his tenure as Chief Justice.

∾

CHAPTER NINE

FROM THE ACELA CORRIDOR
TO THE BELTWAY

Justice John McLean's father, Fergus, was a Scotch-Irish Uls-
terman who emigrated to the United States sometime around
1775.[1] He landed in Wilmington, Delaware, and eventually settled
in New Jersey, where John, his first son, was born in 1785. My
study of the of pre-Court lives of Justices also measures the years
each spent living in any particular place. Gathering this data was
relatively easy for modern Justices, but precise data for earlier
Justices, and especially those from impoverished backgrounds,
is much harder to locate. John McLean is a good example. After
McLean and his brother were born in New Jersey, the family
moved several times in search (literally) of greener pastures. From
1789 to 1797, I simply made my best guess as to how many years
McLean lived in each state.[2] McLean is also a great example of
how geographical experiences can have a real effect on the Court.

McLean's family moved from New Jersey to Morgantown,
Virginia (now West Virginia), then to rural, frontier Kentucky in
Jessamine County, and then to Mason County. Eventually they
settled on land outside Cincinnati, Ohio, as part of a federal land
grant to settle the Miami River Valley.

McLean's story is typical of the American frontier experience. In 1796, the McLean family and some of their Northern
Kentucky neighbors heard word of fertile land becoming available in the Northwestern territory of Ohio. They pooled their
money to buy a large tract of land. The next year, John (then 11
years old) and his father set out to explore their new home. They
carried rifles, butcher knives, and provisions, floating down the
Ohio River from Maysville, Kentucky, to the provincial outpost
of Cincinnati, where they left the River and trekked north to
present day Warren County, Ohio. They stayed with one Mr.
Richardson, who had already started clearing land for a farm of
his own. They were greeted with a welcome dinner of fresh bear
meat and the promise of corn next summer. John and his father
stayed in Ohio over the winter to clear a farm for themselves
and returned to Kentucky the next summer. The family moved
to Ohio permanently in 1798. How roughhewn was McLean's
childhood? His biographer, Francis Weisenburger, entitled the
chapter on McLean's early years "Reared in the Wilds."

Finally settled in Ohio, John helped with the family farm and
attended a neighborhood school taught by a minister. He earned
extra money by clearing land for his neighbors. He eventually
saved enough for room and board to study under the tutelage
of two local Presbyterian Ministers. In 1804 McLean leveraged
his education into a two-year apprenticeship with the clerk of
the Hamilton County Court in Cincinnati and began to read the
law with two different lawyers in town. Cincinnati was a boom
town in the early-nineteenth century, and thus a promising spot
to launch a legal career.

By the end of his apprenticeship, McLean was a recently married twenty-two-year-old. He had originally planned to finish his
legal studies and begin the practice of law, but instead he seized
an opportunity to buy a printing press and establish a local paper.

He moved back nearer to his family in Warren County and started the *Lebanon Western Star* in 1807. Like virtually all newspapers of the day, the *Western Star* was explicitly political. Given the rural setting, McLean wisely chose to support the Jefferson administration. For example, the first issue, from Friday, February 13, 1807, includes some fantastic slander against Aaron Burr. The paper reprints "a long and interesting letter from Natchez" that details a conspiracy to "unite Kentucky, Tennessee, Louisiana, the Floridas, and part at least of Mexico into an independent empire" supported by Spain and under "the protection of Great Britain," all with Burr "at the head of this conspiracy."

Burr was, of course, arrested by the Jefferson administration in early 1807 for treason. He was tried before Chief Justice John Marshall (presiding while riding circuit in Virginia) and was eventually found not guilty, so whether Burr actually planned on stealing half of America's territory is still unknown. Regardless, this was all typical fare for a Jeffersonian paper in 1807. Any time you decry the current politicization of the media remember that our first newspapers existed primarily to deliver slander and puffery to angry partisans.

(McLean's *Lebanon Western Star*, like so many local and regional papers, met a heartbreaking end in 2013, just six years after its two hundredth anniversary.[3] Ohio's oldest weekly newspaper had become a free weekly in the early 2000s, and in 2013 the Cox Media Group closed the paper for good and folded it into a three-town paper called *The Journal-News Pulse*. Sigh.)

After handing off the paper to his brother, McLean moved back to Cincinnati in 1811 and immediately found work as an Examiner for the Congressional Land Office. The next year, aged twenty-seven, McLean ran for Congress as a Democratic-Republican and won. He served in Congress until 1816, when he resigned to join the Ohio Supreme Court. He served on the court for six years.

Ohio was still America's western frontier, and McLean and his fellow Justices spent most of their time riding circuit. Current practice required at least two Justices to hold court in *each* of Ohio's eighty-eight counties every year, a crushing travel- and court-load. As biographer Frank Gatell wryly noted, "[t]hese conditions and a salary of $1000 a year did not make a seat on the Ohio Supreme Court one of the legal-political plums of early nineteenth century America."[4]

By 1822, McLean was ready for a new challenge. He unsuccessfully pursued a U.S. Senate seat but found satisfaction when President Monroe appointed him Commissioner of the U.S. Land Office, an extremely powerful position in a country expanding and granting land rights all throughout the West. A year later, Monroe named McLean Postmaster General, another critical role. McLean was himself a western frontiersman, so he understood and respected the special needs of newly settled Americans. McLean opened more post offices in his first two years than had been opened in the last twenty. By 1828, the post office had nearly 28,000 employees, making it the biggest employer in the U.S. government.

McLean served as Postmaster General until 1829, under three presidents (Monroe, Adams, and Jackson), before Jackson named him to the Supreme Court. McLean was Jackson's first nominee and fit the bill in three important ways: Ol' Hickory had a soft spot for plainspoken frontiersman; he wanted to appoint someone from the Seventh Circuit (Kentucky, Ohio, and Tennessee); and he hoped to eliminate McLean as a possible future candidate for president.

Jackson succeeded on the first two criteria but failed to eliminate McLean as a future presidential candidate. McLean was in the mix for almost every election from 1832 until his death. He eventually was rumored as a candidate for three different parties:

the Anti-Masonic Party in 1832, the Whigs in 1836, and finally the Republican Party in 1856. Imagine a modern Supreme Court Justice repeatedly flirting with a third-party presidential run, and you'll have a sense for just how different the Court was in the nineteenth century.

Geography played an important role in McLean's pre-Court experiences in a number of ways. First, he joined the Court in what scholars refer to as the "seventh seat." The Seventh Circuit Act of 1807 added a seventh Justice to the Court and also reorganized the federal circuit courts by creating a Seventh Circuit comprising Ohio, Kentucky, and Tennessee.[5] Appointing the initial occupant of the seventh seat, Jefferson chose a resident of the Seventh Circuit—Kentucky's Thomas Todd. When circuit riding was a key part of a Justice's duties, presidents generally nominated locals. Justices would hear cases throughout the circuit every year, so appointing well-known local lawyers made sense logistically and legally, and it had the added benefit of hewing closely to public opinion.[6]

For roughly a century there were seats on the Supreme Court that were associated with geographic regions. The early legacy of the seventh seat is a prime example. When Justice Todd died in 1826, President John Quincy Adams replaced him with another Kentuckian, Robert Trimble. The unlucky Justice Trimble died two years later of a "bilious fever," just past the age of fifty.[7] President Jackson chose McLean partially because Ohio was in the same circuit as Kentucky. The sense of geographic ownership over the seat was strong enough, however, that Jackson first sought approval from the Kentucky delegation in Congress before nominating McLean.[8]

McLean is emblematic of a whole subcategory of Supreme Court Justices: frontiersmen and women. These individuals lived part or all of their lives on some version of the frontier as it moved progressively west. Multiple Supreme Court Justices started somewhere in the east and migrated west for a new life and greater opportunity. Examples abound: McLean's family moved from New Jersey to Ohio. Another Jackson nominee, John Catron, was born in Pennsylvania and ended up in Tennessee. Samuel Miller was born in Kentucky and practiced in Iowa. Melville Fuller grew up in Maine and moved to Chicago to seek his fortune. Both Joseph McKenna and Steven Field grew up on the East Coast and moved to California in the earliest days of its statehood. The last example is Sandra Day O'Connor, who grew up on "the Lazy B," a cattle ranch in Southeastern Arizona without running water or electricity. Needless to say, it requires a certain type of person to leave home and seek their fortune in an unknown wilderness far away. Privations and adventures necessarily ensue. Frontier life naturally encourages rugged and entrepreneurial individuals, but also tightknit communities in which one must rely upon the kindness of neighbors to survive. It is a particularly American experience.

McLean's experience in Cincinnati as a lawyer and a judge certainly affected his most famous act on the Court: penning the iconic dissent in *Dred Scott*. When McLean was on the Ohio Supreme Court, he heard an 1817 *habeas corpus* case from a black man named Lunsford. Lunsford had been owned as a slave in Kentucky, but he was illegally sold to Thomas D. Carneal who lived in Cincinnati where slavery was banned. Carneal forced Lunsford to perform slave labor in Cincinnati by day and returned Lunsford to Kentucky each night in an attempt to keep him enslaved.

Lunsford brought suit in Ohio to pursue his freedom.[9] McLean granted the writ, freeing the man, noting that he favored granting freedom to all slaves "as a matter of immutable principles of natural justice" and that if a master used slave labor in a free state like Ohio, the master thereby "forfeits the right of property in slaves."[10] McLean considered slavery "[a]n infringement upon the scared rights of man: Rights which he derives from his creator, which are inalienable."[11] This ruling and the experience of growing up across the river from Kentucky certainly had a deep effect on McLean. He was one of only two Justices to dissent in *Dred Scott*, and his life experience of living in a free state directly across the river from a slave state surely influenced his vote.

Unfortunately, many of the Justices in the *Dred Scott* majority were less positively affected by their geography. Six of the Justices who voted in the majority in *Dred Scott* had some connection to slave owning. Roger Taney, James Wayne, Peter Daniel, John Campbell and John Catron all grew up and spent the bulk of their professional lives in southern slave states. All five of them had been slave owners, though Campbell and Taney freed their slaves before joining the Court. The circumstances were varied. Peter Taney's family owned a Maryland tobacco plantation and Wayne's family owned a Savannah, Georgia rice plantation. Tobacco and rice farming were among the most dangerous and labor-intensive types of plantation work, so those families owned a massive number of slaves who were surely treated especially awfully. Daniel grew up on a family farm in Virginia staffed by slaves. Campbell grew up in a less wealthy family. His father was a "lawyer planter," meaning that his income came from both professions. This meant a smaller farming operation and thus fewer slaves. Catron's family was much poorer but still owned slaves when Catron grew older. Regardless of the scope of the practice, each of these Justices was surely affected by his personal experience and profit in slave labor.

The last slave-owner in the *Dred Scott* majority was Samuel Nelson, who grew up in New York State. His family sold one or more slaves to support Nelson's education in the early nineteenth century. New York outlawed slavery in stages. In 1799, New York passed the Gradual Emancipation Act, which emancipated slave children born after July 4, 1799, but indentured them until they were young adults. Existing slaves remained in bondage until their death or emancipation by their owner. Nelson headed to Middlebury College at fifteen in 1808 and graduated in 1813, so if his family sold slaves to cover tuition during those years, Nelson grew up around slavery and profited from it in his education, all well after public opinion in New York had turned against slavery. Amongst the Justices to vote in the majority in *Dred Scott*, only Robert Grier, who was born and raised in Pennsylvania and worked there, had no family or personal connection to slave owning. Geography can deeply effect perception.

Measuring Geography Over Time

My study measures the time each Supreme Court Justice spent in any state or foreign country. I used only full years of experience, and if a Justice lived in multiple places in the same year, I tried to use the location that predominated. Consider this summary of John Catron's childhood from historian Frank Gatell:

> There is a dearth of information about John Catron's early years. Not even the date or place of his birth have been clearly established. The best that can be said is that he was probably born about 1786 in Pennsylvania, of German ancestry on his father's side. He spent some childhood years in Virginia and then moved to Kentucky, where he stayed until 1812. His background was apparently one of poverty, and whatever education he obtained was either self-taught or came later in life. He next went to Tennessee, in the area near the Cumberland Mountains.[12]

Under these circumstances, I just coded as best I could.

Once I recorded where the Justices had lived, I aggregated the states into regions, so I could get a better sense for which regions predominate for pre-appointment experience. The categories are New England, Mid-Atlantic, South, Midwest, Southwest, West, Washington, D.C., and "Abroad."[13] I counted Washington, D.C., as a standalone region rather than lumping it in the Mid-Atlantic or the South, because growing up or working in Washington, D.C., is quite a different experience than growing up in the South, which covers Virginia to Florida, or the Mid-Atlantic, which covers Maryland through New York. Time spent in Washington, D.C., is time spent in an environment dominated by the federal government (thus the "beltway mentality"). When a Justice lived in the suburbs of D.C. but worked in D.C., I coded that experience as D.C., again because living in Bethesda or Arlington is quite distinct from living in the rest of Virginia or Maryland. I also counted D.C. separately because the rise of D.C. as a pre-appointment home was one of our most startling discoveries. Spoiler alert: it has grown *a lot*.

Official Home State

Before turning to the regional statistics by year, we begin by assigning each Justice, from Jay to Barrett, an "official" home state. Table 9.1 on the next page shows the states ranked from most Justices to least.

Given the historical context, it makes sense that three of the top four states would be New York, Massachusetts, and Virginia. These were the wealthiest of the original thirteen colonies (and then states), and thus were hotbeds of lawyers and legal excellence. The relative dominance of New York (it has 50 percent more Justices than the number two state) reflects its role as a

OFFICIAL HOME STATE	Number of Justices
New York	15
Massachusetts	10
Ohio	9
Virginia	8
Maryland, Pennsylvania, Tennessee	6
Kentucky, New Jersey	5
California, Georgia, Illinois	4
Alabama, Connecticut, South Carolina	3
Arizona, Colorado, Indiana, Iowa, Louisiana, Minnesota, Michigan, New Hampshire, North Carolina	2
Kansas, Maine, Mississippi, Missouri, Texas, Utah, Wyoming	1
Alaska, Arkansas, Delaware, Florida, Hawaii, Idaho, Montana, Nebraska, Nevada, New Mexico, North Dakota, Oklahoma, Oregon, Rhode Island, Vermont, Washington, West Virginia, Wisconsin	0

TABLE 9.1

commercial and legal epicenter from 1788 to today. New York has added nine new Justices since 1900. Massachusetts has had six. Virginia, by contrast, has had just three.

Surprisingly, ahead of Virginia's eight Justices are Ohio's nine. Ohio's relative dominance over its neighbors is also somewhat puzzling. To be sure, Ohio is older than surrounding or nearby states, but it's nevertheless odd that Ohio would have nearly five times as many Justices as Michigan, for instance. West Virginia and Wisconsin have none!

Likewise, original colonies like Delaware and Rhode Island have also never had a Justice. George Washington bears much of the blame for this. Remember that Washington was keenly aware of the need for geographic diversity in the early Republic. He appointed Justices from nine of the original thirteen states but chose to start repeating states in his second term rather than finish out the original thirteen.[14] Washington might have set a different precedent in which the states took turns, or every state got a Justice at least once. Instead Rhode Island and Delaware were passed over and remain frozen out, along with the fourteenth state, Vermont. To add insult to injury, all three of these states border much more dominant states in terms of their Justice-counts: Massachusetts or Maryland. There is an excuse for Washington freezing Rhode Island out, as the state was the last to ratify the Constitution. Rhode Island finally joined the Union only in 1790, after briefly flirting with going it alone. Good luck getting a Justice with that attitude.

The relative dominance of Ohio, Kentucky, and Tennessee may surprise modern readers. The seventeenth, fifteenth, and sixteenth states to join the Union, respectively, have twenty Justices between them. The first, thirteenth, and fourteenth states have none. A lot of this has to do with the demise of the Federalists and the rise of the Jeffersonians, especially Andrew Jackson. Jackson was from Tennessee and had a strong preference for frontiersmen like himself. Other strangely underrepresented states include Texas with just one Justice, and Florida, Oregon, and Washington with none.[15]

Geography by Years—D.C. Rises

Tallied by the total years spent in each region, these geographic trends are more pronounced because many Justices who weren't originally from New York or Massachusetts spent a chunk of time in those states, for work or education. For example, time spent at Harvard, Yale, and Princeton are frequent enough that they are relative boons to Massachusetts, Connecticut, and New Jersey respectively.

When you add up all of the pre-appointment time that Justices spent in each state, the list looks pretty similar to the list above with one notable exception. New York remains in first with 805 total years. Washington, D.C., is second, with a total of 535 years. Massachusetts is third at 514 years. D.C. only passed

Massachusetts with the additions of Neil Gorsuch and Brett Kavanaugh. Kavanaugh spent a full forty-four years in D.C., more than any other Justice by a large margin (note that I code the suburbs of Washington as D.C.). Before the appointments of Gorsuch and Kavanaugh, no Justice was coded as having spent any part of their childhood in Washington, D.C., so the great bulk of those 535 years comes from time spent working in the federal government, generally as a politician, lawyer, law clerk, or judge.

On a per-Justice basis, the rise in D.C. experience is quite clear, as Figure 9.1 shows.

FIGURE 9.1 YEARS IN D.C. PER JUSTICE

Given that D.C. only became our capital in 1800, it makes sense that John Marshall was the first Justice to join the Court after having lived in D.C. Marshall lived in D.C. in 1800–01, when he served as an elected member of the House and as Secretary of State under John Adams. From the Marshall 1 Court forward, the Supreme Court has always included at least one Justice who had previously lived in D.C.

Two other eras stand out as low points. Waite 5 and 6 (1882–88) included only one Justice who had previously lived in D.C.—Stanley Matthews, who served four years as a Senator from Ohio before being nominated to the Court by President Garfield. Fuller 5 (1893–94) likewise had only one Justice who had lived in D.C.—Howell Edmunds Jackson, who was a Senator from Tennessee.

There are two periods in history in which the Court was relatively full of Justices who had spent much of their pre-appointment lives in D.C. All nine of the Justices on Vinson 2 (1949) had lived in D.C. before joining the Court, with Fred Vinson himself having spent twenty-one years in D.C. as a U.S. Representative from Kentucky and as a D.C. Circuit Judge. The Vinson Courts were dominated by FDR appointees who had worked in D.C. as part of the New Deal before joining the Court.

Today, however, pre-Court time spent in D.C. by Justices is at an all-time high. This has nearly everything to do with the dominance of pre-appointment experience serving on the D.C. Circuit Court of Appeals and in other high-level (but generally not Cabinet-level) government positions. The huge spike on the graph leading to today reflects the additions of Gorsuch and Kavanaugh, both of whom are among the most D.C.-centric Justices ever.

Roberts 7, clocking in at almost fifteen years per Justice, was the high point for average time spent living in D.C. on the Court. Eight of the nine Justices had some experience living in the nation's capital. Only Sotomayor did not live in D.C. before joining the Court. Brett Kavanaugh had the most with forty-four years, but five Justices had thirteen years or more in the District. Barrett's replacement of Ginsburg in Roberts 8 caused a slight decline from the height of Roberts 7, as Barrett spent only five years in D.C. before decamping to teach at Notre Dame. But even Barrett's relatively short five years is above the all-time average of 3.6.

Geography by Region

Table 9.2 shows the total number of pre-appointment years that Justices spent in geographic regions, from most represented to least:

Region	Total Number of Years
Mid-Atlantic	1624
South	1457
Midwest	1093
New England	882
Washington, D.C.	535
West	348
Foreign	105
Southwest	97

TABLE 9.2

Readers may be surprised at the relative significance of the South on this table. Among Justices today, only Clarence Thomas and Amy Coney Barrett have lived in the South at all. But the region has had historical importance in the earlier parts of our nation's history, starting with its founding in 1789. Until 1947, in fact, time spent in the South was more prevalent on the Court than that of any other region. From 1949 to 1955, however, Southerner Justices Rutledge, Vinson, and Jackson died in office and were replaced by non-southerners Minton, Warren, and the second Justice Harlan. Ever since the South has failed to regain its historical dominance.

Perhaps most surprising is the relatively high number of southern Justices appointed in the period following the Civil War. As noted earlier, one can't explicitly blame geography for case results on the Court, but the prevalence of southerners on the Court before the 1950s may help explain *Plessy v. Ferguson* and other decisions that upheld Jim Crow and the doctrine of "separate but equal."

Like the South, the Midwest has seen a collapse in representation on the Court recent years. Only Roberts, Thomas, Kagan, and Barrett have spent any time at all in the Midwest, with Barrett's twenty-one years in Indiana the most time spent among all four. On a per-Justice basis, the Roberts 6 and 7 Courts represented the Midwest less well than in any time since 1826, before which there was hardly a settled "Midwest" to speak of.

Very few Justices have come from the Southwest. Rehnquist and O'Connor were from Arizona, and Justice Thomas Clark was from Texas. Otherwise no Supreme Court Justice has lived for any lengthy period in the Southwest. Collectively the Justices have spent more time living overseas than in the Southwest.

The combined total for years spent overseas is higher than one might expect. A number of Justices, especially in the early periods of our Nation, were born overseas and spent part or all of their childhoods on foreign shores. These are William Paterson (Ireland), James Wilson (Scotland), James Iredell (England), David Brewer (Smyrna), George Sutherland (England), and Felix Frankfurter (Austria).

Other Justices went overseas for some portion of their education. John Rutledge and John Blair studied law at the Middle Temple in London. Brandeis studied at the Annen-Realschule in Dresden. Stanley Reed studied at the Sorbonne for a year. There have been a number of recent Justices who received scholarships to study at Oxford or Cambridge, typically with Rhodes or Marshall scholarships. These include John Marshall Harlan, Potter Stewart, Byron White, David Souter, Stephen Breyer, Elena Kagan, and Neil Gorsuch.

Yet other Justices have served in a government capacity overseas, often as a treaty negotiators or ambassadors. John Jay spent five years overseas as the Plenipotentiary to Spain and negotiated the Treaty of Paris, ending the Revolutionary War. William Day went to Paris to negotiate the treaty that ended the Spanish American War. John Marshall was the Minister to France, Nathan Clifford was the Minister to Mexico, and Lucius Lamar was the Special Confederate Commissioner to Russia. Frank Murphy and Howard Taft served as Governor of the Philippines, which I've coded as "abroad" despite the fact that the Philippines were an American territory.

If you aggregate the regions into a Northeast measure (a combination of New England, the Mid-Atlantic and Washington, D.C.), an East Coast measure (counting only states bordering on the Atlantic Ocean), or an Acela corridor measure (the states that the Amtrak Acela travels through from D.C. to Boston) the dominance of these variously defined regions in recent Courts becomes clear. Justices spent almost half of their pre-appointment lives in the Northeast or the Acela Corridor, and more than half of their lives on the East Coast. Our current Justices have spent a relatively short amount of time west of the Mississippi.

The three most prevalent geographic areas on the Roberts Courts are Mid-Atlantic, Washington, D.C., and the West, although all of the Justices who served on a Roberts Court except for Barrett spent at least a few years in New England, the only such region on the current Court. This has everything to do with their nearly unanimously shared experience of attending Yale and Harvard.

Why It Matters

For roughly the first 100 years of the Court's existence, presidents sought to appoint Justices that came from the various geographic circuits that covered the nation. Over time this tradition became more of a guideline, but there was still an effort made to match seats on the Supreme Court to particular regions. Yet from the twentieth century forward, geographic diversity waned, culminating in our current Court, in which almost no diversity exists at all.

America is a large and regionally diverse country, and a Court staffed by a majority of Justices who primarily lived or worked in the Acela Corridor is a significant problem. It leaves the distinct impression that the South, Midwest, and Southwest are just unrepresented fly-over country.

Traditionally, time spent in D.C. correlated with experience in elected or high-level government positions of the kind associated with the ideal of the lawyer-statesman I discussed in Chapter Five. More recently, it largely comes from time spent on the D.C. Circuit or in elite and narrow government service like the White House Counsel's Office or the Office of the Solicitor General.

Objections to the dominance of coastal elites on the Court are fairest when D.C. is involved. You can dispute whether growing up and working in New Jersey, as Alito did, or in the Bronx, as Sotomayor did, reflects any kind of geographic bubble. However, the opposite is true of living or working in the D.C. metro area—they call it the beltway bubble for a reason. Simply, D.C. is a one-horse town focusing on politics and lobbying in a way that is unparalleled among any other American city. New York has always been considered America's financial capital and Los Angeles is associated with Hollywood and entertainment, but both of those cities have a lot else going on. By contrast, D.C. is first and foremost a government town.

The problem is not just that spending a plurality of one's adult life in D.C. means that other regions are ignored; it is that living in D.C. teaches a very special set of life lessons about how the sausage is made and what power and influence looks like on the federal level. Again, it may well be a good idea to have a few D.C. hands on the Court, and historically there has always been at least one Justice with such experience. Whether it is a good idea to have such Justices dominate the Court, however, is another matter altogether.

CHAPTER TEN

∾

FROM POLYMATH AUTODIDACTS TO HOOP-JUMPERS EXTRAORDINAIRE

The life of Robert Jackson (1892–1954) is a remarkable American success story. His life story can be easily divided into two acts. In Act One he lives an uber-typical small town American life—an intelligent and hard-working farm boy becomes a successful country lawyer. In Act Two, a solo practitioner from Jamestown, New York, (population 45,155 in 1930) moves to Washington, D.C., in 1934 to work at the IRS. He eventually rose to become U.S. Solicitor General, then U.S. Attorney General, then Associate Justice on the Supreme Court, reaching this last height just *eight* years after leaving his solo practice in a bucolic small town.

Nor did Jackson disappoint on the Court: he is one of America's most admired Justices. On the Court he was known as a staunch protector of individual liberties, a brilliant writer, and a keen legal mind. He is perhaps even more famous for serving as the Chief American Prosecutor in the Nuremberg Trials of 1945–46 while still a Justice. Jackson's is a story that well reflects the benefits of allowing individuals to demonstrate merit over a lifetime of hard work.

Jackson was born on his parents' farm in Spring Creek, Pennsylvania, on February 13, 1892.[1] When Jackson was five, his family moved twenty-five miles north, to Frewsburg, New York, where Jackson spent his childhood. Eugene Gerhart's adulatory biography of Jackson describes a typical rural childhood. He grew up milking cows and helping raise and sell horses. His family made a decent living raising stock, selling lumber, and farming the land. Jackson went to the local public schools, graduating from Frewsburg High in 1910.

Jackson spent the next year commuting by trolley to the nearest "big town": Jamestown, New York. Jackson took an extra year of study at Jamestown High and also read the law with his mother's cousin, local lawyer Frank Mott. At the end of this year, Jackson was set on becoming a lawyer and thought he "ought to go to a law school, not having had any college."[2] In 1911, Albany Law School offered a two-year course of study that granted an LL.B., the functional equivalent of today's J.D., as well as a one-year program for "law office men." The shorter program was aimed at preparing apprentices reading the law for the bar examination and practice, but it did not grant a degree. Because Jackson had already put in a year in Mott's office, he chose the one-year course of study.

Per historian John Q. Barrett, Jackson's father, William Jackson, strongly objected to both law school and Mott:

> [One] lawyer whom Will Jackson particularly disliked was Frank Mott. Mr. Jackson disapproved of how Mott lived—his fancy lifestyle was well beyond his means, he borrowed money and he did not repay his debts. Mr. Jackson knew that Mott was fond of Robert and wanted to take him into his office, and he feared that his son would follow Mott into the law, and into a life of disreputable conduct. Will Jackson thus made it clear to Robert

that if he wanted to study law (as opposed to medicine, which was the career path that Will was encouraging his son to pursue), Robert would pursue it without financial help from his father. (Robert's mother Angelina, who of course was related to Mott by her grandfather's remarriage, had a softer perspective on all of this. For one thing, she liked Mott—as she put it, "maybe Frank did owe people, but he was very nice to his mother.")[3]

Because his father refused to pay, Jackson borrowed the tuition from his bachelor uncle (and his middle-namesake), John Hough-wout. I could not find tuition data for Albany Law School in 1911, but tuition and fees at the much fancier (and likely more expensive) University of Pennsylvania ran $160 that year (roughly $4400 in 2019 dollars).[4] Law school was much more affordable in 1911, but still expensive for a middle-class farmer's son with no parental support.

In 1911, Albany Law School was located in a former church across from the state capital, although as Jackson quipped, the church's façade "suggested a piety that was not fully sustained by the student body."[5] Albany, like many contemporary law schools, had just a few full-time professors; most of its curriculum was taught by adjuncts.[6] It focused on the actual practice of law as much or more than its academic study. Jackson did well: all As except for one B in his first semester (he got an 88 percent in Equity).[7]

After one year of law school, Jackson returned to Mott's law office in Jamestown to finish his three-year apprenticeship.[8] Jackson took, and passed, the two-day written bar examination in the Fall of 1913. He was sworn in as a lawyer that December, at just twenty-one years old. Jackson then split office space with Mott and opened his own practice. Ultimately, Jackson practiced for more than thirty years in Jamestown, taking a typical country lawyer's mix of cases: some criminal defense work and some commercial trials. He drafted wills and contracts. He also served as the corporation counsel for Jamestown for twenty-six years, a position of local prominence that also allowed him to keep an eye on business developments. In small towns like Jamestown, corporation counsel had (and still has) an inside track on advising all sorts of potential clients.

Jackson came to national attention for two reasons. First, he was very active in local, state, and national bar associations. He was one of the founders of the Federation of Bar Associations of Western New York and served as its president from 1928 to 1930. He also rose to become chairman of the National Conference of Bar Association Delegates (the forebear of the ABA's House of Delegates) in 1933–34.[9] Second, he was heavily involved in Democratic politics at the same time that Franklin Delano Roosevelt was rising in the political ranks of New York and the nation. In 1931, as Governor of New York, Roosevelt appointed Jackson to a commission to study and improve the justice system in the state.[10]

When Roosevelt was elected president in 1932, he again turned to Jackson, asking him to become the General Counsel of the IRS. On the one hand, this was a substantial promotion for Jackson. He was serving in an appointed position in the Treasury Department, and for the first time he moved from the relatively small pond of Western New York State to the deeper waters of Washington, D.C.

On the other hand, moving to the IRS was hardly the obvious path, let alone a sure-fire stepping stone to the Supreme Court. If you doubt this, consider just how many more prestigious appointed law jobs FDR ran through before he got to General Counsel of the IRS and said, "how about Jackson? Did we find anything for Jackson yet?" Or ask yourself what new opportunities would the position offer? Presumably Jackson could have left the

IRS to become a tax lawyer in a large firm in D.C. or New York, but nothing in Jackson's background suggested that he wanted to trade in his life and success in Jamestown for this narrower (although likely more remunerative) path.

Nevertheless, Jackson made the most of his opportunity and proved himself to be effective and valuable everywhere he went. From the IRS, Jackson went to the Treasury Department, then the SEC, then to the Tax Department of the Department of Justice. Up to this point, Jackson had done well, but he was ready to return to Jamestown. He had proven himself in Washington, but he earned more in private practice back home and was a bigger fish in a smaller pond. Jackson informed Roosevelt of his intentions, but Roosevelt valued Jackson enough to entice him to stay with the promise of future promotions. FDR followed through and appointed him Solicitor General in 1938 and then Attorney General of the United States in 1940.

By this time Jackson was firmly in line to possibly join the Supreme Court. The previous Solicitor General, Stanley Reed, had joined the Court in 1938, and former Attorney Generals were often appointed to the Court, including Frank Murphy, whom Jackson replaced in 1941. It is also notable that Jackson was appointed towards the end of FDR's run of nominees to the Court: he was FDR's seventh. Clearly, FDR had already run through his initial list of lawyers and supporters.

In 1941, FDR elevated Harlan Stone to the Chief Justiceship and nominated Robert Jackson to take his vacant spot as an Associate Justice. Jackson thus ended a remarkable stretch of just over seven years in Washington, D.C. The whirlwind began in 1934, when Jackson resigned as corporation counsel to Jamestown, New York, and put his western New York practice on hold to travel to Washington, D.C., to help with FDR's New Deal. Seven years later he had worked as a lawyer at every level of the executive branch and found himself on the highest Court in the land, with a limited educational pedigree but an extensive record of practical legal achievement.

Jackson was the last man appointed to the Supreme Court without a law degree. Later in life Jackson knew he was on the trailing edge of a shift in how Americans prepared to practice law, "I suppose I would be one of the last in New York State to receive that kind of training. Shortly after that they adopted a rule requiring three years of law school."[11] Jackson recognized that apprenticeship and law school both had advantages, but he preferred apprenticeship. "If I had my way, I would have [future lawyers] serve a real apprenticeship. These young fellows out of law school aren't fitted to try cases."[12]

Nevertheless, even Jackson's one year of law school is still more formal education than fourteen other Justices who read the law and had limited or no other formal education: James Iredell, Thomas Johnson, Samuel Chase, Alfred Moore, John Marshall, Gabriel Duvall, Robert Trimble, John McLean, Philip Barbour, John Catron, John McKinley, Nathan Clifford, Noah Swayne, and James Byrnes. All told, roughly a seventh of America's Justices had no formal higher education. Many of them share stories of growing up in relative poverty and using an apprenticeship in a lawyer's office as a launching point to a new life as a professional. Each of these Justices distinguished himself otherwise in his career, achieving professional success without any leg up from higher education. Jackson is just one of many autodidacts who rose through the ranks to find themselves at the pinnacle of the legal profession.

Warren Burger

Do not think that just because every Justice appointed after 1941 had a law degree that each of those Justices had the full four years of undergrad and three years of law school. Chief Justice Warren Burger, commissioned in 1969, had just a few night classes at the University of Minnesota as his undergraduate education, followed by four years of night law school at the St. Paul College of Law (later merged into William Mitchell and then with Hamline, currently named Mitchell Hamline).

Night school at the St. Paul College of Law was the opposite of the elite educational backgrounds now adorning the Court. Founded in 1900, the school only offered night classes (generally to students working full-time day jobs) and had no full-time academic faculty. Every class was taught by a practicing lawyer or judge after hours.[13] Faculty were paid $5 a class, but many waived the fee and did it as a public service to the bar. According to Douglas Heinrich's history of the law school, admissions standards were hardly stringent—"entrance requirements were a high school diploma or its equivalent, and to be at least eighteen years of age—and breathing."[14]

The school was inexpensive, with tuition at the beginning of the century running only $60 a year (equivalent to just over $1500 today). As a result, the school teetered on the edge of bankruptcy throughout its existence. Money pressures led inexorably to lax admission policies, which then led to grade inflation and eventually to poor bar exam performances. St. Paul College of Law was not accredited by the American Bar Association until 1943, twelve years after Burger graduated.

Cost was certainly a factor in Burger's attendance. He paid tuition and supported himself by selling insurance for the Mutual Life Insurance Company of New York.[15] After graduating summa cum laude, Burger joined a prominent St. Paul law firm, Boyesen, Otis & Farley, and became involved in Republican politics. He eventually ended up on the D.C. Circuit and then the Supreme Court.[16] When Nixon nominated Burger to the Court in 1969, he called Burger "superbly qualified."[17] The ABA agreed, unanimously granting Burger their highest recommendation, "highly acceptable from the viewpoint of professional qualifications."[18]

Compare the role that law school education played a half a century later, when Anthony Kennedy announced his retirement from the Supreme Court. Before eventually nominating Kavanaugh, President Trump quickly identified four finalists. As decision time neared, *The New York Times* reported on each finalist, noting that Judge Raymond Kethledge was considered to be weak for a reason that would have disappointed Burger: "Judge Kethledge does not have the Harvard or Yale pedigree that Mr. Trump has told associates he would like to see in the next justice."[19] Burger, who served as the fifteenth Chief Justice of the United States Supreme Court for twenty-seven years, would have been shocked to hear that a federal judge who had graduated at the top of his class at the University of Michigan Law School, had clerked on the Supreme Court (for Kennedy no less), and then spent ten years working in big Detroit law firms and for the Ford Motor Company before becoming a Sixth Circuit Judge was *under*qualified to serve on the Court due to the name at the top of his diploma.

Educational Background

Recall Figure 5.2, which showed how much the legal careers of the Justices have shifted over the years. At first solo practice dominated, then small partnerships, and eventually big firms. The last few decades showed an overall collapse in practicing law. The educational backgrounds of the Justices tell a parallel story about the elite bar. Figure 10.1 shows three different measures of years spent in education—years in undergraduate education, years spent reading the law, and years spent in law school.

FIGURE 10.1 YEARS IN UNDERGRAD, READING THE LAW, AND LAW SCHOOL
PER JUSTICE

First note the early dominance of reading the law. The first year in which the Justices had spent more time in law school than apprenticeships was 1909. There were only *two* Justices appointed before 1900 that spent no time in an apprenticeship: John Blair (who studied at the Middle Temple in London from 1755 to 1756) and Benjamin Curtis (Harvard Law class of 1832). Otherwise, each of the other fifty-five Justices appointed before the twentieth century spent at least a year or more reading the law, even if he also attended law school. You can see that the years in law school per Justice starts to rise in the 1880s. In this period, a combination of law school and apprenticeship became common for Justices. Eventually, law school alone came to dominate in the twentieth century.

After the ascendance of Justices with law school experience, it took a long time for today's model of four years of undergrad and three years of law school to become universal on the Court. In fact, the first Supreme Court to fit the current model was not until Rehnquist 1 in 1986. That year, Burger retired, Rehnquist was elevated to Chief Justice, Antonin Scalia joined the Court, and the universalization of today's standard was complete. The swap of Burger for Scalia exemplifies the changes on the Court. Burger was a lawyer's lawyer who had graduated from a middling law school with no undergraduate degree. Scalia was the model elite Justice: Georgetown University for undergraduate and Harvard for law school, followed by a career teaching in some of the best law schools in the country (Virginia, Chicago, and Stanford). And the trade was only a harbinger of things to come.

Finally, consider how much earlier undergraduate education became a standard feature than law school. If you squint at the solid line marking the undergraduate years per Justice in Figure 10.1, you see that for more than a decade in the late-nineteenth century (from Waite 5 in 1883 to Fuller 6 in 1894) *every* Supreme Court Justice had four years of undergraduate education and an undergraduate degree. The first time that law school education hit an average of three years per Justice was the 1940s. While apprentice-trained, self-educated strivers joined the Court as late as James Byrnes in 1942, lacking *any* undergraduate education at all became pretty unusual by the late nineteenth century.

Elite Undergraduate Education

Given that the first year in which every Justice had four years in undergrad and three years of law school was 1986, it seems hard to believe that the Court could become so utterly dominated by elite educational experiences just a few decades later. Yet the Roberts Supreme Courts well reflect the triumph of the Ivy League. Roberts 5, 6, and 7—the period between the death of Scalia (Georgetown) and the appointment of Barrett (Rhodes)—included only *one* Justice that did not attend Stanford or an Ivy League school for undergrad: Justice Thomas, a proud Holy Cross alum. Just as Scalia's replacement of Burger was a harbinger of the elite model, Gorsuch replacing Scalia (Columbia undergrad in lieu of Georgetown) helped the elite grow even more elite. Perhaps when Barrett and Thomas retire we can get Justices with Yale, Harvard, or Princeton undergraduate educations to replace the Rhodes and Holy Cross degrees and continue the upward trend.

The study codes years spent at an Ivy League university or Stanford—what I've determined to be an "elite" undergraduate experience. Figure 10.2 shows just how dominant an elite undergraduate experience has become.

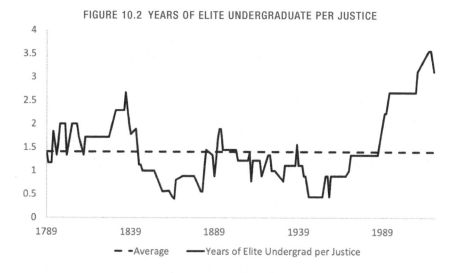

FIGURE 10.2 YEARS OF ELITE UNDERGRADUATE PER JUSTICE

Again we find that the trend is relatively recent. As late as 1986, the representation of elite education was below average for the Court. Over the next thirty years, however, time spent in elite undergraduate institutions roughly tripled, hitting the all-time high that we see with Roberts 6 and 7. Also note that Justice Thomas (appointed in 1991 by George H. W. Bush) was the longest serving Justice on Roberts 7. Thus, every Justice appointed between 1991 and 2020 had a degree from an elite undergraduate institution, easily the longest streak of such appointments. Roberts 8 shows a decline because of Justice Barrett is a proud Rhodes College graduate.

That said, it is fun to see a relative and early peak of elite education in 1836–37 with the Taney 1 Court. Four of the six Justices on Taney 1 graduated from Yale, Harvard, or Princeton. Smith Thompson and James Wayne graduated from the "College of New Jersey" (Princeton's original name) in 1788 and 1808, respectively. Henry Baldwin was Yale class of 1797, and Joseph Story was Harvard Class of 1798. Taney himself was a Dickinson College graduate in 1795, so Taney 1 was an abnormally formally educated nineteenth century Court. Ironically, self-avowed populist and man of the people Andrew Jackson appointed Baldwin, Wayne, and Taney. Between Presidents Trump and Jackson, maybe there is something about populist presidents favoring elite educational backgrounds.

Of course, attending a college at all in that era likely said more about wealth and family connections than it did about academic abilities. In the 1970s, Sonia Sotomayor could earn entrance to and a scholarship from Princeton, whereas John McLean and John Catron (the two other Jackson appointees) had to read the law and make their way as lawyers.

Despite a few low points, there has never been a Supreme Court without at least one graduate from an elite undergraduate institution. So, while the current Court is more dominated by these institutions than any other, the many advantages given to those educated at Harvard, Princeton, or Yale have been illustrated by the Supreme Court (and by American government and business) since the founding.

Yale and Harvard Law School

Compared to their law school degrees, however, the undergraduate degrees of the Justices on the Roberts Courts look like a model of diversity. There are seven different undergraduate degrees on Roberts 8: Yale, Columbia, Princeton (with three Justices), Harvard, Stanford, Rhodes, and Holy Cross. By contrast, for the bulk of Roberts's tenure Yale and Harvard have dominated among law schools. Northwestern Law graduate John Paul Stevens was appointed in 1975. Rehnquist and O'Connor were Stanford Law grads. Between O'Connor and Barrett, Justice Ginsburg's one year at Columbia Law School was the only non–Yale or Harvard law school experience on the Court.

Ironically, Ginsburg's Columbia degree reflected Harvard's intransigence more than her own intellectual powers. As you'll recall, Ginsburg wound up a Columbia graduate because of Harvard's decision to withhold their J.D. when she moved to New York and Columbia to live with her husband Martin Ginsburg during her third year.

Figure 10.3 shows the ever-growing dominance of Harvard and Yale. On our current Court, experience in law school is almost synonymous with time spent at Harvard or Yale Law:

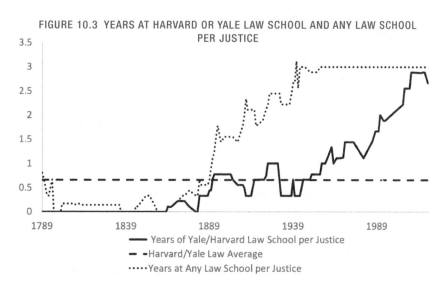

FIGURE 10.3 YEARS AT HARVARD OR YALE LAW SCHOOL AND ANY LAW SCHOOL PER JUSTICE

— Years of Yale/Harvard Law School per Justice
- -Harvard/Yale Law Average
·····Years at Any Law School per Justice

I find this graph astounding. As President Trump himself suggested pre-Barrett, a Yale or Harvard Law degree is now almost a requirement to serve on the Supreme Court. This requirement is unprecedented historically, as the list of law schools represented on the Court below establishes. In fact, the first Justice who attended Harvard Law School (Benjamin Curtis) who was not appointed until 1851. The first Yale Law graduate (David Davis) was appointed in 1862.

Amazingly, Waite 3 and 4 (1881–82) were the last Courts that included no Justices who had studied at Yale or Harvard law schools, over 135 years ago. The most recent low deviation from the general trend was Burger 5 (1981–86), which included two Stanford graduates (O'Connor and Rehnquist), a Howard graduate (Thurgood Marshall), a Northwestern graduate (Stevens), a Washington and Lee graduate (Powell, although he did spend a year at Harvard Law getting an LLM degree), and a St. Paul College of Law graduate (Burger). Incredibly, replacing the two Stanford Law School graduates (Rehnquist and O'Connor) made the Court ostensibly *more* elite.

If you look at Figures 10.2 and 10.3 together, you can see an interesting general trend. Collectively, from roughly 1865 to 1955, the Supreme Court had less elite undergraduate and law school experience than in the ensuing decades. As meritocracy in America took hold after World War II, elite education becomes more prevalent, and really spikes in the late 1980s, when credentialism and contested confirmation hearings came together to create our current Court.

The Most Common Undergraduate Institutions and Law Schools

The rise of these elite institutions is anomalous historically. While Princeton, Harvard, and Yale have always been dominant, there has been an equally long tradition of diverse undergraduate institutions. Here's a list of every undergraduate institution represented on the Court (including at least a year of attendance, but not necessarily a degree), from most common to least:

University (Undergraduate)	# of Justices	University (Undergraduate)	# of Justices
Princeton University (College of New Jersey)	12	Douglas University (now defunct)	1
Yale University	11	The University of Edinburgh	1
Harvard University	10	Emory University	1
Columbia University (King's College)	4	Franklin College	1
		University of Glasgow	1
Stanford University	4	College of the Holy Cross	1
Bowdoin College	2	Kentucky Wesleyan College	1
Brown University	2	Lincoln University (PA)	1
Centre College	2	Middlebury College	1
Dartmouth College	2	Northwestern University	1
Dickinson College	2	Rutgers College	1
Georgetown University	2	University of St Andrews	1
Kenyon College	2	St. Augustine College	1
University of Michigan	2	The University of Tennessee, Knoxville	1
University of Pennsylvania	2	The University of Texas at Austin	1
Rhodes College (Southwestern College)	2	Transylvania University	1
Washington and Lee University	2	Union College	1
College of William and Mary	2	Vanderbilt University	1
Amherst College	1	The University of Virginia	1
Bethany College	1	West Tennessee College (now Union University)	1
University of California, Berkeley	1	Western Reserve (now Case Western Reserve University)	1
Carleton College	1	
The University of Chicago	1	Whitman College	1
College of the City of New York	1	Williams College	1
University of Colorado Boulder	1	University of Wisconsin—Madison	1
Cornell University	1	

TABLE 10.1

I love this list. America's 115 Justices, through Barrett, attended forty-nine different undergraduate institutions. In total it is a strange list: One Justice attended a university that is now defunct. Others attended universities that have been renamed. Some attended small religious colleges and others Ivy League universities. There are some schools that seem under-represented. The list of schools with only one Justice is a who's who of America's elite universities and small colleges, including Amherst, Cal Berkeley, Cornell, Middlebury, Northwestern, University of Texas, Vanderbilt, Virginia, and Williams College. Centre, Dickinson, and Rhodes Colleges educated more Justices! In fact, if we're just judging by Justices, Rhodes College, with two (Fortas and Barrett), has a claim to the title of "Harvard of the South" over Vanderbilt, Duke, and other pretenders.

The top of the list is more predictable. Yale, Harvard, and Princeton have jostled for the top slot for years. In 2003, with John Roberts's appointment, Yale and Harvard were tied at 10 apiece, with Princeton below at 9. But the next three appointments in a row (Alito, Sotomayor, and Kagan) vaulted Princeton to 12. Kavanaugh's appointment brings Yale back up to 11, hot on Princeton's heels, with Harvard wondering when it will get a break. Pour one out for the Crimson. Stanford has had an enviable record in the last fifty years, but the Ivy League's head start makes Princeton, Harvard, and Yale difficult to catch.

The list of law schools is shorter, partially because fewer Justices attended law school than undergrad, but still hearteningly diverse. On the next page is Table 10.2: a list of the law schools at which Justices studied for at least a year.

Harvard is by far the most dominant among law schools, with claim to almost twice as many Justices as its nearest competitor. Among these Harvard Law grads, eight were pure "Harvard men" (and they are all men), having also gone to Harvard for

Law School	# of Justices	Law School	# of Justices
Harvard	20	Alabama	1
Yale (New Haven Law)	12	Cal Berkeley	1
Columbia	7	Centre College (defunct)	1
Michigan	3	Colorado	1
Albany	2	Howard	1
Cincinnati	2	Indiana	1
Cumberland	2	Kansas City School of Law	1
Litchfield (Tapping Reeve) (defunct)	2	New York Law School	1
Middle Temple (London)	2	Notre Dame	1
Northwestern	2	Penn	1
Stanford	2	St. Paul College of Law	1
Virginia	2	Texas	1
Washington and Lee	2	Transylvania (defunct)	1

TABLE 10.2

their undergraduate degree: Benjamin Curtis, Horace Gray, Oliver Wendell Holmes, William Moody, Edward Sanford, Harry Blackmun, David Souter, and John Roberts.

All told, the Justices attended twenty-six different law schools, including three that are now defunct. That law schools such as Transylvania, St. Paul College of Law, Kansas City, Howard, and Centre College are tied with the likes of Penn, Texas, and Cal Berkeley demonstrates the diversity of the list. It is also heartening that Albany, Cincinnati, and Cumberland law schools have a claim to six different Justices between them.

The educational diversity reflected above is hardly limited to the type of law school—the diversity in experiences among the Justices who read the law is even richer. There is no way to quantify the types of apprenticeships that were their day's equivalent of either Harvard or taking night classes at the St. Paul College of Law, but they certainly existed. For example, George Washington's well-connected nephew, Bushrod Washington, read the law in the Philadelphia office of the prominent lawyer and future Supreme Court Justice James Wilson.[20] In an era well before there was such a thing as a Supreme Court clerkship to set one's course for prominence, an apprenticeship like Washington's must have been the functional equivalent. Similar to the way that Kavanaugh replaced Justice Kennedy (who he clerked for) and Roberts replaced Rehnquist (who he clerked for), Bushrod Washington was appointed to replace James Wilson himself when Wilson died.

By way of comparison, however, Justice John Catron apprenticed briefly under a lawyer named George W. Gibbs in Sparta, Tennessee, before Catron volunteered to fight in the Second Tennessee Regiment.[21] Catron eventually fought under Andrew Jackson in the War of 1812, kick-starting Catron's eventual prominence. Suffice it to say that Gibbs offered a substantially less helpful apprenticeship than did James Wilson, and yet both Washington and Catron eventually found themselves on the Supreme Court.

Why It Matters

College and law school are foundational experiences in every Justice's life. College is frequently a place of personal and intellectual discovery. Law school may be even more formative, as it is often the birthplace of a budding lawyer's professional identity and legal philosophy. Just listen to what various Justices have said when they return to their alma maters. To a person, they credit undergraduate and law school education as transformational times of intellectual and personal growth. Thus, each Justice's higher education really matters. Accordingly, it is not a good idea to have them all come from the same institutions, even if those institutions are the "best." Just as a matter of intellectual and experiential diversity, allowing the similarly situated institutions of Yale, Harvard, and Princeton to dominate is unhealthy, even if there is some level of diversity between the schools and within the walls of each.

These three schools are, and have always been, "elite"—in terms of not only the formal educations they provide, but also the social connections they offer. Historically, and especially today, the value of a Harvard, Yale, or Princeton degree has at least as much to do with the networking opportunities as it does with the education itself. From the day that a future Justice walks onto one of these campuses, he is likely to have a circumscribed set of future acquaintances and friends. The odds that your circle of friends and colleagues will be largely made up of Ivy League graduates is drastically higher if you yourself are an Ivy League graduate. If we are searching for practical wisdom and contact with ordinary people as a baseline expectation for our Justices, graduates of the most elite educational institutions are hardly fertile soil.

Consider also the skill sets we are privileging by emphasizing elite educational achievement. Not every student who goes to Yale or Harvard has been entirely focused on attending these schools since they were fourteen years old, but many were. The students at Harvard, Yale, and Princeton have frequently arranged their lives around this goal. In high school they took the most challenging classes and got the best grades. They were extremely engaged in extracurricular activities, often with an eye for how they would look on a college application. Again, this is not to denigrate this hard work. It is, in fact, very impressive. That said, it is hardly conducive to gaining practical wisdom and a broader set of experiences.

Requiring an elite law school education compounds this effect. In order to stay on track, these super-strivers must follow up on a dominant performance in high school with an even more impressive performance in their undergraduate classes and activities in order to compete against the best in the law school admissions game. The individuals we are selecting are obviously motivated and intelligent, but many have also, in some senses by necessity, lived a narrow and extremely goal-oriented life from their early teenage years.

Many people I've talked to have pushed back on these ideas. Americans are very attached to meritocracy, and many simply cannot believe that there is any downside to selecting Justices with the very best educational credentials. Part of the problem is that I present most often to relatively elite audiences of law professors, lawyers, or judges, who cannot for the life of them understand why I would advocate against hiring the "best" to be on the Supreme Court.

I have three standard responses to these objections. First, I am not arguing that none of the Justices can or should have attended Harvard or Yale. Historically, those schools have always been represented one way or another. That does not mean that *all* of the Justices should have attended these schools.

Second, I ask my interlocutors to reconsider their overly narrow conception of "merit." As noted above, it is silly to choose every Supreme Court Justice based on whether they aced every class in high school or college. Should we really eliminate a potential Justice based upon a C in ninth-grade Algebra or in Organic Chemistry sophomore year of college? Moreover, is there nothing a person can do in their adult life to demonstrate comparable merit? Bravery in battle? Getting elected to the Senate? Becoming an exceptional practicing lawyer?

Lastly, and on a personal note, I'm offended that we're limiting the Supreme Court to just book-smart, type-A, overachievers. There is more to life than building the perfect resume. I worry about a society that places so much emphasis on a series of ever-narrowing hoops. Our current version of meritocracy creates so many more "failures" to advance on the path than successes, and at such a young age. Healthier societies recognize multiple routes to success and many fewer paths to failure.

~

CHAPTER ELEVEN

LET'S MAKE THE JUSTICES
WEIRD AGAIN

Joseph P. Bradley was born March 14, 1813, in Berne, New York, a tiny farming village situated in the Helderberg Mountains.[1] Bradley's family struggled to scrape a living off of the rocky, mountainous land. Bradley was the eldest of twelve children, and his family survived as borderline subsistence farmers. They raised their own food, including grains, vegetables, and livestock. The farm animals were slaughtered for food and tanned for shoes and harnesses. They grew flax and spun linen, and harvested wool from their sheep. Later in life Bradley arrived at college in a homemade suit.

Bradley and his siblings worked hard. He later remembered that by the time he was eleven he worked all day in the fields "with scythe and harrow and driving the plow" over their steep hillsides. When he was fourteen, his family bought a new piece of land; he and his father led the clear cut. They used the lumber to make charcoal, which Bradley then peddled in downtown Berne.

Bradley attended some church schools as a youth, but he was largely self-taught, spending every free minute traveling into town to read in the public library. Bradley's story is the perfect testimonial to how a public library can change a young person's life. His autobiography contains a short description of how he availed himself of the library's collection:

> I was an incessant devourer of every mental aliment that could possibly be obtained…Many and many a Saturday night, when I could get away, would I tramp down to this mecca and during the entire Sunday revel in the intellectual treats which it offered. The stock books of this library were such as Josephus's works, Bollin's Ancient History, Hume and Smollett's History of England, Mavor's Collection of Voyages and Travels, and the like.…In my Father's collection was an old copy of Moore on Surveying, and Wilson's old book on navigation. These were favorites. I learned the art of practical surveying before I was sixteen.[2]

Bradley maintained this voracity for knowledge, and especially detailed and specialized knowledge, his entire life.

When he turned eighteen, Bradley begged his father for the chance to pursue a formal education, really any formal education. His father well knew that his son was an exceptionally smart and motivated young man, but he was also the eldest male in a struggling family of 12 children. Indeed, in Bradley's autobiography he recognizes just how large a gift he was requesting:

> At length, in December 1831, an event occurred which changed the whole current of my existence and determined my future destiny. Whilst my father and I were threshing out the buckwheat crop one day in the month of October or November of that year, the desire for an education became so vehement that I broke out in a way I had never done before to my poor father. I told him that my life was being wasted. That what I was doing amounted to nothing. That I felt I *must* have an education. He said, "I cannot afford to

give you an education." I said, I did not expect him to do it; but if he would let me go (I was then over 18) I would somehow obtain an education myself; and I would fully make up to him the loss of my unexpired time before coming of age....He finally consented to my proposition, only stipulating that I should help him get in the balance of the Fall crop. He further gave me a small amount of money (about twenty dollars) to start with.[3]

Bradley spent the next two years teaching school and saving his money for college tuition. What little education Bradley had in Berne came from a Dutch Reform Church school. One of the ministers recognized Bradley as an exceptional young man and eventually arranged for him to attend the then–Dutch Reformed associated Rutgers University in New Brunswick, New Jersey. Like many other young Americans, Bradley's admission to college changed his life forever. Bradley enrolled in 1833, originally to study theology, but eventually he focused on law and mathematics. Bradley completed a four-year program in three years. He finished at the top of his class and as the best math student in the college.

Bradley also had the great fortune to attend Rutgers with much wealthier and more well-connected classmates who became lifelong friends. Bradley's best friends at Rutgers were Frederick Frelinghuysen (later a U.S. Senator and Secretary of State) and Cortland Parker (later a decorated lawyer and the sixth President of the ABA), both from well-connected New Jersey families. After graduation, these two friends read the law with Theodore Frelinghuysen, Frederick's uncle and one of the best-known lawyers in New Jersey. This was an exceptionally propitious clerkship. During his career Theodore Frelinghuysen was the Attorney General of New Jersey, a U.S. Senator, and the Whig vice-presidential nominee with Henry Clay for president in 1844.

At first it looked like poor Bradley might be frozen out. He was unable to procure an apprenticeship in law, so he worked for a stretch as a schoolteacher and as the legislative correspondent for the Newark *Daily Advertiser*. His friends Cortland and Frelinghuysen kept their eyes out, however, and in November 1836 they found him an apprenticeship with Archer Gifford, a Newark lawyer who was also Collector of the Port. Bradley jumped at the opportunity.

Bradley basically supervised his own legal education, reading and re-reading Blackstone, Kent, Coke, and Justinian's Institutes—generally covering all of the subjects with characteristic fervor. I will spare you the long quote, but Bradley's autobiography (written when he was a much older man) has a hilariously detailed list of subjects and books studied. Unsurprisingly, when Bradley was orally examined for admission to the New Jersey Bar in 1839, he "had no difficulty in answering all questions propounded."[4]

Bradley's career as a lawyer was blessed by his involvement with two growing industries: railroads and insurance. In 1840, Bradley entered into a partnership with John Jackson, who was the secretary and attorney to the New Jersey Railroad and Transportation Company. From then forward Bradley was a railroad lawyer.[5] In 1850, he became the lawyer to the Camden and Amboy Railroad, one of the biggest and most successful companies in New Jersey and Bradley's most important client going forward. Bradley eventually served as their general counsel, a director, and a member of the executive committee, tying his professional life to a leading company in an exploding industry. Bradley and the railroad prospered in tandem.

At the same time that Bradley was vociferously defending the interests of railroad clients all over the country, he became interested in the math underlying actuarial science and the insurance business. In 1857, Bradley started working as an actuary for the Mutual Benefit Life Insurance Company of Newark, the insurance company that eventually became Prudential. He worked for the company as an actuary from 1857 to 1863, serving a purely mathematical and statistical role. In 1865, he became the President of the New Jersey Mutual Life Insurance Company and served in that role until 1869.

Consider the breadth of Bradley's interests and career. He became an actuary for a growing life insurance company during the very birth of that industry. The "Historical Background" section of the American Society of Actuaries website suggests that in 1889, forty years *after* Bradley's work and during the post–Civil War industrial and professional boom, there were just eighty to one hundred actuaries in the entire country.[6] There were surely fewer in 1857. All of Bradley's calculations were done by hand and required an advanced understanding of probabilities and math. But the *really* crazy thing here is not Bradley's mathematical prowess, it's that he decided to do all this *on top* of his thriving career as a railroad lawyer.

Bradley's specialized legal career resembles those of many corporate lawyers today. He became the "go to" expert to a rapidly growing industry that kicked up a lot of legal work. Bradley was a predecessor to today's specialist, right down to his narrow corporate client base and very healthy remuneration. The real difference is that Bradley's interests were broad enough to encompass a multitude of areas of work and study simultaneously. In a sense, Bradley's work as an actuary was actually his hobby. He certainly didn't need the money, and his legal career could have filled two lifetimes of interesting and highly paid work.

Yet even still, recounting Bradley's professional breadth gives us just a small slice of his overall intellectual curiosity. Bradley's eulogist and old college friend, Cortland Parker, marveled:

> I am free to say that it has never happened to me to meet a man
> informed on so many subjects entirely foreign to his profession
> and informed not slightly or passably, but deeply—as it seemed,
> thoroughly on them all. Literature, solid or light, in poetry or
> prose; science; art; history, ancient and modern; political economy;
> hieroglyphics; modern languages, studied that he might acquaint
> himself with great authors in their own tongues; the Hebrew and
> kindred tongues that he might perfect himself in biblical study;
> mathematics, in knowledge of which he was exceled by few—all
> of these were constantly subjects of his study.[7]

Bradley's own library became legendary. He had over six thousand volumes of non-law material and another ten thousand law books "filling his home to overflowing."[8] His law library was apparently so exceptional that Prudential Insurance bought and maintained the entire collection for their legal department after his death.

Bradley's son Charles gathered and published a posthumous collection of Bradley's various writings, and their breadth matches that of Bradley's library.[9] The essays include a translation of the Roman poet Lucan, a history of the first American steam engine, a discussion of standard weights and measures, long diatribes about reformatting the calendar, and a full schematic of Noah's Ark.

In some ways, Bradley was a product of his times. Professions were much less specialized before the Civil War, and a brilliant and hard-working individual like Bradley could be both a decorated corporate lawyer who argued six different very complicated railroad cases before the Supreme Court *and* a mathematician able enough to serve as an actuary in the nascent life insurance business. He accomplished these professional feats all while remaining a polymath who wrote with equal passion on "The Force of Water as Used in Hydraulic Machinery in Mining" and more personal essays on "Happiness," "Time," "Freedom of

Thought," and "the Moral Faculty." Bradley himself summed up his variety of interests and its connection to his professional life nicely: "The lawyer ought, indeed, to know almost everything, for there is nothing in human affairs that he may not, some time or other, have to do with."[10]

Bradley joined the Court in 1870 and served until his death in 1892. Bradley was among the most decorated Justices in the post–Civil War era, although he is probably best known for his unfortunate majority opinion in the *Civil Rights Cases* of 1883.[11] He specialized in technical areas of the law such as patents, railroad law, and insurance, and worked hard to clarify obscure or confused areas of the law. Biographer Charles Fairman tells a long story about Bradley's work riding circuit in Texas as a Justice. At that time there were a large number of land disputes stemming from the mishmash of competing land grants from Spain, Mexico, and the Republic of Texas. Bradley became an expert in the "intricate system of land titles and . . . our Spanish and Mexican grants." Bradley became such an expert in this arcane area of Texas law that he was revered as a *trial judge* in Texas.[12]

He was also known as a tremendous colleague on the Court, offering guidance to Justices as different as Lucius Lamar and John Marshall Harlan. A letter and gift from Harlan to Bradley tells you a lot about both men and their relationship:

> You know that I greatly rely upon you, while you are on the bench (and I hope your departure from it is far in the future), to keep me *straight*. But it is important that you be kept straight—and to that end I send you an article from Kentucky—"straight"—It is 21 years old. A small quantity of it will produce delightful sensations, and make you wonder why every sensible man is not an adherent of the Presbyterian or the Dutch Reformed Church. Too much of it at one sitting may do harm.[13]

Entrepreneurs and Newspapermen

Here we cover a selection of some of the varied, non-law business interests pursued by Justices over the years. Recall that three of the first ten Justices spent a great deal of their time working as business owners and entrepreneurs, with decidedly mixed results. Justice Wilson owned an iron works and engaged heavily in land speculation. His business gambles led eventually to bankruptcy, debtor's prison, and a grim, penniless death from malaria. Samuel Chase attempted to corner the flour market during the Revolutionary War, leading to his own bankruptcy and significant political damage. These two are hardly an advertisement for the life of an entrepreneur.

More successfully, Thomas Johnson also owned an iron works and a large amount of land along the Potomac and died a wealthy man. John Marshall himself spent a large portion of his career in land speculation, eventually coming to own almost all of the fantastically valuable land in the Northern Neck of Virginia when *Martin v. Hunter's Lessee* settled title to the land in Marshall's favor.

Several Justices owned and operated heavily biased and partisan newspapers. Recall that John McLean founded the Jeffersonian *Western Star* in Lebanon, Ohio, just outside of Cincinnati. The very next Justice appointed by Andrew Jackson, Henry Baldwin, had *also* helped run a pro-Jefferson newspaper, a Pittsburgh paper entitled *The Tree of Liberty*.[14] (While the *Western Star* was a fine name, *The Tree of Liberty* was better yet.)

Nor was owning a newspaper necessarily a sedate business in the early-nineteenth century. If there was a pro-Jefferson paper in town, it was just a matter of time before a competing, anti-Jefferson paper sprung up. A young Philadelphia transplant named Ephraim Pentland obliged, and founded a Pittsburgh paper named *The Commonwealth* in July 1805 to compete with *The Tree of Liberty*.[15] Pentland and *The Commonwealth* quickly laid into *The Tree of Liberty* and its principals. In a Christmas Day 1805 screed, Pentland called Henry Baldwin and the *Tree of Liberty*'s editor, Tarleton Bates, "two of the most abandoned political miscreants that ever disgraced the state."[16] Pentland likewise suggested that *The Tree of Liberty* should change its name to the "Weekly Recorder of Apostacy," which is admittedly also a snappy title for a newspaper.[17] The battle between the two papers got so far out of hand that Bates, the editor of *The Tree of Liberty* and Baldwin's dear friend, was shot and killed in an honor duel that began in the pages of the two newspapers.[18] Like the more famous Burr–Hamilton duel, Bates's death led to widespread denunciation of duels, and it was apparently the last recorded duel in Pennsylvania.[19]

Samuel Miller (1816–90) was another newspaper founder, albeit for different reasons. Miller is the only former medical doctor to serve on the Court. He graduated from Transylvania University in 1838 with an M.D. and settled to practice in Barbourville, Kentucky, a small town in the Cumberland Mountains. Barbourville had barely two hundred inhabitants, and life as a country doctor was financially and physically challenging, not to say somewhat boring. Miller thus started his own newspaper, *The True American*, to argue for the abolition of slavery and to speak on other issues of the day.[20] Miller's boredom also led him to read the law on his own. He passed the Kentucky bar in 1847 and practiced in Barbourville until he moved his family to Keokuk, Iowa, in protest of the new pro-slavery Kentucky Constitution of 1850. Here Miller flourished as a lawyer and was eventually nominated to the Court by Abraham Lincoln in 1862.

Several other Justices had substantial experience with newspapers. Stanley Matthews edited the *Tennessee Democrat* and the

Cincinnati Herald during the 1840s.[21] Melville Fuller was the editor of the *Augusta Age* in Maine before decamping to Chicago, where he eventually found success as a lawyer. Fuller also worked as a Chicago correspondent for the *New York Herald*.[22] John Clarke was the publisher of the Youngstown, Ohio, *Vindicator*.[23] James Byrnes was the owner and editor of the *Aiken Journal and Review* in Aiken, South Carolina.[24]

Private Enterprise per Justice

Figure 11.1 shows the per-Justice years of non-law experience in private enterprise.

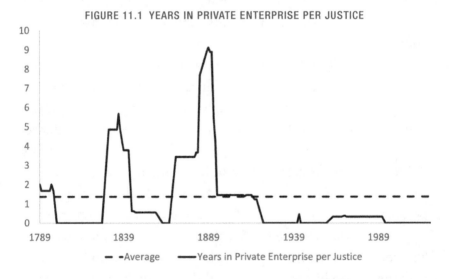

FIGURE 11.1 YEARS IN PRIVATE ENTERPRISE PER JUSTICE

- ‐Average ——Years in Private Enterprise per Justice

There are two noticeable peaks in private enterprise experience. The first peak, in 1830–44, reflects the appointment of the newspapermen Henry Baldwin and John McLean discussed above. The second and highest peak is the Fuller 1 Court of 1889. Four different Justices on that Court had significant non-law experience: Joseph Bradley (insurance), Stanley Matthews (newspaper), Samuel Blatchford (publisher of Blatchford's Circuit Court Reports, an early aggregator of case law), and Lucius Q. C. Lamar (Latin and math professor).

Private entrepreneurial experience basically left the Court with the retirement of Chief Justice Edward White in 1921, who had spent a large chunk of his adult life as a sugar farmer in Louisiana while also practicing law. After White, just two other Justices spent time in private enterprise. James Byrnes (covered above) is the short bump in 1941. The longer bump, from the 1960s into the 1980s, registers Byron White's experience as a decorated NFL running back on the Court, which we covered at length in Chapter Two. Besides these two figures, since 1921 the Court has had virtually no private-enterprise experience outside of law.

Military Service—Oliver Wendell Holmes, Jr.

As a younger man, Oliver Wendell Holmes, Jr., must have seemed an unlikely future soldier, coming as he did from a wealthy and well-connected family of Boston Brahmins. Holmes himself boasted about his decorated lineage: "All three of my names designate the families from which I am descended. A long pedigree of Olivers and Wendells may be found in the book called *Memorials of the Dead in Boston*.... Of my grandfather Abiel Holmes, an account may be found in the biographical dictionaries."[25]

Oliver Wendell Holmes, Senior, was actually the most famous of Holmes's forbears. Twice a Harvard graduate, Holmes, Senior, was a professor of Anatomy at the Harvard Medical School and also one of the most famous American writers and poets of his generation. He wrote the still-famous poem "Old Ironsides" and penned three very popular collections of essays entitled "The Autocrat at the Breakfast Table," "The Professor at the Breakfast

Table" and "The Poet at the Breakfast Table." Holmes, Senior, also helped found and edit *The Atlantic Monthly*. Of course, this hyper-literary, scholarly, and almost aristocratic background hardly screamed "future foot soldier in the Civil War."

Nor did Junior's time as an undergraduate at Harvard presage soldiering. Holmes graduated as the class poet in 1861, a sign that he was at least interested in his following his father's literary footsteps. He was a diffident and sometimes difficult student. Holmes finished somewhere in the middle of his class and encountered disciplinary problems, including breaking dorm windows and "repeated and gross indecorum" in a moral philosophy class.[26] One of the frustrations of researching this book is the many opaque references to youthful indiscretions. When I read that Oliver Ellsworth was dismissed from Yale for "mischievous incidents" and Holmes was nearly dismissed for "gross indecorum" I dearly wished contemporary sources had been more willing to spill the beans on what are surely uproarious stories. This is part of why Thurgood Marshall's biographies are such a great read—he seemed to revel in his past life as a rascal.

Holmes and many of his Harvard classmates were abolitionists and romantics. When Abraham Lincoln called for seventy-five thousand troops to be raised from state militias at the outset of the Civil War, Holmes and his friends left Harvard before graduating to enlist in the Union Army. Holmes, Senior, had to intercede so that Junior could take his final exams while in the militia, allowing him to graduate in 1861 before taking up arms.

At first, Holmes saw limited battlefield action. He was initially assigned to the Fourth Battalion of Massachusetts Volunteers, which was not scheduled to see combat. Holmes then agitated to join the 20th Battalion, which was headed south to Washington, D.C. By Fall 1861, Holmes and the 20th Battalion had marched south to Camp Kalorama, in the Georgetown section of Washington. For a time, Holmes and the regiment stayed on the D.C.

side of the Potomac and had limited engagements with Confederate soldiers.

Things changed radically during the battle of Balls Bluff. The 20th Massachusetts was sent into Virginia to discourage the Confederate Army from advancing closer to D.C. They camped for the night in Balls Bluff on the Virginia side of the Potomac, with the steep, impassable bluff in front of them and the Potomac behind them and with few boats to bring reinforcements across from Union territory or the wounded back from the Virginia side. Holmes's friend and fellow soldier Henry Abbott called the camp "one of the most complete slaughter pens ever devised."[27]

The Confederate Army ambushed the 20th and drove them back across and into the River, wounding or killing more than half of the 1,700 Union Soldiers, many via drowning. The scene was pandemonium. The title of a recent book on the battle succinctly describes the options Holmes and his compatriots faced: *Swim, Surrender, or Die.*[28] Holmes was shot in the chest and placed in a boat with other wounded soldiers and sent back to Maryland. Given the paucity of Union boats and the fate for most of the wounded, this was a best-case scenario for Holmes.

From there Holmes almost died in the military hospital at Camp Benton. A doctor described a harrowing scene after the battle. "Many of the wounded were crying and shrieking and the whole floor was covered in blood."[29] It was a miracle that Holmes did not die. He was shot in the chest, and the bullet somehow managed to miss his heart or lungs, and he did not bleed to death or drown, as so many others had.

Holmes's wound was serious and his convalescence long enough that he returned home to heal. He returned to active service in March 1862, just in time to march south with the Army of the Potomac on the ill-fated Peninsula Campaign. The plan was for Union soldiers to march through the Tidewater area of Virginia towards Richmond, with the hope of eventually capturing the Confederate capitol. Instead, they marched in swamps, got stuck in the mud, and were besieged by both dysentery and strong Confederate resistance. Holmes described a hellish scene in a letter home: "As you go through the woods you stumble constantly, and... perhaps tread on the swollen bodies already fly blown and decaying, of men shot in the head, back, or bowels."[30]

In August 1862, Union command abandoned the Peninsula Campaign and called the 20th back to D.C. to defend against Confederate incursions. On September 17, 1862, Holmes and the rest of the Army of the Potomac met the Confederate soldiers at the bloody battle of Antietam Creek. More than six thousand Union and Confederate soldiers died, along with another seventeen thousand wounded. Holmes was among them, having been shot through the back of the neck. This shot also missed any vital organs, and Holmes was again extremely fortunate to survive. Six inches higher and he would have been shot in the head. A bullet going through a different part of his neck could have torn through his windpipe. Holmes had been shot in the chest facing forwards at Balls Bluff, but he was shot in the back and in full retreat at Antietam, "bolting as fast as I can," a fact that Holmes dryly noted was "not so good for the newspapers" that reported on the battle and Holmes's role.[31] Holmes commemorated Antietam's anniversary every year for the rest of his life with a drink and a toast to his fallen comrades.

Holmes was again sent home to recuperate. Two months later he rejoined the 20th, and soon thereafter he came down with dysentery. In May 1863 he was wounded in battle for the third time, this time from a cannonball fragment in his heel. Another cannonball blew his pack off of his back. Holmes was, yet again, lucky to be alive, having narrowly avoided death, and he was again sent home to convalesce. It was seven months before he could march and return to combat. By this point he was understandably demoralized and a "nervous man." When he returned to service in January 1864, he did so as an aide to General Horatio Wright of the 6th Corps and saw less direct combat for the balance of his service. Holmes's three-year enlistment ended in July 1864. He declined a promotion to colonel and returned home to Boston.

Like most veterans of the Civil War, Holmes was haunted and deeply affected by his service. When he died in 1935 at the age of ninety-four, his final effects included several grim mementos including two musket balls with a note in Holmes's own writing stating "these were taken from my body in the Civil War" and two blood-stained Union uniforms with another note stating "[t]hese uniforms were worn by me in the Civil War and the stains upon them are my blood."[32]

But Holmes's Civil War service left more than just physical scars. In Louis Menand's excellent book, *The Metaphysical Club*, he details a reading and social group started by Holmes and his friends after the war while he was at Harvard studying law. Here Holmes, Charles Sanders Pierce, William James, and John Dewey (among others) came to the conclusion that pragmatism rather than dogmatism was the secret to governance and life itself. Holmes's experiences in the Civil War "made him lose his belief in belief." Given his traumatic war experience, is it any wonder he lost faith?

The war led Holmes to rethink fundamentally the nature of truth, and more importantly for our purposes, the nature of law, pragmatism, and judging. Holmes concluded that intellectual surety itself was the primary danger: "When you know that you know, persecution comes easy."[33] Plus, "to have doubted one's own first principles is a mark of a civilized man."[34] This philosophy extended through Holmes's masterwork *The Common Law* ("the life of the law has not been logic; it has been experience"), and his jurisprudence ("a Constitution is not intended to embody a

particular economic theory.... it is made for people of fundamentally differing views").

Stephen Budiansky's new biography of Holmes, subtitled
A Life in War, Law, and Ideas, argues that the Civil War was the
foundational experience of Holmes's life, and led to his life-long
commitment to pragmatism and skepticism:

> The war confirmed [Holmes's] deep belief that life is a gamble
> and there are no certainties; and by the same token it taught him
> to be extremely wary of ideological certainty. It really confirmed
> his philosophical skepticism, which in turn was the bedrock of
> his judicial philosophy. He often warned that law is not some
> moral abstraction or lofty ideal, but at root a statement of where
> society will kill you rather than have its proscriptions disobeyed.
> A brutal realism, but one that underscored the absolute need for
> tolerance and compromise over ideological zealotry. Before we
> try to inflict our moral certainties on the world, he was saying, we
> ought to pause and reflect first that we may well be wrong—and
> second that certainty all too often leads to violence.[35]

Holmes learned other lessons from the war, of course, including respect for the common man, the importance of a continuous
hard work and effort, and the great "passion and irony" of life.
Yet, for our purposes, the key takeaway is how the Civil War
shaped and molded Holmes's pragmatism and eventually, his
greatness as a Justice.

It is also worth noting that two of the all-time great Justices,
John Marshall and Holmes, are also the two Justices who had the
most intense experiences of war. John Marshall spent a frozen
winter with George Washington at Valley Forge and repeatedly
saw combat. Holmes's war record is second to none on the Court.
Of course, Holmes was also a two-time Harvard graduate, a
Harvard law professor, and a brilliant scholar before joining the

Court, so there is an argument that he is the proto-elite Justice. Nevertheless, Holmes himself would likely disagree about whether those academic experiences or his three years at war were most important to his intellectual growth and future success.

Military Service Declines

The amount of military service on various Supreme Courts tends to rise and fall depending on the wars America fought and the percentage of the population at large that served. For example, most Justices who were of fighting age during the Revolutionary War, the Civil War, and World War II appear to have fought, as shown by the spike in judicial military experience following those wars. Veterans of other wars, and especially all of the wars after World War II, were less prevalent on the Court, reflecting that legal elites were much less likely to serve (let alone see combat) in the Korean, Vietnam, Afghanistan, or the two Iraq Wars.

Even at the historical high points for time spent in military service on the Court, its prevalence is relatively low because no Justice has ever spent the bulk of his career in the military. Most

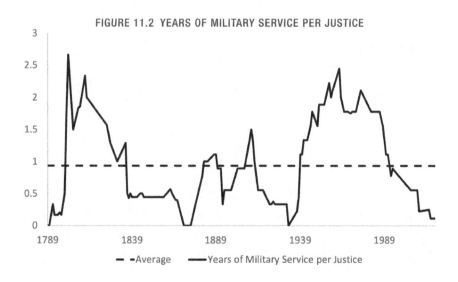

FIGURE 11.2 YEARS OF MILITARY SERVICE PER JUSTICE

of the military experience reflected in Figure 11.2 below came from stretches in active warfare.

Figure 11.2 shows that throughout most of its history the Court has had at least one Justice who had served in the military. Strangely, the first two Jay Courts had no military experience. This is because the first six Justices named to the Court were middle aged and generally powerful politicians or judges during the Revolutionary War. So, while these individuals were often very engaged in the war effort (it would be hard to find many civilians who were more engaged in the war than John Jay), they served in a different capacity, and are thus not coded as war veterans. When Thomas Johnson joined the Court in 1791, the Court had its first Justice with military service, reflecting Johnson's two years as a Brigadier General in the Maryland Militia.

The Roberts 6, 7, and 8 Courts have almost no military experience. Justice Breyer served six months active duty in a strategic intelligence reserve unit while at Stanford and then eight years in the reserves. I only counted his active service time and coded this experience as a year of active service.[36] Justice Alito was an ROTC candidate in college, but there is no record of any active service.[37] This small amount of experience is also pretty limited in scope. No current Justice has seen combat or been deployed overseas. Further, it is unclear whether any Justice has even lived for an extended time in military housing. Yet America has been involved in five different large-scale conflicts since the 1950s.

Why It Matters

Earlier chapters have covered experiences shared by a great number of Justices over the years. Almost every Justice has been in private practice at some point, for example. Many Justices have attended Harvard or Yale Law Schools or served as a judge before joining the

Court. This chapter covered rarer and more unique experiences.

It is remarkable just how many weird, and seemingly *sui generis*, characters made it onto the Court over the years. Professionally, the Court once included hustlers, entrepreneurs, newspapermen, a disillusioned doctor, and an actuary. It also used to hold true polymaths—individuals who came from nothing and were self-taught in a great many areas along with law.

The current Court does not lack in Justices that came from poverty and impressively triumphed over tough circumstances. Both Thomas and Sotomayor undoubtedly fit that bill, and this book does not mean to degrade their tremendous achievements. Their stories are actually an advertisement for our current meritocracy. Thanks to that meritocracy, extraordinarily smart and hard-working young people like Thomas and Sotomayor can place themselves on the path to the Supreme Court by attending elite colleges and Law Schools, regardless of their family income. Once admitted, they have a chance to grab the golden ticket, just as their wealthier and better-connected classmates do. Nevertheless, once that ticket is firmly in hand, it is undeniable that these uniquely American success stories today follow a more inflexible plot line. Thomas and Sotomayor certainly faced discrimination and hardship in college and beyond, but the structure of their paths to the Court is remarkably similar to that of their Court-mates. It is not that they did not struggle or overcome tremendous odds. Rather, it is that they did so precisely through the same, narrow system of meritocracy as their better-heeled colleagues.

Earlier self-made Justices took a much more varied path to the Court—often marked by detours, failed businesses, political excursions, etc. The more varied experiences of those old Courts reflect a less specialized time in which multi-talented generalists rose to the top in wholly unpredictable ways. To quote Tolkien, "not all those who wander are lost." If we hope to return practical wisdom to the Court, we should consider finding individuals who have taken the winding road through life.

Bradley, Byron White, and Holmes are emblematic. All three of them resemble other Justices in important ways: Bradley was a lawyer's lawyer, with a life of excelling in private practice. Both Byron White and Holmes had an educational pedigree that resembles those of today's Justices. Nevertheless, all three held a breadth of interests, and they were demonstrably willing to jump off the beaten "path" to the Supreme Court, or to elite achievement generally.

Consider William Gillette's almost poetic description of doctor, lawyer, and abolitionist Samuel Miller:

> What was Sam Miller like? He was a genuine product of the frontier. Not only was he rugged, but his zest for living made him love his family, work, and play. He liked to ride horse, dance a jig, sing a song. His physical energy propelled his intellectual vigor. He was direct and spoke and wrote as he thought. He was bored with indirection, annoyed with "highfalutin'" sham, intolerant of genteel sophistication, impatient with both pretentious legal nonsense and stuffed shirts who talked too long.... Such blunt, sometimes brutal, frankness won him some temporary enemies but more permanent friends. For beneath the buffalo was a good and generous friend and a fine storyteller with a robust sense of humor. He was a laughing, loving, hating, feeling man, with the fire of youth and the courage of the warrior. Indeed, Miller had the gift of the gods: joy of living life to the fullest.[38]

Within this flattering encomium to Samuel Miller, we might also recognize the personal qualities of Thurgood Marshall, Sandra Day O'Connor, and other former Justices. Where have these dazzling characters gone? Our nation turns its lonely eyes to them.

CHAPTER TWELVE

BRING BACK PHRONESIS AND RANGE

Brown v. Board of Education is the twentieth century's most important Supreme Court case, and it is not particularly close. In May 1954, a unanimous Court overruled *Plessy v. Ferguson* and reversed more than a half-century of law that held the doctrine of "separate but equal" to be constitutional. A recap of the story, and especially of Chief Justice Earl Warren's prominent role, is instructive. Like Justice Marshall's unanimous triumphs in the nineteenth century, perhaps we can glean some broader lessons from the Warren Chief Justiceship about how a Court attains success. My retelling is largely drawn from Richard Kluger's excellent history of the decision, *Simple Justice.*[1]

But before we turn to the case itself, a moment on the Court's position when Warren arrived as Chief Justice. Chapter Eight of this book began with a description of the crippling dysfunction and internecine battles of the Stone and Vinson Courts of 1941–53. During this period, either most or all of the Justices had been appointed by Democratic presidents: Roosevelt and Truman. In theory, these Justices should have easily found common ground. And yet the Courts of the period were notorious for non-unanimous decisions and splintered opinions. By the 1951–52 term, the Court failed to reach unanimity in a shocking 81 percent of their decisions.[2] That was, by far, the lowest point for unanimity between 1944 and 2019, and it remains a historical low. (To compare, in 2012, the recent high point for unanimity, more than 60 percent of the Court's cases were unanimous.)

Personal animosity was unusually pitched. Robert Jackson never forgave Hugo Black and William Douglas for advocating against his ascension to Chief Justice. Douglas and Frankfurter legitimately hated each other. Black, Frankfurter, Douglas, and Jackson reportedly thought little of Vinson's intellect, and freely expressed their disdain. Kluger offers a colorful description:

> The tension lines ran every which way. Minton found Jackson pompous and Black prone to demagoguery. Douglas remained aloof from nearly everybody save Black. Black and Frankfurter thought Reed often lacked the courage of his convictions. Burton, a straight-laced teetotaler who never smoked or cursed, found his neighbor on the bench, the Rabelaisian Minton, somewhat on the uncouth side and did not enjoy having his robe sprayed when the tobacco-chewing Hoosier missed the spittoon provided for him behind the bench. And so it went.[3]

Brown v. Board of Ed. and its sister cases arrived against this backdrop of universal animosity. The cases were first argued on December 9, 1952. Vinson was still Chief Justice and the cases arrived in great uncertainty. The Vinson Court had chipped away at segregation around the edges in the previous years, but it had never come close to overruling *Plessy v. Ferguson* nor its odious holding that "separate but equal" was constitutional. Here that precedent was directly challenged.

Moreover, the chances of a truly disastrous result, an explicit upholding of *Plessy*, were very real. In the run-up to *Brown*, the NAACP legal team led by Thurgood Marshall faced withering criticism in certain quarters for pushing too early to overrule *Plessy*. An adverse result, it was thought, risked guaranteeing another sixty years of legal segregation. These critics urged an incremental approach that worked within the framework of *Plessy*—picking off various institutions that were facially and obviously unequal against blacks, and thus in violation of the separate-but-equal standard. This more conservative approach could change lives in the near term and also build the groundwork for overturning *Plessy* when public and judicial opinion improved at some point in the future. Nevertheless, Thurgood Marshall and the NAACP bravely pushed their chips to the middle of the table and went all in, hoping to dismantle legalized segregation in one fell swoop.

The 1952 argument was inconclusive, and many were not sure what to make of the NAACP's gamble. The Court itself was likewise torn. As per usual, the Justices met in conference to discuss the cases and their disposition. There is no official record of the meeting; apparently no votes were taken. Nevertheless, the handwritten notes and recollections of the various Justices give us some idea where the Court was headed.

Vinson was skeptical of a broad ruling on school desegregation. Kluger describes Vinson as a "shrewd politician and a legal pragmatist," and thus "exceedingly wary of brushing aside the long-standing traditions of the South—his South—no matter what constitutional justifications could be assembled in behalf of overturning *Plessy*."[4]

Vinson was not alone. Justice Frankfurter's notes from the conference list another three likely "no" votes: Clark, Reed, and Jackson. If this speculation was correct (and Frankfurter was rarely wrong in guessing how his colleagues might vote) a Vinson Court might have overruled *Plessy* in a 5-4 decision in which each Southern Justice except Black (i.e., Vinson, Clark, and Reed) dissented. Douglas's notes from the conference speculated that Frankfurter, a "small-c" conservative who might hesitate to overrule any precedent as old and well established as *Plessy*, might vote to uphold segregation, creating a possible 5-4 majority *in favor* of segregated schools.[5] Frankfurter's own notes and recollections suggest that this result was always unlikely; still, contemporary observers guessed there might have been as many as nine separate opinions from the case. The end result was far from certain: historian Jim Newton accurately characterized the Court as "flummoxed" by the cases.[6]

Frankfurter worried that the Court was headed towards a divided and disastrous result, so he pushed for a new set of questions and a re-argument in the next term. The other Justices agreed, and on June 8, 1953, the desegregation cases were re-calendared. The parties were tasked with answering a series of new questions about the history of the Fourteenth Amendment, the power of the Court to end segregation, and what a remedy ending such a wide ranging and ingrained practice might look like.[7]

On the one hand, the decision to reargue pushed off the oncoming train-wreck possibility of a bitterly divided Court narrowly striking down, or narrowly upholding, school segregation. On the other hand, the delay was only that—a delay—and didn't carry with it any certain promise of a more unified Court. The answers to these new questions could have moved different Justices in or out of any potential majority.

In the meantime, fate intervened. Chief Justice Vinson died on September 8, 1953, of a heart attack. His death further delayed the case, but it raised the chance of a different outcome and perhaps a more unified Court under a new Chief justice. To get a taste of the contemporary state of vitriol on the Court, consider the reported comment by Justice Frankfurter, an avowed atheist, to a former clerk that Vinson's death was "the first indication [he] had ever had that there was a God."[8]

President Eisenhower set to work in selecting a new Chief Justice. Kluger describes Eisenhower's criteria: "character and ability" first, then "high ideals, a moderately progressive social philosophy—a middle-of-the-roader, in other words, in his own image—and a substantial ration of common sense." Judicial experience would be "helpful but not necessary," and the nominee should add "geographic and religious balance" to the Court.[9]

Eisenhower settled on Earl Warren, a man who "seemed to reflect high ideals and a great deal of common sense."[10] Warren was the sitting governor of California who had unsuccessfully run as the vice-presidential candidate with Thomas E. Dewey in the election of 1948. He was certainly an admired politician, having been re-nominated as Governor of California in 1946 by both the Republican *and* Democratic Parties, but he was hardly a giant intellectually or in the broader public imagination. Kluger quotes at length from a 1947 *Inside U.S.A.* article on Warren that painted him as a "genial second-rater" who was "honest, likable, and clean" and had "little intellectual background, little genuine depth or coherent philosophy; a man who has probably never bothered with abstract thought twice in his life." In sum, a man who "will never set the world on fire or even make it smoke."[11]

Contemporary observers decried the selection as a missed opportunity to appoint a "first-rate" Chief Justice and noted that Warren had "never sat on a bench in his life, not even for five minutes in police court."[12] Frankfurter was reportedly "outraged that Eisenhower would name a mere politician to the Court."[13]

Warren is exactly the sort of Justice that has been completely eliminated from the Court. A list of Warren's life experiences reads like a list of what we're currently missing. Warren worked his way through the University of California at Berkeley for both his undergraduate and law degrees. He was a fine student but hardly top of his class. He served in the Army during World War I, rising to the rank of first lieutenant, although he never was deployed overseas. After the war he spent the rest of his career in government, working as a city attorney in Oakland, and then 18 years in the District Attorney's Office in Alameda County, serving as the District Attorney for thirteen years. He became the Attorney General of California in 1938 and was elected Governor in 1942, serving until his appointment to the Court in 1953.

Warren brought these experiences with him as Chief Justice and managed to unify a divided Court and deliver a unanimous opinion where none seemed possible. After the second argument in December 1953, the Court again convened to discuss the cases. Initially there was a bare five-Justice majority with the possibility of drawing more support, but much disagreement as to the nature and scope of any possible majority opinion. Justice Reed, Vinson's fellow Kentuckian and closest friend on the Court, seemed to be a firm "no" vote. Kluger summarizes the situation:

> Thus, the Court's array showed Warren that he had a piece of work to do. A solid five-man bloc was apparently ready to declare against segregation on principle. But even its members were not entirely agreed on just how it should be done. Douglas and Minton seemed to favor a short, simple statement of principle which did not try to face the varying problems that would arise in different areas. Black apparently wanted to narrow the scope of the opinion to something less than a cosmic declaration of human rights. Burton and Warren seemed flexible on the timetable that would be laid down for implementing the Court's action.
>
> Beyond the openly committed group, Warren could apparently count on Clark—but only if the opinion of the Court assured the segregating states a good deal of latitude and enough time

to respond in as painless a fashion as possible; whether such an opinion could be fashioned without yanking out all of its teeth first remained to be seen. Frankfurter sounded as if he would go along, but he was known to savor writing concurrences that often served to dilute the impact of the majority opinion. And Jackson had all but promised to write a concurring opinion if the majority did not acknowledge that it was acting in a frankly unjudicial way—a scarcely reasonable request to make of the brethren. Reed, finally, seemed fixed on voting to uphold segregation while insisting that every state was obligated to equalize its colored schools straightaway.[14]

Warren desperately wanted to avoid dissents and concurrences if possible, and he hoped beyond hope for "a single, unequivocating opinion that would leave no doubt that the Court had put Jim Crow to the sword."[15] As such, he declined to push for a single yes/no vote in the first conference after the re-argument. He and the other Justices agreed to keep talking and working, and Warren hoped to be able to bring some or all of them around.

Note Warren's political acumen on two different fronts here. At the time, the school desegregation cases had dragged on for years; there must have been a temptation for Warren to consider the opinions of his fellow Justices fixed and to take 5-4 or 6-3 and move on. Replacing Vinson with Warren had not replaced the other eight Justices, and there was little suggestion that they were open to compromise. In fact, all evidence pointed to the contrary. Nevertheless, Warren knew that a massive decision sat in front of them and took its political and logistical ramifications more seriously than its legal implications. Warren had spent too long as a politician to care overmuch about the legal niceties of any particular decision; he just wanted a decision that would move the country forward on perhaps its central dividing issue.

Second, Warren knew not to press against these Justices. Instead, he gave the entire Court breathing room. This, in turn, gave him time to work on each of the different personalities and positions. He was deferential to the Court's intellectual heavyweights—allowing Black to preside over the Court's first conference as the senior Justice, and working closely with Frankfurter, Douglas, and Jackson in drafting his opinion. He was also solicitous to the Court's lesser lights, getting to know them and earning their respect.

In the end Warren wrote a simple and short decision, joined by all other Justices, that relied as much on logic and common sense as it did on law. Warren circulated the opinion and then adjusted it to meet edits, while still keeping others on board. Jackson's top law clerk that term, Barrett Prettyman, remembers his reaction to Warren's opinion: "I wished that it had more law in it but I didn't find anything glaringly unacceptable in it. The genius of Warren's opinion...was that it was simple and unobtrusive. He came from political life and had a keen sense of what you could say in this opinion without getting everybody's back up."[16]

This description suits the decision quite well. It clocks in at a tidy 13 pages in the U.S. Reports, with just 14 short footnotes. It is exceedingly light on citations to other cases and certainly does not try to build a grand case either way that all of the Court's earlier proclamations led to this result, nor that the Court was required to overrule or rethink large swaths of older cases, with the notable—and, of course, critical—exception of *Plessy v. Ferguson*. Consider the Court's stirring conclusion:

> We conclude that in the field of public education the doctrine of "separate but equal" has no place. Separate educational facilities are inherently unequal. Therefore, we hold that the plaintiffs and others similarly situated for whom the actions have been brought

are, by reason of the segregation complained of, deprived of the equal protection of the laws guaranteed by the Fourteenth Amendment. This disposition makes unnecessary any discussion whether such segregation also violates the Due Process Clause of the Fourteenth Amendment.[17]

The closest stylistic parallels to Warren's opinion here are the opinions of Chief Justice Marshall quoted at the outset of Chapter Two. Rather than ostentatiously flaunt its own technical legal excellence, Warren's opinion challenged the reader to disagree with its fundamental and simple logic and decency. I mean no disrespect to Barrett Prettyman, Jr., by all accounts a brilliant lawyer, but the idea that "more law" would have improved the opinion is emblematic of our misguided focus on technical legal excellence. "More law" brings more infighting over narrow legal questions. More infighting over narrow legal questions brings concurrences and dissents. More concurrences and dissents weaken the precedent and fan the flames of public objection. More law can thus prove self-defeating and obfuscating rather than clarifying.

Warren managed to draft a unanimous opinion, bringing even Reed on board. When it came time to convince Reed, Warren did not try to defeat him with legal reasoning or to browbeat him on the facts. Reed's clerk recalls that Warren asked Reed simply "to decide on whether it's really the best thing for the country" to dissent. The clerks described Warren as "not particularly eloquent and certainly not bombastic. Throughout the Chief Justice was quite low-key and very sensitive to the problems that the decision would present to the South. He empathized with Justice Reed's concern."[18]

Reed came around, and the Court announced its unanimous decision on May 17, 1954. Kluger is quite clear in his assessment of this achievement, describing Warren as a "judicial statesman and political tactician of the most formidable sort" and a direct descendent of John Marshall.[19]

There are a few ironies to this version of the story. As Kluger makes clear, Warren's insistence on unanimity came at a price. Most notably, the Court declined to rule on a remedy in its first opinion, and its second opinion only guaranteed desegregation at "all deliberate speed." As students of desegregation well know, "all deliberate speed" varied widely by geographic region, with some areas leaning more heavily on "deliberate" than on "speed." Some would argue that certain areas of the country have never fully implemented *Brown*. In celebrating Warren's achievement, it is still reasonable to second-guess the actions of the Warren Court. Maybe a 5-4 decision enacting an immediate federal court takeover of Southern schools would have resulted in faster and deeper reforms. Or maybe that would have caused popular backlash, harming the prospects of the Civil Rights movement and its key legislative victories: the Civil Rights Act of 1964 and the Voting Rights Act of 1965. These are legitimate questions that are impossible to answer.

Second, because Warren's decision relied upon common sense and sociological research as much as law, it faced attacks from some august corners of legal academia. The famous Columbia Law School professor Herbert Wechsler, for example, assailed *Brown* for failing to act "Toward Neutral Principles of Constitutional Law," to take the title of his famous 1959 *Harvard Law Review* essay.[20] Wechsler did not object to the result in *Brown*. To the contrary, his essay offers multiple preferable (and more technically legal) avenues for reaching the same result.

All fair concerns, to be sure. But re-reading Wechsler's argument today, it is hard to imagine that a more technical opinion could have succeeded outside of the halls of academia. To the contrary, Wechsler seems to under-consider the sheer magnitude of the moment, causing him to propose a kind of opinion that would have been wholly unsuitable. It is also worth considering the possibility that "neutral principles of constitutional law"—or, really, any other technical legal conception of the Court's job—do *not*, in fact, offer much useful constraint on the Court. Recent decades of highly divided and politicized decisions stated in ornate and beautifully drafted technical legalism show this to be exactly the case.

Last, some may argue that Warren's own pre-Court and post-*Brown* record was deeply flawed. As Governor of California during World War II, he was instrumental in the creation and operation of the Japanese internment camps—hardly an advertisement for practical wisdom. Likewise, Warren has become a controversial Chief Justice because he led a liberal revolution in multiple areas of jurisprudence after *Brown*, most notably redesigning the American constitutional law governing race, poverty, and criminal justice.

Some disagree with Warren's entire project and so are unlikely to ascribe much practical wisdom to the Chief Justice. Others are more sympathetic but note that the Warren and Burger Courts seeded their own destruction. There's a particular irony to highlighting Warren as the last great Justice to have come from a different, older sort of background that encouraged practical wisdom. The Warren Court, along with the post-Warren liberal majorities of the early Burger Court, charted the activist judicial path on which the Court now finds itself. Warren's decisions unquestionably brought intense political attention to the Court and its Justices. Conservative dissatisfaction with these decisions, and with the liberal drift of Republican appointees of presidents from Eisenhower to George H. W. Bush, led to a search for more "reliable" Justices, and thus to the model we now see adopted by both Democratic and Republican presidents. It also presaged the bruising confirmation fights that have become ever more common.

Still, I love the example of Warren and *Brown*. As discussed below, practical wisdom, or what Aristotle called *phronesis*, is not about the rightness of any particular result. This is important because the *Brown* example is *not* about the result, although the result was and is obviously correct. To the contrary, *phronesis* is about the *process* of making hard decisions, and here Warren shines like few other Chief Justices. He kept the biggest picture in mind and worked to gather a unanimous Court behind one of its most important and controversial decisions ever. Warren also recognized the actual audience for the Court's writings: the American people. Unlike more intellectually decorated Justices, Warren had little concern for how law professors would evaluate his work, or whether his opinion demonstrated a mastery of the underlying law and precedent. Instead, he wrote practically: first to gather a unanimous Court; and second to persuade a skeptical public. In these regards Warren displayed an uncommon share of practical wisdom.

Moreover, the connection between Warren's life experiences and his approach to this case demonstrate just what we've lost in adopting the new model of Supreme Court Justice. We have privileged technical legal ability over a range of experiences that generate practical wisdom, and we are all the poorer for it.

Elite, Neutral, and Cloistered

Hopefully you are now convinced that the kinds of backgrounds we find in today's Justices are quite different than those found in the Justices of the past. The point of my empirical study was to establish the existence of this difference. In this chapter, however, I aim to convince you that the changes have been bad. The more

I study these trends the more concerned I have become. This is because we have replaced experiences that bring the Justices into contact with ordinary Americans with experiences that I consider to be elite, neutral, and cloistered.

Start with our bygone pre-Court experiences: practicing the law, holding elective office, fighting in the military, serving as a trial judge, etc. In each of these activities you are directly answerable to third parties: Lawyers work for clients. Politicians serve the voting public. Soldiers work within a strict hierarchy. Trial judges work with juries and face the litigants before them, putting human faces to the ramifications of their decisions. State court judges and justices are often elected.

These working relationships have powerful psychological effects. Lawyers, politicians, soldiers, and trial judges must frequently suppress their own natural preferences to follow the will of their clients, the public, a commanding officer, or a jury. Politicians and lawyers must often temper their own beliefs to match those of their audiences. These experiences in self-control and self-denial can prove useful to a Justice whose preferences clash with his perception of the correct legal decision. Federal appellate judges and law professors, by contrast, are instructed to be "neutral." Tuning out the "noise" of the outside world is their modus operandi. Yet sometimes whole swaths of our shared human experience can be found in this "noise." We want Justices to take a fresh and unbiased look at every case, but treating the work of the Court as narrowly legal is foolishly myopic.

Politicians, soldiers, trial judges, and practicing lawyers operate in busy and complicated real-life situations. They cannot be neutral or cloistered. They must get elected, find clients, follow orders, or make legal or political arguments. Trial lawyers and politicians must also make their arguments in a manner ordinary people—jurors and voters—can understand and appreciate.

Same with trial judges. Trial judges must explain the law in plain language that jurors and litigants can understand—though they don't always succeed, as anyone who has heard jury instructions will know. Each of these jobs encourage the translation of the complicated into the explicable—an essential skill for Justices that is nevertheless absent on the present Supreme Court. Lastly, politicians and lawyers frequently must learn the art of compromise. Politics is a messy business that requires give and take from all parties involved. Likewise, much of lawyering involves negotiation, settling, and deal making—again, all activities that are essential to a well-functioning Supreme Court.

Conversely, consider the elite, neutral, and cloistered experiences that now dominate. Today's Justices spent an inordinate portion of their pre-Court life as appellate judges or legal professors. The jobs share much in common: Both are notoriously and proudly independent. Both deal with law in a highly abstract manner. Both are intentionally cloistered from public opinion. Both tend to encounter litigants on the written page. Both involve a great deal of contact with law students or recent law school graduates (in their role as judicial law clerks). Both jobs thus involve the continual affirmation of smart young people genuflecting to their ideas.

Both jobs are extraordinarily difficult to attain, requiring a high level of technical legal excellence. Unsurprisingly, elite academic credentials are required for the jobs. How elite? One must be continuously at the top of the class, and more. Even straight "A"s in high school and scoring a perfect SAT doesn't guarantee admission to Princeton. Getting into Princeton does not guarantee admission to Yale Law School. Attending Yale Law School does not guarantee a clerkship on the Supreme Court, and so it goes.

Because of the nature of today's elite legal competitions, these Justices have also spent more time living in Washington,

D.C., than any previous Court. Insofar as there is an "inside the beltway" mentality, these Justices surely have it.

Even their limited experiences practicing law run more towards the elite, cloistered, and neutral. These Justices specialized in appellate-heavy work at law firms and the Solicitor General's Office; or they engaged in highly politicized work for the White House Counsel's Office and for Congress, with little time spent in the more traditional litigation or transactional practices of law.

Some may object that these experiences have actually made the current Justices uniquely qualified for their seats on the Court. It is surely true that these D.C.–centered experiences have taught the Justices more about the workings, output, and nature of the Supreme Court than any prior group of Justices. Many of today's Justices have spent a lifetime studying the Court as law professors, or practicing before it as lawyers. This chapter argues that what at first might seem to be a strength is, in fact, a crippling weakness.

Why It Matters—Specialists and Range

At heart this argument comes down to one's belief in specialization. Earlier Courts reflected an American tendency towards generalization and a very broad conception of merit. The Justices took winding and diverse roads onto the Court. Current Justices have all seemed to follow a narrow and more specialized path. Which is superior?

David Epstein's excellent book *Range: Why Generalists Triumph in a Specialized World* offers a persuasive case for generalists, especially on decision-making bodies that deal with unpredictable issues.[21] Epstein's overarching argument is that those with broad experiences and training are better than specialists at addressing complex, real-world problems. Epstein highlights the work of psychologist Robin Hogarth, who describes two different types of learning environments: "kind" and "wicked."[22] Kind environments involve situations where there are bounded rules and a positive feedback loop between specialization and solutions. Chess, classical music instruction, and golf are examples of this sort of learning environment. In wicked environments, however, "the rules of the game are often unclear or incomplete, there may not be repetitive patterns and they may not be obvious, and feedback is often delayed, inaccurate, or both."[23] Complex, real-world problems tend to be wicked, not kind.

Computers and specialists tend to shine in "kind" environments, because expertise and mastery is tightly connected to correct answers. By contrast, humans and generalists operate better in wicked environments. Epstein notes that AI has mastered chess and *Jeopardy!* but has struggled in more open-ended challenges like curing cancer: "The difference between winning at *Jeopardy!* and curing all cancer is that we know the answer to *Jeopardy!* questions. With cancer we're still working on posing the right questions in the first place."[24]

It is not just that generalists are better in areas of uncertainty. Experts are actually worse: "highly credentialed experts can become so narrow-minded that they actually get worse with experience, even while becoming more confident—a dangerous combination."[25] Experts tend to jump to the "inside view" of every problem. "We take the inside view when we make judgments based narrowly on the details of a particular project that are right in front of us." Generalists take the "outside view" and probe "for deep structural similarities to the current problem in different ones...a mindset switch from narrow to broad."[26] Experts frequently fall prey to the Einstellung effect: "a psychology term for the tendency of problem solvers to employ only familiar methods even if better ones are available."[27]

Computer programmers use the term "premature optimization" to describe a common mistake that occurs when programmers indiscriminately apply previous solutions to new problems without first fully understanding their different root causes.[28] These attempts at increasing efficiency actually produce worse and more cumbersome results, as yesterday's solution is misapplied to today's different problem. It's an apt analogy for the current Supreme Court. There is probably no legal institution in America that more regularly considers "wicked" learning environments—real-world problems—than the Supreme Court. And yet we have staffed the Court with legal technocrats, ready, willing, and able to find a narrow and legalistic answer from yesterday to a broad and complicated question of today.

Epstein also discusses Philip Tetlock's groundbreaking research into the science of prediction-making. Tetlock describes how a broad base of knowledge helps humans make more accurate predictions:

> If we want realistic odds on what will happen next, coupled with a willingness to admit mistakes, we are better off turning to experts who embody the intellectual traits of Isaiah Berlin's prototypical fox—those who "know many little things," draw from an eclectic array of traditions, and accept ambiguity and contradiction as inevitable features of life—than we are turning to Berlin's hedgehogs—those who "know one big thing," toil devotedly within one tradition, and reach for formulaic solutions to ill-defined problems.[29]

"Foxes" outperform "hedgehogs," despite seemingly knowing *less* about the topic at hand, because hedgehogs "tend to see simple, deterministic rules of cause and effect framed by their area of expertise."[30] The hedgehog's deep knowledge actually works against them, blinding them to the broader context foxes are able to consider. On a different but related topic, studies have shown that crowdsourced predictions on the outcomes of Supreme Court cases are often more accurate than expert predictions.[31]

How does one become a fox rather than a hedgehog? Broad experiences and exposure to all sorts of different areas of expertise. Successful predictors "were excellent at taking knowledge from one pursuit and applying it creatively to another, and at avoiding cognitive entrenchment."[32] As Epstein notes when talking about educational models, "breadth of training predicts breadth of transfer."[33]

As the world grows more complex, and as we ask the Supreme Court to answer ever more freighted and difficult questions, we have decided to abandon breadth for depth and to replace foxes with hedgehogs. Worse yet, these hedgehogs are all experts in the same narrow area: Supreme Court decision-making. Focusing on technical legal excellence over all else is exactly backwards. Is it any wonder that opinions have grown longer and more complex?

Why It Matters—Practical Wisdom

Believing that a breadth of experiences leads to better decision-making is, of course, not a new idea. Consider Aristotle, whose conception of virtue ethics is having quite a comeback moment. What other concept of philosophical virtue has inspired a hit NBC sitcom? Mike Schur, showrunner of *The Good Place*, has noted that "traditional Aristotelean virtue ethics" is "the show's overarching statement."[34] Likewise, the Harvard law professor and political philosopher Michael Sandel has settled on his own version of virtue ethics as the solution to age-old debates over how to create a just society. Sandel's account is particularly salient because, like *The Good Place*, it brought these debates outside the philosophy classroom and into the public square. In 2009, WGBH Boston and PBS filmed and aired twelve one-hour videos of Sandel's lectures and caused a sensation. His 2009 book based on the class, *Justice: What's the Right Thing to Do?* was likewise a *New York Times* bestseller.[35] The book is extremely readable, especially for a work of moral philosophy, and the lectures are gripping (and still available for free on Harvard's website).[36]

Why has virtue ethics seen a comeback roughly 2,300 years after Aristotle first outlined the theory? Part of it is dissatisfaction with the two other main schools of moral philosophy: consequentialism and deontology. To radically oversimplify, there are three main branches of moral philosophy: consequentialism, deontology, and virtue ethics. These categories overlap; some disagree that they are separate at all. Nevertheless, please work with me here.

As its name might suggest, consequentialism judges a moral act by its consequences. Utilitarianism is the best-known version of consequentialism. To determine which is the most correct or moral act, we simply ask, "what act will maximize utility?" Deontology judges a moral act according to an external set of rules, regardless of its consequences. Kant's moral imperative is an example of a deontological alternative to utilitarianism. John Rawl's *A Theory of Justice* is a newer version of deontology.

The nice thing about both consequentialism and deontology is that they attempt to answer directly the ultimate questions, "what is a just act?" or "what is a just society?" Theoretically, these approaches offer a single and universal answer to those questions. The devil, naturally, is in the details. The "trolley problem," and other more concrete real-life examples, show the many challenges of applying over-arching theories of justice to specific cases.

Virtue ethics, by comparison, focuses on the character of the actor and the process of decision-making rather than the justness of any particular action. Aristotelean virtue is the key to moral decision-making.[37] Virtue ethics is a "third way" around the eternal battle between the consequentialists and the deontologists. This is because virtue ethics deals with *process* rather than results.

Michael Sandel summarizes the three approaches thusly:

> Over the course of this [book], we've explored three approaches to justice. One says justice means maximizing utility or welfare—the greatest happiness for the greatest number. The second says justice means respecting freedom of choice—either the actual choices make in a free market (the libertarian view) or the hypothetical choices people *would* make in an original position of equality (the liberal equalitarian view). The third says justice involves cultivating virtue and reasoning about the common good.[38]

Sandel chooses the third path because it avoids the pitfalls of the first two and because it replaces ends-related thinking with means-related thinking. Instead of arguing about the nature of just ends, virtue ethics asks how one might make just decisions. Good and virtuous decision-making, theoretically, leads naturally to just results.

Aristotle is the progenitor of virtue ethics, and his term *phronesis* is its key. Book VI of Aristotle's *Nicomachean Ethics* discusses four intellectual virtues: science, theory, philosophy, and practical wisdom.[39] Unlike science, theory, or philosophy, *phronesis* is not "concerned with universals only—it must also recognize the particulars; for it is practical, and practice is concerned with the particulars."[40] *Phronesis* is primarily "concerned with things human and things about which it is possible to deliberate."[41] Deliberation on the particulars is the heart of *phronesis*.

Sandel's popularization of virtue ethics relies on this principle. Each lecture is packed with real-life examples of ethical dilemmas, including affirmative action, abortion, and other contemporary debates. Sandel does this to make the theoretical real, but also because here his form matches the substance. Moral philosophy cannot, and should not, be divorced from particularized factual examples. We learn about justice by looking at it in real life, not by reasoning from first or universal principles.

Phronesis is thus a uniquely practical concept. Aristotle explicitly differentiates the fact-dependent nature of practical wisdom from "scientific knowledge" or "skill in conjecture."[42] Scientific knowledge (*episteme*) is theoretical and builds from universal principles. Aristotle naturally respects this sort of thinking, but explicitly rejects it as a basis for his theory of ethics.

Conjecture, says Aristotle, "involves no reasoning and is something that is quick in its operation." Practical wisdom, however, requires long deliberation: "[R]eadiness of mind is different from excellence in deliberation."[43] Practical wisdom is not gained by cloistered study and contemplation. It is gained in living a varied and challenging life.[44] *Phronesis* is "practical, and practice is concerned with particulars.... [T]hose who have experience are more practical than others who know."[45] Aristotle questions whether the young are capable of practical wisdom:

> [W]hile young men become geometricians and mathematicians and wise in matters like these, it is thought that a young man of practical wisdom cannot be found. The cause is that such wisdom is concerned not only with universals but with particulars, which become familiar from experience, but a young man has no experience, for it is length of time that gives experience.[46]

Aristotle also quite pointedly differentiates between practical wisdom and what he calls "mere cleverness." *Phronesis* often resembles cleverness, but its ends are quite different. Practical wisdom leads to correct decisions, cleverness alone is flashy and insubstantial.[47]

Fans of America's burgeoning obsession with "happiness" or the "good life," will probably already know that Aristotle explicitly attaches *phronesis* to the good life. For Aristotle the goal of life is not fleeting or momentary happiness, but *eudemonia*: a state of excellence and well-being. Consider the following definition of *eudemonia* and how it connects to *phronesis*: "Eudemonia—well-being; A person's state of excellence characterized by objective flourishing across a lifetime and brought about through the exercise of moral virtue, practical wisdom, and rationality."[48] To Aristotle, *phronesis* is not just a pillar of moral philosophy; it is the key to a well-lived life. It is not a route to excellence or justice; it is excellence and justice itself.

Practical Wisdom and Judges

Aristotle's understanding of virtue ethics is universal, but it is particularly well suited to judging. This is partially tautological. Judging naturally involves judgment, and virtue ethics offers a comprehensive analysis of *how* a judge might reach just decisions. Virtue ethics also has the advantage of avoiding the unanswerable theoretical debates of consequentialism and deontology, which have very little to do with the real concerns of judging. Indeed, looking at judging through the lens of virtue ethics offers a practical way to focus on questions of much greater import: what processes and which characteristics lead to justice?

Virtue ethics can, theoretically, cut the Gordian Knot of argument over the "rightness" of liberal or conservative outcomes. Rather than asking whether a decision accords with one's utilitarian or Kantian framework, which will naturally be freighted by how one sees the politics of any case, we can ask whether or not the Justices first approached the case wisely and then reflected the best version of decision-making before coming to their final decision.

Some will argue that this move is reductive and unhelpful. Critics will argue that we have no neutral way of determining whether a decision is just or not, so virtue ethics just dodges the hard questions. Besides a list of virtues and the description of a process, virtue ethics offers arguably no details as to what justice really entails. Nevertheless, consequentialism and deontology are also riven by disagreement over the meaning of "justice." It is easy to say that decisions should benefit the greatest number of people or reflect some universal rule of morality, but the application of these rules inevitably leads to disagreement and confusion. As such, virtue ethics can actually be more concrete than these universal systems, because at least it offers clarity on the processes and traits that lead to just decisions.

Virtue ethics thus applies nicely to the best versions of common law judging—fact-based, pragmatic, and often modest. Lawrence Solum has specialized in what he calls "virtue jurisprudence," the application of Aristotelean ethics to American law.[49] As Solum notes, "the notion of a just decision cannot be untangled from the notion of a virtuous judge grasping the salient features of the case. Virtue, in particular the virtue of phronesis, or judicial wisdom, is a central and ineliminable part of the story."[50] Solum's work is echoed by Karl Llewellyn's argument that judging is best described as a craft. Craft value and virtue ethics are close cousins.[51] Judges as varied as Frankfurter, Holmes, and Richard Posner have likewise pressed for judicial pragmatism and humility for similar reasons.

Virtue also more closely matches the American conception of a "fair" judge, especially in a time of political polarization, than other philosophical systems. While there may be little agreement on the politically charged issues before the Court, there is (hopefully) still general agreement that Justices should approach each case by its merits and come to the best decision possible based on the law, facts, and context. This common-sense hope for our judiciary is a restatement of virtue ethics. We are hoping for a certain type of judge to use a certain type of process to come to the best decision he can.

Consider Robert McCloskey's wisdom about what we might look for in Justices: "[The work of the Court] requires judges who have what a great poet called 'negative capability'—who can resist the natural human tendency to push an idea to what seems its logical extreme or have done with half-measures and uncertainties."[52] Here McCloskey refers to John Keats's praise of Shakespeare as a writer "capable of being in uncertainties, mysteries, doubts" and not bound solely to "irritable reaching after fact and reason."[53] In other words, we need Justices who can accept "half-knowledge" and uncertainty in their work, rather than attempting to iron out every technical legal issue presented.

You Don't Have to Like Virtue Ethics to Agree That Practical Wisdom is a Good Thing—And Currently Lacking on the Court

Some of my readers, perhaps many, will read the above and find themselves utterly unpersuaded. Or perhaps they agree with Richard Posner's attack on the entire field of moral philosophy:

> I do not derive my economic libertarian views from a foundational moral philosophy such as the philosophy of Kant, or Locke's philosophy of natural rights, or utilitarianism, or anything of that sort. I regard moral philosophy as a weak field, a field in

disarray, a field in which consensus is impossible to achieve in our society. I do not think it provides a promising foundation for a philosophy of government.[54]

Nevertheless, hopefully all can agree that common sense—*phronesis*—is a desirable attribute for Supreme Court Justices. Yet practical wisdom is not gained by cloistered study and contemplation of the neutral principles of law. It is gained by living a varied and challenging life.

Remember that *phronesis* is the opposite of "mere cleverness." Yet the current trend in Justice selection seems to be focused *uniquely* on exactly that trait.

What the Court Now Does

Nevertheless, is it possible that our new model of Justice is, in fact, the proper fit for our new kind of Court? The nature of the Supreme Court has, of course, morphed over time, but recent decades have marked particularly consequential changes. The Court's caseload has shrunk while the size of its potential *certiorari* pool has grown.[55] This means the Court is deciding fewer cases as an absolute number and as a percentage of petitions. The Court thus limits itself to cases of national impact: cases in which it can announce broad rules or decide critical constitutional issues.[56] While the overall percentage of constitutional cases in the Court's docket has not risen, the salience of those decisions (and the public backlash) has grown significantly since the 1950s.[57] In the eighteenth and nineteenth centuries, a large chunk of a Justice's job was riding circuit and actually trying federal cases in local courts. Later the Court's work was narrowed to Supreme Court appeals. Then we narrowed which cases were even considered. Every few decades we have moved further away from the particulars and into the universal.

Each of these decisions has been politically charged. The decision to rarely grant review itself is political. The Court has essentially limited its own power by choosing to address fewer cases. Commentators have speculated about the reasons, ranging from a desire "to reduce the role of the judiciary in the nation's political life,"[58] changes in the Court's mandatory jurisdiction,[59] the power of the court clerks in the process,[60] advanced age,[61] or sloth.[62] Arthur Hellman has concluded that the Court's shrunken docket reflects an "Olympian" Court that issues fewer, but more monumental decisions.[63] Richard Posner (among others) describes the current Court as a superlegislature that sits chiefly to proclaim broad new law, rather than a more traditional appellate court, which aims to create legal uniformity and correct errors.[64]

Here it is helpful to compare America's judicial structure to civil law judiciaries like those in France or Germany.[65] In civil law systems, the kind of work done by our Supreme Court is often divvied between two very different judicial bodies. As noted earlier, most civil law countries have a separate constitutional court which handles *only* constitutional challenges. These courts are often staffed by individuals, including former politicians and non-lawyers, who have not been career judges. These countries have a separate highest court (and sometimes several "highest courts" for different areas of the law—commercial law, criminal law, etc.) that serves as the final word on issues of statutory interpretation and other more clearly "legal" issues.

Supporters of the civil law system might find our own judiciary, in which a single Court handles these very different tasks, to be utterly bizarre. Settling narrower legal disputes like how to read the word "wetland" in the Clean Water Act, or whether a tomato is a fruit or a vegetable under an import tariff scheme, is well suited to judicial technocrats who have spent years answering these sorts of questions. Constitutional debates over gay marriage or illegal search and seizures are quite different, and they require a different—and arguably broader and more political—set of skills.

This is why France's constitutional court is hardly even really a court. The French purposefully call it a council (*conseil*), not a court (*cour*). The council includes all living former French presidents and nine other members. Because the number of former presidents shifts over time, there is no set number of members, and not all of the members appear at every sitting. The arguments and decisions are purposefully political. Everyone understands that the council is not answering its questions based solely upon legal arguments. In our own country, these two very different responsibilities have fallen under a single Supreme Court at least since *Marbury v. Madison*, and it is likely too late to restructure. That said, it is always worth remembering that the Court does at least two very different jobs, and that those suited to one job may be incompetent in the other.

It hardly bears repeating that technical legal excellence is extremely well-suited to the Court's narrower responsibility. To again borrow from Hogarth, issues of statutory construction tend to be "kind" learning environments, whereas broad constitutional issues are transparently "wicked." In the narrower area there are long traditions and precedents to follow, making a technical mind more apt for the job. (Arguably even those issues would be better solved by foxes than hedgehogs. Consider Karl Llewelyn's astute observation that for every canon of statutory interpretation there is an equally well-cited and established counter-canon, so that the main work of statutory interpretation is to choose the outcome first, and then mix and match the precedents and canons that support the end result, rather than the other way around.[66])

Technical legal excellence, however, is clearly a bad quality for those charged with broad constitutional policymaking. The fruits of technical legal excellence—lengthy multipart tests and tortured analysis—do little to increase public confidence or understanding. To the contrary, they make confusion and cynicism more likely. Consider areas like standing, or race and gender discrimination, which are now complex to the point of incoherence.

As the Court has involved itself more in hot-button constitutional issues, the public has decried Justices who act like politicians. The self-defeating solution? Pick Justices who resemble the very best legal technocrats we can find, i.e. former appellate court judges and the winners of our hyper-elite competitions. Surely these exceptional legal minds will find a way to settle difficult constitutional disputes "legally" rather than "politically."

These Justices Are a Particularly Bad Fit for This Court

Not so much, actually. But first, let's give the current Court its due. Supporters can argue that this Court is the most qualified of any Court in history—they have spent more time considering and studying constitutional theory than any previous group of Justices. Likewise, one person's elitism is another person's highly functioning meritocracy. The current Court arguably evinces a salutary desire to have the best of the very best serve in government and staff the Court.

Supporters might also argue that the Court tends to be an elitist and anti-democratic body by design. Thus, arguing that "ordinary people" who have "real-life experience" should staff the Court misunderstands its fundamental nature. Institutional and constitutional design suggest we should embrace this elitism by finding the smartest and most able Justices possible to serve critically important life tenures. Perhaps Justices who have extensive experience as appellate judges and law professors and who are well versed in abstract thinking on constitutional issues are the only people we should even consider for the Court.

I argue that this trend is exactly backwards. As the Court begins to resemble more closely a policymaking "Olympian" body, it is especially important to appoint individuals with real-life experience. This is because the current Supreme Court makes many decisions that are not "legal" at all, so technical legal expertise and excellence is not particularly useful. To the contrary, as Epstein suggests, it may actually be harmful. Next, we cover some specific harms.

Complexity

Although writing judicial decisions or law review articles may sharpen analytical reasoning, excellence in that style of writing and reasoning frequently leads to obfuscation rather than clarification. Evidence abounds that the Court's output has grown less accessible and more complex. Consider the opinions themselves. Majority opinions have grown substantially longer.[67] The prevalence of dissenting and concurring opinions also grew for 1960–2010, although the recent trend has been towards greater unanimity.[68] The most confusing and complex type of decision—those decided by a plurality rather than a majority—has also become more common.[69] As professor Suzanna Sherry put it, the Court "is deciding half as many cases as it did a generation ago, and using twice as many pages to do so."[70]

Empirical and doctrinal legal scholarship evinces increased complexity. Laura Little's study of the Supreme Court's use of linguistic devices for obfuscatory purposes found "increased splintering" within the decisions and "increased opinion length and complexity."[71] Joseph Goldstein argues that even "professional interpreters" would struggle "to unravel what the Court has to say, often at great length in heavily footnoted multiple opinions."[72] Robert Nagel described the writing as "formalized" and characterized by "elaborately layered sets of 'tests' or 'prongs' or 'requirements' or 'standards' or 'hurdles' [and] standing amidst a welter of separate opinions and contentious footnotes."[73] Commentators have criticized the Court's treatment of conflict of laws and federal jurisdiction as complex and incoherent.[74] Complexity and nuance have also led to "stealth overruling," situations where the Court discards a disfavored precedent piece by piece, rather than by clear overruling.[75]

Stephen M. Johnson's excellent comparison of the grade-reading level of cases from the 1930s and those from the twenty-first century showed that more recent opinions are longer and less readable:

A comparison of the Supreme Court's opinions issued during the 1931–1933 terms and the 2009–2011 terms confirms that the Court's opinions are, indeed, less readable and much longer today than they were three-quarters of a century ago. Based on the Flesch Reading Ease formula, the opinions issued during the 2009–2011 terms were, on average, about twenty-five percent less readable than the 1931–1933 opinions. Kincaid Grade Level Formula showed that the 2009–2011 opinions were written at about a grade level higher reading level than the 1931–1933 opinions. The average opinion length has more than tripled from about nine pages for all the opinions in the case (majority, concurring, and dissenting) during the 1931–33 terms to about twenty-eight pages during the 2009–11 terms.[76]

The actual process of writing the opinions also reacts to

political salience, with higher-profile cases drawing longer, more complex opinions and more dissents and concurrences.[77]

This group of Justices seems particularly ill situated to reverse the trend. Insofar as the current group of Justices can take their jurisprudence of standing or the Establishment Clause seriously (just to use two particularly galling examples), it is a sign that we are placing too much stock in technical legal excellence and too little in common sense. Finding the smartest people to try to untangle the thorniest problems does not necessarily result in elegant solutions. Instead it often results in over-thinking, over-writing, and brutal complexity. This trend is especially discouraging in the highest-salience cases. This Court decides cases that have a massive effect on the entire nation in opinions that few can even read and understand.

The Court's Regulatory Role

The Chief Justice of the United States is the titular head of the Federal Judiciary and carries a special regulatory role that extends beyond merely deciding cases. Chief Justices have approached this task with variable enthusiasm. William Howard Taft is widely considered the gold standard. He used his tenure to reformat the federal judiciary, creating the Judicial Conference and modernizing the Court's *certiorari* system.[78] Frankfurter argued that Taft deserves a place in history "next to Oliver Ellsworth," the federal judiciary's original architect.[79]

By contrast, consider Chief Justice John Roberts's 2014 Year-End Report on the Federal Judiciary. These reports are usually pretty dry, presenting some statistics about the workload of the courts and an anodyne essay by the Chief Justice. In 2014 Chief Justice Roberts surprised many by including a lengthy explanation of why American "courts will often choose to be late to the harvest of American ingenuity."[80] Why "choose" to move slowly on technology? Because, "like other centuries-old institutions, courts may have practices that seem archaic and inefficient—and some are. But others rest on traditions that embody intangible wisdom."[81]

Roberts compares the push to adopt new technologies to the race between the tortoise and the hare, with the losing hare symbolizing advocates of new technologies and the victorious tortoise our wisely reticent judiciary. It is pretty amazing for any twenty-first century leader to proudly embrace the role of the techno-turtle, but if you have paid any attention at all to recent management of the federal courts it is not particularly surprising. Unlike Taft or Ellsworth, recent Chief Justices have been more interested in defending the status quo than adjusting to changing circumstances. Using technology to update a judicial branch that still largely operates like the federal courts of the twentieth or even nineteenth century seems like an uncontroversial and wise idea. It has also been suggested as a solution to America's yawning access-to-justice crisis. Nor is Robert's attitude shared globally. The Chief Justice of Canada, Richard Wagner, has been a bold and outspoken leader on access to justice and technology.[82] England has created Her Majesty's Online Courts to replace some physical courts and has deregulated large swaths of its legal profession in a sweeping modernization effort.

The Supreme Court also leads the process for drafting the Federal Rules of Civil Procedure, Evidence, Criminal Procedure, Bankruptcy, Appellate Procedure, and Admiralty, although Congress generally retains the power to revise or reject.[83] Unless proposed rules are rejected, modified, or deferred, they automatically become law, provided that Congress has had at least seven months to consider them.[84] While the Court has ceded some of the rulemaking responsibility to the Judicial Conference, the Justices are still key players in the process.[85]

The Court thus plays a large role in managing a gigantic bureaucracy and its rules, all with very limited experience outside of appellate courts, which are of course the tiniest sliver of the judicial branch. Practical wisdom and experience does not only affect case decisions, it's a part of running the judicial branch. These Justices have one—and only one—view of our vast judicial machinery.

The Court's lack of trial and litigation experience shows itself in case results. In a pair of decisions—*Bell Atlantic Corp. v. Twombly* and *Ashcroft v. Iqbal*—the Court held that Rule 8 of the Federal Rules of Civil Procedure requires plaintiffs to present a "plausible" claim for relief in the complaint, a significant tightening in pleading standards.[86] The text of Rule 8 requires only a "short and plain" statement of facts and claims and has done so since that Rule's inception.[87]

Commentators have pilloried *Twombly* and *Iqbal*, noting that these cases evince hostility to, and ignorance of, litigation practice.[88] These cases are of a piece with a Supreme Court's general "litigation reform" project, through which the Court has attempted to head off a perceived "litigation crisis."[89] These reforms have tracked with the continuing collapse in the number of federal court trials.[90] Whether Justices with more trial experience might have respected juries more is an open question.

Waning Public Confidence

If the point of selecting the "best" Justices for the Court is to boost public confidence, the returns are in, and they are not positive. In 2015, a Pew Research Center poll showed that 43 percent of Americans had an unfavorable opinion of the Supreme Court, the highest level of dissatisfaction since the poll began in 1985.[91] A 2014 Gallup poll showed a thirty-year low in public confidence in the Supreme Court, down to just 30 percent.[92] In 2015, Gallup found that only 53 percent of Americans had "a great amount" or "a fair amount" of trust in the judicial branch of the federal government.[93] This result represented a substantial decline from 76 percent in 2009.

Some of this decline might be seen as part of our nation's overall trend towards polarization. Republican and Democrat views began to diverge in 2001, and confidence in the Supreme Court has continuously grown more polarized.[94] This trend explains why public approval of the Court by Republicans fell dramatically under President Obama and then increased under President Trump (despite his vociferous attacks on Supreme Court decisions and individual Justices he disliked).[95] Democratic approval likewise fell under Trump, although not as much as Republican approval rose.

Still, the overall trend is not promising. Instead of appearing to the public as a neutral institution applying the law to the cases before it, the current Court is seen as yet another polarized political body, though better educated and more verbose. It is almost as if appointing the very smartest people with the very narrowest experiences has eroded public confidence and trust. Who could have guessed?

A Last Word on the Nature of Elite Competition

In presenting this research I have found law professors, especially law professors at elite institutions, to be by far the most hostile audience. Sometimes the critiques imply or even state outright that I am jealous of my betters. I take this critique seriously and I am self-aware enough to know that as a competitive person and law professor myself, I am indeed "behind" (and *laughably* behind) these Justices. Where I faltered in these elite competitions, they triumphed.

That said, my objection to these Justices is not based on their ability to triumph on a very clear career path packed with challenging competitions. These Justices have ploughed an unimaginably long and hard road to get where they are. They have worked relentlessly and tirelessly from their earliest days in school to be the very best of the best. Forgive a brief summary of the triumphs represented on Roberts 8 already outlined in Chapter One, but the sheer weight of these accomplishments is worth revisiting.

The Justices competed for admission to the very best universities and law schools. The great majority attended Stanford or an Ivy League undergrad and Harvard or Yale for law school. Three Justices received fellowships to study at Oxford.[96] *Six* Justices served as clerks to Supreme Court Justices— Breyer (Goldberg), Roberts (Rehnquist), Kagan (Thurgood Marshall), Barrett (Scalia), Gorsuch (Kennedy), and Kavanaugh (Kennedy). Three of the Justices were tenured faculty at elite law schools— Breyer (Harvard), Kagan (Chicago and Harvard), and Barrett (Notre Dame). Five Justices held a high-level law and policy job with either the executive branch or the Senate—Kagan and Breyer worked for the Senate Judiciary Committee. Kagan was Associate Counsel to the President. Roberts worked in the White House Counsel's Office. Kavanaugh was the Assistant to the President and Staff Secretary. Three worked in the Solicitor General's Office (Kagan, Alito, and Roberts) and four had argued cases before the Supreme Court before becoming Justices themselves.[97] Eight of the Justices secured jobs as federal appellate judges and the ninth was Dean of Harvard Law School. In sum, at each level of their professional careers these Justices have competed against their peers for accolades and jobs that were very, very difficult to obtain, and they won.

Nevertheless, there is a dark side to this path. These competitions encourage a particularly narrow focus upon achievement, to the exclusion of all else. This certainly predicts an ability to work hard and to complete difficult and complicated tasks. It does not, however, tend to correlate very strongly with a broader sense of perspective.

Lastly, many of these achievements show a potentially overweening desire to be on the Supreme Court. To paraphrase Plato and quote Douglas Adams, "it is a well-known fact that those people who most want to rule people are, *ipso facto*, those least suited to do it."[98] It is quite unlikely that the politicians or lifelong lawyers who used to become Supreme Court Justices were angling for a Court appointment from the start of their careers. Consider Justices, like Taft or Jay, who left the Court to pursue other interests. It is unimaginable that a Justice would do so today. Reaching the Court is not just a life achievement, it is *the* achievement, the apotheosis of their life's work. Many of these Justices have been competing to join the Court their whole lives; how could they leave?

CHAPTER THIRTEEN

∿

THE NARROWING OF LIFE'S RICH PAGEANT

Experiential Diversity Shrinks

On May 26, 2009, President Barack Obama nominated Sonia Sotomayor to the Supreme Court as a replacement for retiring Justice David Souter. Roughly a year later, Obama nominated Elena Kagan to replace John Paul Stevens. These two nominations were historic on multiple fronts. Sotomayor became the first Latina Justice and Kagan raised the number of women on the Court to an all-time high of three—both massive leaps forward for a body that featured only white men for almost two centuries. Likewise, when President Trump appointed Amy Coney Barrett to replace Justice Ginsburg he made history by choosing to replace a female Justice with another woman for the first time.

A picture speaks a thousand words, so consider two different portraits of our first four female Justices. The first, a lovely and naturalistic 2012 portrait by the artist Nelson Shanks, recently hung in the National Portrait Gallery as an homage to the historic changes on the Court:

Not to be outdone, writer and documentarian Maia Weinstock memorialized the first four female Justices in a custom-made LEGO portrait:

My favorite features are Justice O'Connor's arched eyebrows, Justice Ginsburg's iconic ruffled collar (not to scale) and of course the depiction of Sotomayor's lustrous curly hair.

If portraits fail to persuade, consider another eyeball test. There's a gripping YouTube video of every Supreme Court "class photo" from 1892 until 2019 that just scrolls through the pictures with no commentary. You get a masterclass in changing hairstyles and the improvements in photography, along with a front row seat to history. Thurgood Marshall arrives at minute 1:44 of the video, ironically in the last black and white photo. It is not until 1967 that we have a photo of the Court that includes anyone other than white male Justices. In 1981 Sandra Day O'Connor arrives, signaling the Court's first female. Thomas replaces Marshall in 1991, Sotomayor arrives in 2009, and last, a smiling Kagan appears in 2010, completing the most diverse Court ever in terms of race and gender. This Court is coded as Roberts 4 and is the most visibly diverse Court ever.

Seated from left are: Justices Thomas and Scalia; Chief Justice Roberts; and Justices Kennedy and Ginsburg. Standing from left are Justices Sotomayor, Breyer, Alito, and Kagan. *Credit*: Photograph by Steve Petteway, Collection of the Supreme Court of the United States.[1]

Compare these portraits to the one of the earliest known photographs of the Supreme Court, which displays nine of the ten Justices from the Chase 1 Court, helmed by Salmon P. Chase (John Catron is not pictured; he died in 1865 and was not replaced due to the Judicial Circuits Act of 1866 shrinking the size of the Court). This photo (next page) was taken February 23, 1867, by the Civil War photographer Alexander Gardner. The portrait shows the dourest group of white, protestant, males possible.

This Supreme Court does win in one area of diversity: facial hair. Samuel Nelson (sixth from the left) sports an iconic pair of mutton chops, a bare chin, and a neck beard covering his Adam's apple. James Wayne has a good-looking pair of mutton chops as well. David Davis and Stephen Field likewise sport healthy looking beards that might shame a modern hipster in a Brooklyn coffee shop. But it certainly lacks the visible diversity of the modern Court.

From left to right: The Clerk of the Court, D. W. Middleton; Justices Davis, Swayne, Grier, and Wayne; Chief Justice Chase; Justices Nelson, Clifford, Miller, and Field.
Credit: Photograph by Alexander Gardner, Collection of the Supreme Court of the United States.[2]

The eyeball test for diversity, however, does not capture the whole story. Using a broad measure of diversity of experiences, the Roberts 4 Court was the least diverse Court since the early-1950s. In fact, using a broader measure of diversity of experience, Roberts 4 was actually less diverse than the Chase 1, pictured above. How is that possible? Because outside of race and gender, the Chase 1 Justices lived more varied lives.

We'll use a comparison between these two Courts as an introduction to the categories studied, partially to show how a modern Court could be less diverse than one from 1864, and also to unpack how the diversity study works.

The first category considered is race and gender, and, you guessed it, all of the Chase 1 Justices were white males of northern European descent. So, there was no diversity in this category at all. Roberts 4, by contrast, was the most diverse Court for race and gender ever (tied with Roberts 5, 6, 7, and 8). Chase 1 is not alone in lacking racial or gender diversity. White males of northern European descent dominated the Court from the start and did not become a minority on the Court until the twenty-first century. Just to demonstrate how dominant northern-European white males were, Justice Cardozo, whose ancestors were Sephardic Jews from Spain and Portugal, was appointed in 1932. Cardozo was the first Justice of southern-European stock (Italian, Spanish, or Portuguese) on the Court.

The second category studied is religious affiliation. Here Chase 1 is actually relatively diverse, if you consider their denominational diversity within Protestantism. The Court included three Episcopalians (Chase, Nelson, and Wayne), three Presbyterians (Catron, Davis, and Grier), two Unitarians (Clifford and Miller), and the Supreme Court's only Quaker Justice (Swayne). By comparison, Roberts 4 had three Jewish Justices (Ginsburg, Breyer, and Kagan) and six Roman Catholics (Roberts, Alito, Thomas, Kennedy, Sotomayor, and Scalia).

Any nineteenth century Court that included Unitarians and Quakers was religiously diverse for that era. Episcopalians *dominated* the early Court. The early dominance was such that more than half of all the Justices have been Episcopalians, even today. That said, the diversity amongst protestant denominations is interesting to track over the years, with Unitarians, Quakers, Disciples of Christ, and the Dutch Reform Church joining larger and more expected denominations like the Episcopalians, Baptists, and Presbyterians.

The third category is professional experience pre-appointment. Here Chase 1 was relatively diverse, but Roberts 4 slightly more so. The dominant experience on Chase 1, as is typical of every Supreme Court before the twenty-first century, was time spent in the private practice of law, with Noah Swayne's twenty-nine years in practice leading the way. All ten of the Chase 1 Justices had practice experience as private lawyers, working as solo practitioners or as part of a small firm or both. Chase 1 had five former politicians, including a former Senator, a former Governor, two former members of the House of Representatives, three state legislators, and a former Mayor of Savannah, Georgia. Chase 1 also included a former Secretary of the Treasury, U.S. Attorney General, an Attorney General for the State of Maine, and a former Postmaster for tiny Cortland, New York (one of Samuel Nelson's first jobs). Seven of the Justices had experience as a state court judge and six Justices worked as trial judges. Two had fought in the war of 1812 (Wayne and Catron). The Chase 1 work experiences clustered around working as a private lawyer, sitting as a judge, and serving as a politician.

Roberts 4 has seven Justices who practiced law in law firms or as corporate counsel, and two who only have government experience. There are no former politicians or former state court judges, and only one former trial judge. Five Justices taught law full time and eight of them served as federal appellate judges. Diversity is higher for Roberts 4 here because there is no single dominant experience like the private practice of law on Chase 1.

The fourth and fifth categories cover the Justices' childhood circumstances, considering, first, whether they grew up in farm communities, towns, or cities; and, second, how wealthy their families were. Chase 1 is more diverse than Roberts 4 on both of these measures, and especially for the type of community the Justices experienced as children. Chase 1 had three Justices from family farms or plantations, five from rural areas, and two from small towns. The rural and agrarian bent is pretty typical for the nineteenth century, reflecting a largely agrarian economy before the Civil War. From the Industrial Revolution forward, urban settings came to dominate on the Court, as in American life generally.

Chase 1 had Justices who grew up across the economic spectrum: one upper class (Wayne, raised on a Georgia plantation), two upper-middle class (Nelson and Davis), four middle class (Chase, Swayne, Grier, and Catron), one lower-middle class (Miller) and two from especially poor families (Catron and Clifford). This mix of childhood backgrounds is somewhat unusual, especially having two Justices from the least privileged category. Only seven Justices have ever come from abject poverty, so having two on the same Court is quite unusual.

Roberts 4 had a whopping seven Justices from urban areas (Ginsburg, Breyer, Alito, Kagan, Sotomayor, and Kennedy) and two from small towns (Roberts and Thomas). Roberts 4 had three Justices from the upper-middle class (Roberts, Breyer, and Kennedy), four from the middle class (Ginsburg, Alito, Kagan, and Kennedy), one from the lower-middle class (Sotomayor) and one from deep poverty (Thomas).

The sixth category asks what geographic region Justices called home during the majorities of their pre-Court lives. Chase 1 was again more diverse than Roberts 4. Chase 1 Justices spent a roughly equal amount of time pre-appointment in the South and the Mid-Atlantic, with some significant time in both the Midwest and New England, and a decent showing for the West Coast due to Stephen Field. Chase 1 had one Justice who had lived in another country. Justice Clifford spent (roughly) a year as U.S. Envoy Extraordinary and Minister Plenipotentiary to Mexico in 1848–49. We need to bring back that title. "Ambassador" is far too dry.

Roberts 4 was dominated by time spent in the Mid-Atlantic, mostly the New York and D.C. areas, with Breyer and Kennedy adding some West Coast flavor. Roberts 4 has more foreign experience due to time spent studying at Oxford (Breyer and Kagan). Overall, the dominance of the Mid-Atlantic meant limited geographic diversity for Roberts 4.

The seventh category considers educational background, and here again Chase 1 was more diverse. As was typical in the mid-nineteenth century, almost all ten of the Justices read the law and only one studied at a law school at all (Davis studied for a year at the New Haven Law School, later absorbed into Yale as its Law School). Swayne, Clifford, and Catron had no formal undergraduate or graduate education at all. They read the law and then joined the bar. Seven other Justices went to a wide variety of undergraduate institutions, including College of New Jersey (later Princeton), Middlebury, Dickinson, Transylvania (for an M.D. degree!), Kenyon, Williams, and Dartmouth.

Roberts 4 reflects much less diversity. Every Justice attended Yale or Harvard Law School (with only Ginsburg's one year at Columbia as an outlier). Every Justice except Thomas (Holy Cross) and Scalia (Georgetown) attended an Ivy League university or Stanford for undergrad.

The eighth and final category is political affiliation. Chase 1 had six Justices nominated by Democratic presidents and four by Republicans. Roberts 4 had five Justices appointed by Republican presidents and four by Democrats, so the diversity was roughly the same here.

The Diversity Study—Methodology

This chapter is a simplified version of the study that biologist Emily Moran and I published in the *Journal of Empirical Legal Studies* in 2013.[3] I will keep the methodology discussion here as basic as possible; the details are all in the original article if you want more.

The study considered the same categories as those discussed in previous chapters, plus identitarian categories such as race, gender, and religion. In total we studied eight different categories: gender and racial, religious, professional background, childhood family setting, childhood economic background, geographic, post-secondary educational, and political affiliation. Each of these contained multiple subcategories. The data collection resulted in a massive spreadsheet of over 382 different possible experiences. We then took the eight categories listed above and combined them into a single comparative measure of the diversity of experiences on each natural Supreme Court from Jay 1 to Roberts 8. The point of this measure is to see whether the change in Justice backgrounds demonstrated in the years study has resulted in a concomitant decline or increase in overall diversity of experiences.

The Simpson Diversity Index and a Short Biodiversity Detour

The study compares relative diversity of experience across time. Given our society's current focus on increasing the diversity of schools and other institutions, I assumed there would be a commonly accepted measure for multivariate diversity. Otherwise how would a corporation or admissions office measure diversity in a sophisticated manner, as opposed to relying merely on racial or gender quotas? Yet despite general agreement on the advantages of diversity in groups from university classrooms to corporate boardrooms, it turns out there is not an agreed upon measure of multivariate diversity among humans. This may actually tell us more than we would like to know about the difference between an institution that says it is in favor of broad diversity, versus actually trying to increase diversity. Often what doesn't get measured doesn't get addressed.

Regardless, rather than trying to create my own measure of comparative diversity, I decided to work by analogy. After poking around a little, the study of biodiversity seemed like a natural fit. Biologists have long investigated whether the overall diversity of different species within a specific ecosystem is waxing or waning. Pro tip: as human populations boom, biodiversity retreats.

Why biodiversity? It may seem strange to think that the mix of attributes and experiences on the Supreme Court is analogous to the number of different plant species in a rain forest, but as a matter of logic and math, biodiversity measures are a great fit for trying to map human diversity. Basically, the study treats each different attribute or experience as if it were a separate species in an ecosystem. As the range of experiences or attributes decline on the Court, the measure shows lessening diversity. As new experiences are added, that boosts the measure. Using the same formula over the entire course of the Court allows us to decide whether diversity is trending up or down, or remaining level.

Fortuitously, the University of Tennessee, where I teach law, is the host institution for one of the premier statistical biodiversity centers in the world: the National Institute for Mathematical and Biological Synthesis ("NIMBioS").[4] So, I had the good luck to be a five-minute walk from a world class biodiversity center! I eventually found my co-author on the original diversity study, Dr. Emily Moran, in the NIMBioS program. I gathered the data and we used two different widely respected measures of biodiversity to measure multivariate diversity in background experiences on the Supreme Court.

Common use of the word "biodiversity" is actually only about thirty or forty years old, having been popularized in the 1980s, but the general study of the number and types of species in a particular area is, of course, much older.[5] The Bible includes the story of Adam naming the animals, making him the first biologist. Aristotle categorized animals and plants into more than five hundred species.[6]

Darwin's theory of evolution sparked a revolution in interest in the classification of plants and animals. Extinction and adaption were also suddenly important areas of study. Later, an explosion in human population led to a great loss of biodiversity, engendering more study. By the middle of the twentieth century, the field of biodiversity had advanced such that scientists were comparing different ecosystems around the world and over time. The most basic method was simply to count the number of species found in an ecosystem. The more species, the more diverse the ecosystem.

This measure came to be seen as too rudimentary. For example, which of these forests strike you as more diverse:

1. Forest 1 has 100 trees. It has 90 maple trees and one each of pine, spruce, oak, birch, sequoia, redwood, beech, willow, sycamore, and magnolia.
2. Forest 2 also has 100 trees. But it has 8 species of tree (all of the above species except for oak, birch, and pine). Each species has 12 or 13 trees in the forest.

A species count considers Forest 1 almost 30 percent more diverse than Forest 2, even though a hike in Forest 1 would be much less interesting than Forest 2 (depending on your feelings about maple trees). Thus, statisticians added diversity measures to capture the representation of each species within the ecosystem. There are two primary measures of biodiversity, one called the Simpson Diversity Index and the other the Shannon Diversity Index. These two indexes were coincidentally created a year apart by two different data scientists, neither of whom were trained naturalists (both men worked as codebreakers during World War II). Here we use the Simpson Diversity Index.

Edward H. Simpson was a British statistician and cryptanalyst who worked with Alan Turing in the famous Bletchley Park facility, attempting to crack the Nazi codes.[7] Later in life he worked as a statistician and civil servant in the United Kingdom. He is actually best known for "Simpson's Paradox," a statistical anomaly by which an aggregated dataset suggests one statistical conclusion and the disaggregated parts suggest the opposite.[8]

The Simpson diversity index is described in a one-page article in a 1949 issue of the academic journal *Nature*.[9] The basic idea is to count the examples of each species and then use their squared proportions to define diversity. Leaving the math aside, the diversity index answers a very simple question: given an ecosystem of different species, if two examples are chosen from within the system, what are the chances they will be the same species? The index runs from 0 (every time you take two samples they are the same) to 1 (every time you take two samples they are different). As the number rises, the measured diversity within the ecosystem is considered greater. If you care about the math, I reproduce it in the attached endnote.[10]

Caveat—We Treat These Categories as Equally Important, Your Mileage May Vary

Please note a significant caveat: the Simpson Diversity Index score will be at its highest when there are more categories and when the totals for each category are equal. As a mathematical principle, this is sound, but as applied to humans it means that each category of diversity is weighted equally, which raises two important possible concerns.

First, each reader likely holds a unique idea of which diversity categories are most important. Some, for instance, will find gender or ethnic diversity to be more important than professional experience or education. Deciding how to differently weight the categories, however, would have been politically and ethically impossible (although not mathematically). Thus, for the aggregated diversity score, we made the decision to weight all types of experience equally. As a hedge against this objection we also present the diversity results within each category, so a reader can focus on any particular area of diversity.

Second, there is the argument that ideal diversity does not imply across-the-board equality in representation among groups, but rather a representation that matches the demographics of the United States. Adopting this demographic standard of diversity would, for instance, give us a gender diversity baseline of about 50/50 for gender, but a racial baseline that matches the more complex racial breakdown of the country. Given that these demographics shift constantly over time, attempting to track these different moving targets would inject another possible source of bias in the results, so it was not adopted.

The Results

Figure 13.1 shows the overall diversity result from every Supreme Court from Jay 1 in 1789 through Roberts 8 in 2020:

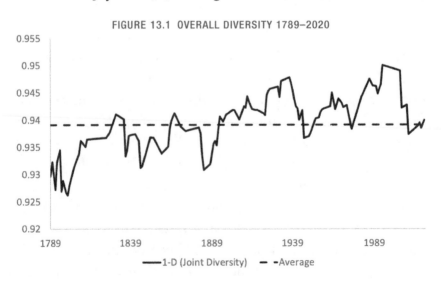

FIGURE 13.1 OVERALL DIVERSITY 1789–2020

First, note that overall diversity on the Court has always been relatively high. A score of 1 means perfect diversity and a score of 0 means no diversity. The average of all the Courts is .939, so overall diversity on the Court has always been much closer to 1 than 0. The high point was Rehnquist 6 from 1994 to 2005 at just a hair over .95 and the low point was Ellsworth 3 from 1800 to 1801, at .926. Still, every Supreme Court has come in above .925 in diversity score, representing a relatively diverse group.

Some of this is due to the sheer number of categories considered, as more categories naturally leads to a higher overall diversity result, but part of it is a general reflection of the diversity of experiences in America's legal profession. Compare this to France's highest legal (as opposed to Constitutional) court, *la cour de cassation*, which deals with civil and criminal cases. This court is staffed by lifelong judges who have worked their way up the ladder in France's bureaucratic court system. Given that the vast majority of the judges on this court entered the judiciary directly after graduating from university, their experiences would likely be less diverse than their American counterparts.

Second, and unsurprisingly, for the Court's first one hundred years or so, diversity was mostly below average. Since 1894 it has generally been above average. The Court was smaller for stretches of the first 100 years, which naturally depresses diversity. Likewise, the Justices themselves were uniformly white males and often from Northern European stock and Episcopalian.

Third, despite its significant volatility, the aggregated diversity graph nevertheless illustrates an overall trend towards greater diversity over the course of our entire history. Yet, since the relative collapse in diversity after 1994, we are undoubtedly at a relative low point within this trend. The recent downward trend in overall diversity has occurred even as gender and racial diversity has grown steadily in the same period of time.

Last, since 1954 there have been only three stretches when the Court was below average for diversity: Burger 4 (1975–81), Roberts 4 (2010–16), and Roberts 7 (2018–20). These Courts are still more diverse than the typical nineteenth-century Court, but that's hardly a point of pride given America's overall changes since then. Diversity has declined considerably in the last quarter century as Justice backgrounds have coalesced into our current hyper-elite model. This is not a salutary trend.

Race and Gender Diversity

Some areas of diversity are obviously up, most notably gender and race. In fact, in terms of this kind of diversity, the Supreme Courts since Sotomayor's appointment have been the most diverse in history, with three women (an all-time high), two total people of color (another record), and one Latina (for the first time ever). As one might expect, the graph measuring gender and racial diversity is hilariously unidirectional, as Figure 13.2 shows:

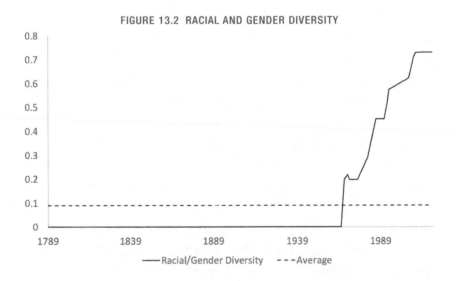

FIGURE 13.2 RACIAL AND GENDER DIVERSITY

This chart makes me laugh every time I look at it because of almost two hundred years of *zero* diversity. There are three obvious takeaways: First, diversity on race and gender has been low historically, as shown by a long running score of zero and an overall average score of under .1. Second, things took off in 1967 with the appointment of Thurgood Marshall and we've never looked back. Last, we are not done here, of course, but progress is progress, and we've clearly seen a massive amount of positive growth in just the last fifty years.

Religion

Astute readers will likely have guessed another area in which historical discrimination has given way to at least some acceptance of diversity: religious affiliation. Here we measure Protestantism, Catholicism, and Judaism. Figure 13.3 shows that religious diversity is, indeed, higher than it has been historically, but also that the recent trend has been away from greater diversity.

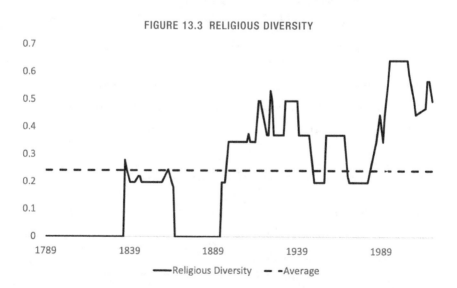

FIGURE 13.3 RELIGIOUS DIVERSITY

Like gender and race diversity, there were long stretches when the Court reflected a single category, protestants. As noted above, Episcopalians dominated within this group, but there was some inter-protestant diversity that is not reflected above. Unlike gender and race, religious uniformity was overcome sooner and more often. For example, the positive growth in the mid-nineteenth century reflects the appointment of Chief Justice Taney, the first Roman Catholic Justice. Likewise, the appointment of Joseph McKenna in 1898 to join Justice Edward White doubled the number of Catholics on the Court from one to two and launched a long stretch during which the Court was relatively more religiously diverse due to its Catholic and Jewish Justices.

Ironically, when Alito replaced O'Connor on the Court in 2006 we saw a reversal of the historical trend. Religious diversity shrunk with the loss of that Court's only protestant, and the two religions that had historically boosted diversity against a baseline of Protestantism (Judaism and Catholicism) came to dominate the court. Before the appointment of the protestant Gorsuch, the Court consisted of only Jewish and Roman Catholic Justices.

The addition of Gorsuch is showed in the steep, late uptick, followed by another fall with the replacement of Ginsburg with the Roman Catholic Barrett. Roberts 8 is dominated by its six Catholic members. Religious diversity is above historical norms, but still not at its peak because it remains dominated by just two religious affiliations.

Diversity of Professional Background

Diversity of professional background on the Court is relatively high. The study uses thirty-two different categories of professional work—city mayor, U.S. Senator, solo law practitioner, Attorney General, etc.—to reflect the variety of experiences of Supreme Court Justices throughout history. This approach allows us to recognize the full breadth of professional experiences, but it does mean that our diversity scores in this area will be necessarily much higher than, say, those of racial and gender diversity, for which there are far fewer categories. Likewise, for professional background we allowed fractional responses for Justices to reflect each of their various different pre-Court jobs. Religion deals with only whole numbers, reflecting that the Justices were Jewish or Protestant their whole lives. Both the sheer number of categories and the changes in profession for each individual Justice necessarily boost this diversity measure.

Yet even looking at professional diversity in relation to this elevated baseline, Figure 13.4 shows that diversity of professional background is at an all-time high on the Roberts Courts:

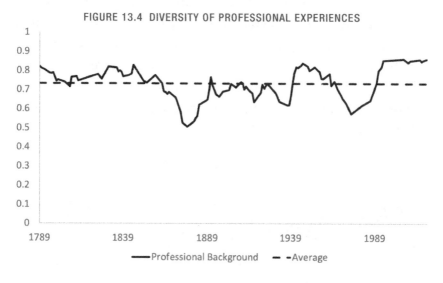

FIGURE 13.4 DIVERSITY OF PROFESSIONAL EXPERIENCES

Frankly, this result surprised me. I expected the focus on hyper-elite experiences to result in lowered diversity for professional background. I was obviously wrong. Diversity of professional background is up and at an all-time high. It turns out that the current crop of hyper-elite lawyers found a diverse mix of jobs before they became appellate judges—as law professors, partners in corporate firms, former members of the White House Counsel's Office, or Solicitors General. The overall effect is still hyper-elite, but the individual inputs are pretty diverse.

It is also interesting just how high the diversity in professional background was in the first Supreme Courts, despite their relatively fewer total Justices. Even as small a Court as Jay 1, with only five Justices, reflected a remarkable amount of professional diversity.

Childhood Background

The study measured two different types of childhood experiences: the geographic setting of the Justice's childhood (farm, small town, etc.) and the level of family wealth (upper class, upper-middle, etc.). If you know these two facts, and then consider the historical era, you can get a pretty good picture of what any Justice's childhood looked like. Interestingly, one of these measures is at a relative high point for diversity, and the other a relative low point. Before reading on make a guess which is which.

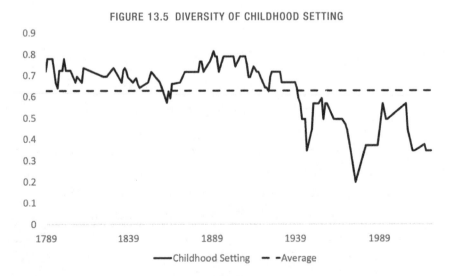

FIGURE 13.5 DIVERSITY OF CHILDHOOD SETTING

Figure 13.5 shows that childhood setting is near an all-time low point and well below average. The average diversity score for childhood setting is .63 and the Roberts 8 score is .35. Seven of the Roberts 8 Justices came from an urban area (Breyer, Alito, Sotomayor, Kagan, Gorsuch, Kavanaugh, and Barrett) and two from a small town (Thomas and Roberts). This makes childhood setting among the least diverse categories in the study.

Childhood setting is also one of the few categories in which diversity started high and has declined in the last one hundred years or so. From 1790–92, the Jay 2 Court scored .78 on this measure. Likewise, from 1909 to 1910, the Fuller 12 Court scored .79. From that point forward, diversity shrank, pretty much continuously. This is strange just as a matter of math. The Court did not have nine members until 1838, so the first fifty years of the Court should naturally be below average, and certainly not continuously above average. Nevertheless it is a reflection of the continuing urbanization of the United States, as well as the disappearance of the family farm, and the much-discussed brain and population drain from rural areas. Those wondering why residents of rural America feel underrepresented in our nation's institutions would do well to consult this finding.

Yet figure 13.6, childhood economic circumstances, on the next page, tells the opposite story.

For most of the first half of the Court's existence, the diversity of childhood economic circumstances falls below the average. This measure has almost always been above average since 1925, reflecting that social mobility, at least in the legal profession, has been greater in the last century than earlier. On a relatively less diverse Court overall, it is heartening to see a long above-average streak here.

Thomas is coded as indigent, and if you've read his biography

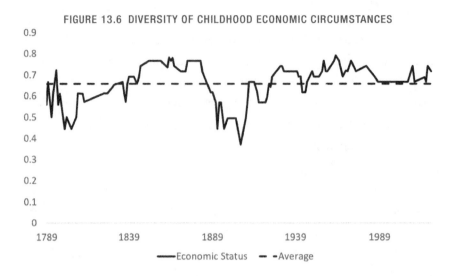

FIGURE 13.6 DIVERSITY OF CHILDHOOD ECONOMIC CIRCUMSTANCES

you know why. Sotomayor grew up in a lower-middle-class family. Kagan and Alito grew up middle class. Gorsuch, Roberts, Breyer, and Barrett are coded upper-middle class, and Kavanaugh upper class. (Note that these are rough estimates, given the difficulty in precisely coding a family's wealth relative to overall society at any given time. Some might argue that Sotomayor's childhood looks more like Thomas's than Warren Burger's, who was also coded lower-middle-class. Or some might argue that there's little to distinguish Kavanaugh's upbringing from Gorsuch's. While there is certainly merit to these and other arguments in this necessarily subjective category, any individual decision does not really change the big picture.)

As an aside, I strongly recommend studying the biographies of all seven Justices who grew up destitute: from most to least recent, Thomas, Goldberg, Byrnes, Douglas, Clifford, Catron, and Wilson. Like many American rags-to-riches stories, these biographies are gripping and exceedingly unlikely tales of depravation and triumph. Each is heartening and worth your time.

Geography

Here the study measures diversity by time spent living in different geographic areas: New England, Mid-Atlantic, South, Midwest, Southwest, West, foreign countries, and Washington D.C. Like professional background, we also allow for fractions here. Each Justice's pre-Court life is counted proportionally within these categories and adds up to 1 for each Justice. This means that like professional background, diversity naturally runs a higher here.

Figure 13.7 shows that geographic diversity is below some recent peaks and even fell below average on Roberts 7.

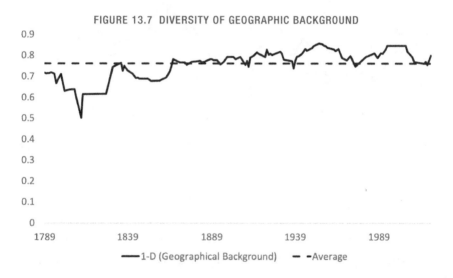

FIGURE 13.7 DIVERSITY OF GEOGRAPHIC BACKGROUND

——1-D (Geographical Background)   ‑ ‑Average

Figure 9.1 (which marked the prevalence of experience living in D.C.) back in Chapter Nine helps explain why diversity fell before the addition of Amy Coney Barrett. The Roberts 7 Justices spent the vast majority of their lives in the Mid-Atlantic or D.C. If we coded D.C. as part of the Mid-Atlantic geographic diversity would be in a full collapse.

Educational Background

Here we measure the highest level of education that each Justice on the Supreme Court reached, separately coding for: J.D. at Yale or Harvard; J.D. at another Ivy League school or Stanford; a J.D. at a non-Ivy League school; undergraduate education plus reading the law; or no formal higher education/read the law. The results in Figure 13.8 are not surprising, educational diversity on the pre-Barret Roberts Courts was at a jaw dropping low:

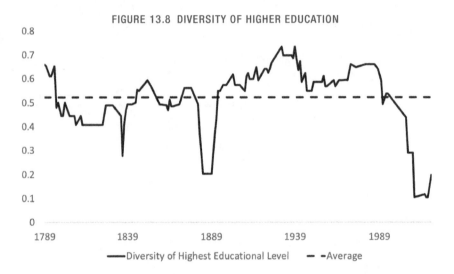

FIGURE 13.8 DIVERSITY OF HIGHER EDUCATION

This is one of my favorite charts in the whole book and it alternatively makes me growl or giggle depending on my mood. Justice Stevens was appointed in 1975 and retired in 2009 as the last Justice to graduate from a non-Ivy League law school. The "diversity" of Roberts 6 and 7 was reflected solely in Justice Ginsburg's Columbia J.D., which is especially ironic since she only attended Columbia for one year. If you're looking for a single factor that has caused overall diversity to shrink on the Court, here you are. Barrett again raises diversity here, as a graduate of a non-Ivy League law school.

Some readers may object to my spin on this data, noting that diversity naturally shrank when we eliminated reading the law as training for the profession. The last Justice coded for "read the law" was James Byrnes in 1941, and unless we have the good fortune to see Justice Kardashian join the Court someday (presumably as President Kanye West's first appointment) we're unlikely to see any new entrants in that category. Fair enough. But the study separately codes for three different types of J.D. experiences (Harvard or Yale, other Ivies and Stanford, and non-Ivy). Is it really OK to have such limited diversity even among three types of law school experiences? Supporters of the current meritocracy (a.k.a. elitists) may say yes, but for my money the answer is a hard no. Consider how relatively diverse the educational experiences of the Jay and Ellsworth Courts were, despite having fewer Justices. Surely we can attempt emulate those Courts.

Political Affiliation

Diversity of political affiliation has been volatile throughout the Court's history, but it has remained relatively high since the creation of the Democratic-Republican party and the arrival of our two-party system. In 1804 Thomas Jefferson nominated William Johnson to join the Court as its first non-Federalist appointee, launching a long period in which there was typically *some* diversity of political affiliation. In the mid-nineteenth century there were brief stretches of Democratic domination (which helps explain some of the disastrous pre–Civil War decisions).

Note that we coded for the Justice's own political affiliation and *not* that of the appointing president. So, for example, Justice Frankfurter counts as an independent and not a Democrat, because that was Frankfurter's own political designation, despite his being appointed by the Democratic president Franklin Roosevelt. This explains why the Courts of the mid-twentieth century still reflect political diversity despite the long string of appointments by Roosevelt and Truman. Figure 13.9 (the last graph in this book!) shows the trend.

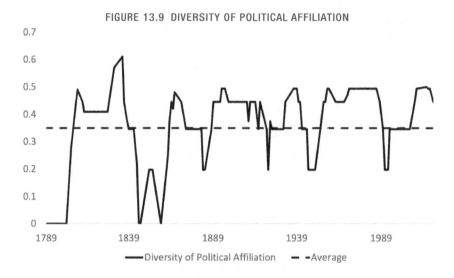

FIGURE 13.9 DIVERSITY OF POLITICAL AFFILIATION

The eight-member Roberts 5 Court marked a relative high-point for political diversity, reflecting the 4-4 split Democratic and Republican appointees. Barrett's addition marked a downturn, as the split became 6-3 Republicans. That said, do not mistake lower diversity in political affiliation with ideological consistency. Consider Rehnquist 4 and 5 (1991–94), Courts that were Republican-dominated but probably less ideologically conservative than other more evenly split Courts.

Why It Matters

Aggregate diversity on the Roberts 8 Court is close to the overall average for the Supreme Court's total history. On the one hand this is reassuring. While experiences are shifting, diversity still remains close to average. On the other hand, a finding of average experiential diversity in 2020 is pretty remarkable, given how much has changed since 1789.

Supporters of the current Court might argue that sacrificing diversity to find the "best" Justices is a beneficial trade-off. I disagree: boosting the diversity of Justice backgrounds will itself result in better decision-making and serve other, broader societal purposes. Let's start with the question of whether a more diverse Supreme Court will make better decisions.

The Supreme Court is a small decision-making body—currently just nine individuals—that makes difficult decisions on legal, social, and moral issues. Would a larger group be preferable? Studies show that large groups of humans make better decisions on average than small groups, even small groups comprising so-called "experts." This is the so-called "wisdom of the crowds" effect. As one example among many, Consider the long-term performance of stock market index funds against portfolios picked by experts or the relative success of crowd-driven Supreme Court prediction models.[11]

Why do large groups outperform small groups? Part of the answer is diversity of experience and viewpoints. There is natu-rally less diversity in a smaller group, especially in a smaller group of "experts." Humans gain expertise in study or work or both, so experts in a field tend to have very similar work and educational experiences, leading to similar decision-making processes, biases, and viewpoints. These tend to be repetitive and self-reinforcing, leading to worse results. Psychologists call this danger "groupthink." Homogenous groups of experts tend to approach problems in the same or similar manner, leading to cohesion but also substantively poorer decisions.[12]

Why is diversity of experience and knowledge so helpful? Multivariate diversity is an antidote to groupthink because injections of disparate views and experiences create cognitive conflict.[13] Small group diversity also has a positive effect on "integrative complexity," the recognition of multiple dimensions of an issue and placing these dimensions in context. Diverse groups do a better job of revealing false assumptions and prejudices. Diverse groups are better at brainstorming additional strategies and finding novel solutions. Multiple studies establish that diversity in decision-making bodies results in greater creativity, innovation, and problem-solving.[14]

Other studies describe three broad benefits of diversity: improved workforce quality; market sensitivity; and organizational agility.[15] David Carter and his co-authors studied diversity on Boards of Directors and found a positive relationship between diversity and firm value.[16] There have also been a bevy of educational studies on the benefits of diversity in the classroom and at the podium. A diverse learning environment fosters relational and cooperative learning environments and increased civic awareness and openness to other cultures.[17] Two recent studies found that gender and racial diversity in law firms is associated with higher profits.[18] Basically, decision-making, investigation, and deliberation all improve in diverse groups.

Diversity has likewise proven helpful in legal decision-making. Psychologist Samuel Sommers has made a career of studying the effects of diversity on jury decision-making.[19] For example, in one series of experiments Sommers created a mock trial for a criminal case designed to potentially raise issues of race and racism.[20] He then assigned two different types of juries—one set of all white juries and another set of mixed race juries—and then videotaped the deliberations. The mixed-race juries were substantively superior. The discussions took longer, included more case facts, included fewer factual errors, and included more explicit discussions of racism. Note that the improvements were not limited to racial sensitivity. The deliberation on non-racial issues also improved.

Of course, the jury itself is, by design, an institution that favors diverse viewpoints and the wisdom of the crowd. Our Constitution places juries at the heart of American justice. The founders thought that a randomly selected group of one's peers would do a better and fairer job of deciding criminal and civil cases than a single expert (the judge).[21] Nor were they ignorant of the shortcomings that the jury system inherently presents. The great majority of the founders were lawyers who had experience trying cases to juries, so if any group of early Americans knew the many shortcomings of juries, these lawyers did.

Diversity models for the Supreme Court come to an analogous conclusion. Adrian Vermeule created a model for Supreme Court decision-making that took different types of expertise into account.[22] The model is based upon pretty basic and relatively noncontroversial assumptions about expertise and good decision-making. His conclusion? The Supreme Court could use at least one non-lawyer, and maybe more. Choosing only lawyers for the Court necessarily creates a large swath of identical experiences and expertise. Lee Epstein and her co-authors likewise have argued against the norm of prior judicial experience because it privileges only one professional background over other important experiences.[23]

Diversity's Expressive Value

This book considers diversity broadly, including visually obvious factors such as race and gender as well as harder-to-spot matters like education and professional background. I've already discussed the logistical benefits of this more inclusive notion of diversity, but we should not ignore the expressive value of a Supreme Court that looks like the composition of America at large.

Unlike Congress or the presidency, the Supreme Court is an appointed body staffed by Justices with life tenure. As the Court has become more important in the daily lives of Americans, it is more critical than ever that that the Court look and feel representative of the country as a whole.

CHAPTER FOURTEEN

∾

LET'S GET THIS SHOW BACK ON THE ROAD

Article I of the Constitution covers the legislative branch, and clocks in at 2,268 words, roughly 52 percent of the entire text of the Constitution. Article II, covering the executive branch, is the next longest at 1,025 words, roughly another 23 percent of the Constitution. Combined, Articles I and II comprise three quarters of the Constitution. Presumably the third branch is the other 25 percent? Ha, no. Article III, which covers the judicial branch, clocks in at a tidy 377 words, or just 8 percent of the Constitution. Even those few words are pretty bare-boned. For example, here's what Article III has to say about the structure of the federal judiciary: "The judicial Power of the United States, shall be vested in one Supreme Court, and in such inferior Courts as the Congress may from time to time ordain and establish." Article III is silent on huge swaths of logistics. How many Justices? Of what backgrounds or training? Sitting where? And doing what exactly? Presumably exercising "the judicial Power." But what exactly is that? Article III was even fuzzier on "inferior courts," which Congress "may" (not must!) "from time to time ordain and establish." The "from time to time" here makes me laugh every time. No rush Congress. Now, later, never, it's your call.

For the first eleven months of our new government there was no federal judiciary whatsoever, as Congress worked to design the judicial branch on a blank canvas. Senate Bill Number One eventually became the Judiciary Act of 1789, the founding document of our federal courts.[1] Future Justices Oliver Ellsworth and William Paterson were the primary architects. The Act created a six-person Supreme Court—one Chief Justice and five Associate Justices. It also created thirteen districts, one for each of the new states. Each district court had a district judge. These districts were then grouped into three circuits: the eastern, middle, and southern circuits. The Act required that every year a "circuit court" should be held in each district and that Supreme Court Justices should ride circuit twice a year to preside in these circuit courts. These circuit courts would consist of the local district judge sitting with two Supreme Court Justices. The circuit courts would handle some appeals from the district courts, but they also had significant original jurisdiction, most notably over any civil dispute that involved claims of more than $500 and federal criminal trials. Basically, the most important federal cases were meant to be handled by the circuit courts with the direct involvement of the Justices. The Supreme Court itself had some cases of original jurisdiction and also served as the last level of appeal, generally as of right.

When you read the first Judiciary Act you are struck by how much of it is focused on the circuit and district court systems, and especially the circuit courts. It seems unimaginable now, but the primary focus of the Supreme Court's original design was utilizing the Justices to staff the lower levels of the nascent federal judiciary rather than in deciding appellate cases. One sure sign is the original number of Justices. Who creates a six-member voting body if the primary goal is orderly voting on contested cases? The possibility of tie votes and gridlock on any judicial body with an even number of members was obvious then as now. So why were there six Justices? Because there were three circuits and we needed two Justices to ride in each of these circuits. Three times two equals six. Tada, six Justices!

The Act was controversial from the start. Many supporters of the Constitution expected a much smaller federal court system, possibly consisting of only a few admiralty courts and a Supreme Court that would do relatively little. Remember that the drafting of the Constitution was contentious, took months, and resulted in a document that faced a very real chance of not being ratified. In this atmosphere the drafters tried to find compromise where they could, often by leaving things purposefully vague. Article III is an obvious example. Article III was purposefully light on details, so some supporters of the Constitution were surprised and disappointed that the power to "from time to time" ordain new inferior courts was used so quickly and expansively. Likewise, opponents of the Constitution had objected that Article III was an obvious attempt to usurp or fully displace state court authority. As such, Paterson and Ellsworth faced several interlocking challenges. They wanted to create a national system of courts that handled more than the bare minimum of admiralty law. But they also did not want an overly large or expensive federal judiciary, and they certainly did not want to threaten the primacy of state courts.

Aside from these broader concerns, there were some wonky logistics in the new structure. The Act allowed district court judges to hear appeals of their own cases as part of the circuit court system, and then allowed Supreme Court Justices to hear appeals of their own circuit court cases—an obvious source of potential bias. Again, this design reminds us that the primary role of early Justices was to ride circuit. Paterson and Ellsworth knew that this appellate structure was unwieldy and possibly unfair, but they thought that the advantages of circuit riding outweighed these obvious downsides.

The diary of Pennsylvania Senator William Maclay, a member of the first Senate judiciary committee, does a nice, if somewhat dyspeptic, job of outlining these objections.[2] There are pages of complaints, but here are a few highlights:

June 29, 1789: I made a remark to Ellsworth [that] his diction had varied from the Constitution. This vile bill is a child of his, and he defends it with the care of a parent, even with wrath and anger... [using the] most elaborate harangue [and the] thorny thicket of law forms.

July 2, 1789: The bill for the judiciary was taken up. I really dislike the whole of this bill, but I have endeavored to mend it in several places and make it as perfect as possible, if it is to be the law of the land. But it was fabricated by a knot of lawyers, who joined hue and cry to run down any person who will venture to say one word about it.

July 7, 1789: The judiciary was taken up for a third reading. I can scarcely account for my dislike of this bill, but I really fear it will be the gunpowder-plot of the Constitution. So confused and obscure, it will not fail to give a general alarm.

July 17, 1789: I opposed this bill from the beginning. It certainly is a vile law system, calculated for expense and with a design to draw by degrees all law business into the Federal courts. The Constitution is meant to swallow all the State Constitutions by degrees, and thus to swallow, by degrees, all the State judiciaries. This, at least, is the design some gentlemen seem driving at. O sweet Candor, when wilt thou quit the cottage and the lisping infant's lips and shed thy glory round the statesman's head? Is it inscribed on human fate that man must grow wicked to seem wise; and the path of politics be forever encumbered with briers and thorns?

By the way, if you were wondering if Maclay's ire was limited to the Judiciary Act, the very next paragraph in Maclay's July 17 diary entry includes a long screed about a boring dinner that night with the Governor of the Western Territory (presumably Arthur St. Clair, the first Governor of the Northwestern Territory). The Governor was "tediously talkative" and "dwelt much on the fooleries of Scottish antiquity" and "worse [yet] showed ill nature when he was laughed at." Maclay's entire journal goes on in this vein and is a treasure. It is a great reminder to those who ask why today's politicians cannot be more like the founders. People have always been people, and politics has always been politics.

The district and circuit court systems were defended on several grounds.[3] The first was cost for litigants. Holding federal district and circuit courts in every state would save money on travel for litigants. A smaller federal judiciary located only in the federal Capital would be inaccessible to most citizens.

Circuit riding also saved money on the system itself. Placing courts in every state was expensive. How to save money? Make the Justices pull triple duty. Justices would serve locally as the trial judges for the most important federal trials, as circuit court judges for some intermediate appeals, and then finally as the appellate court of last resort in the Capital. This design defrayed the costs of a larger federal system. Again, Justice circuit riding was not a byproduct of this system; it was its central feature.

The second defense was the importance of creating uniform federal law. By having the Justices out in the states and trying cases, uniformity was much likelier than waiting for rules of law to be announced from a distant Supreme Court in Philadelphia or New York (or wherever the Capital settled). This issue was especially pressing in federal criminal trials, since they were originally not appealable to the Supreme Court.

The third was that riding circuit matched the British practice of sending judges located in Westminster to conduct trials all over the country. Paragraph 18 of the Magna Carta itself required the King or the "chief justice [to] send two justices to each county four times a year [to] hold the assizes in the county court."[4] The similarities between this British practice and the First Judiciary Act were purposeful and meant to quell concerns about the Supreme Court. It was likewise very common for state supreme court justices to ride circuit and hold trial courts.

The last and perhaps most important consideration was to keep the Justices familiar with the various local laws and to have direct contact between the Justices and the citizens of the states. Many are surprised to hear that, in its initial form, the Supreme Court was meant to be among the *least* cloistered branches of the federal government. As Senator William Paterson argued, riding circuit would bring the law to the people—to "carry Law to their homes, to their doors [and to] meet every citizen in his own State."[5] Congressman Roger Sherman argued that "Justices can acquire a knowledge of the rights of the people of these states much better by riding the circuit, than by staying at home and reading British and other foreign laws."[6]

For the first few decades of its existence, the Supreme Court's primary job was to get out into the country, decide cases, and evangelize for the new constitution and federal judiciary. For many citizens, these first Justices were the face of the new federal government. George Washington understood this. He wrote to each Justice on the eve of their first trips riding circuit to request that they send along any "information and remarks" they learned in their journey through such "an unexplored field."[7] Imagine an America in which the Justices have more insight into local goings-on than the president. This was the case in the late eighteenth century.

Historian Ralph Lerner described the early Supreme Court Justices riding circuit as "republican schoolmasters," ambassadors for the new Constitution and federal judiciary.[8] One of the primary tools was the initial charge to the grand jury in each district, which formally opened the circuit court proceedings.[9] It is super fun to read these charges today. In modern times, a grand jury charge might consist of the presiding judge briefly welcoming the jurors and explaining their duties. These issues were covered back then too, but the earliest tradition also included a rambling and potentially extemporaneous speech by the Justice on a wide variety of topics, including the nature of the new federal judiciary, the jury, and the republic as a whole.

Were these speeches strictly necessary? Well, in his April 12, 1790, speech to the Grand Jury of the Circuit Court for the District of New York, Jay himself noted that "these remarks may not appear very pertinent to the present occasion, and yet it will be readily admitted that occasions of promoting good-will, and good-temper, and the progress of useful truths among our fellow-citizens should not be omitted."[10] Based on the transcript of Jay's remarks, he did not stint on this occasion to promote good will: his comments continue on for pages.

These charges open a window into not only the political and legal concerns of the early Justices, but also life before radio, television, and the internet. When you read these interesting (but, frankly, rambling) speeches, you are struck that the grand jurors and the Justices really didn't have much else to do than speechify or listen. In fact, we have these transcripts because local newspapers would print them in their entirety as "news."

Jay and the other Justices used the occasion to defend the new constitution, calling it a "noble experiment" of "a government of reason" pursuing "the cause of liberty."[11] Of course, the Justices faced the potential danger of becoming too political in their civics lesson. Remember Samuel Chase, the only Supreme Court Justice to ever be impeached. A key part of the impeachment was an exceptionally intemperate opening charge to a Baltimore grand jury, in which Chase decried new Democratic-Republican laws as examples of "mobocracy, the worst of all possible governments."

The Justices may have enjoyed giving these speeches, but they did not like riding circuit. They *hated* it. From the very first time they rode circuit until the practice was made voluntary (and essentially abolished) in the Circuit Court of Appeal Act of 1891, the Justices uniformly and vociferously despised the practice.

In some cases, the complaints were fair. Justice James Iredell, an assiduous letter writer, was the first Justice to regularly ride the southern circuit, and he wrote often about his travel woes.[12] Iredell traveled almost 2,000 miles a year on horseback or in carriages. He spent ten months a year away from his family, traversing "execrable" roads through parts unknown and dangerous. Iredell's biography does a masterful (and hilarious) job of marshalling Iredell's many complaints about his "severe rides" on "very bad roads" in "violent torrents of rain." In one episode a heavy rain caused flooding on the Tar River; Iredell almost drowned trying to traverse the Conetoe Swamp.

The lodging was often substandard. Iredell wrote to his wife of one "very rascally" public house, in which he had to endure drinking, gaming, cursing, and swearing all night. On a different occasion he was forced to share a room with five other lodgers, including "a bed fellow of the wrong sort, which I did not expect." He suffered several injuries from the travel, caused by two different overturned carriages. Disease was a constant companion, including the 1793 yellow-fever epidemic. Iredell justifiably complained of being "heartily tired" or "fatigued to death" by the schedule. Some commentators ascribe Iredell's death at the age of forty-eight to the rigors of circuit riding.

Nor was Iredell alone. William Cushing complained of sharing a room in a public house with twelve strangers. John Jay complained of riding the eastern circuit through rain and snow. In the winter of 1800, Justice Samuel Chase fell off his horse while attempting to ford the Susquehanna River and nearly drowned.

Congress would change and slightly ameliorate the system over time, but Justices were required to ride circuit for almost one hundred years after the Judiciary Act of 1789. This was not due, needless to say, to quiescence by the Justices, who in fact continuously lobbied against circuit riding. Nevertheless, Congress remained convinced that, despite its hardships, circuit riding was a necessary hedge against the possibility of a Supreme Court cloistered in the capital. As Senator William Smith wrote in 1819,

> [I]n a country like this, it is of some importance that your judges should ride the circuits, not only to become practically acquainted with the different rules that govern the decisions in the different States of the Union, but that they may not forget the genius and temper of their government. Adopt the system now before you, and your supreme judges will be completely cloistered within the City of Washington, and their decisions, instead of emanating from enlarged and liberalized minds, will assume a severe and local character.[13]

In 1826, Representative James Buchanan wrote that

> If the Supreme Court should ever become a political tribunal, it will not be until the Judges shall be settled in Washington, far

removed from the People, and within the immediate influence of the power and patronage of the Executive.[14]

Senator George Badger in 1848:

[If circuit riding is banned] we shall have these gentlemen as judges of the Supreme Court...not mingling with the ordinary transactions of business—not accustomed to the "forensic strepitus" in the courts below—not seeing the rules of evidence practically applied to the cases before them—not enlightened upon the laws of the several States, which they have finally to administer here, by the discussion of able and learned counsel in the courts below—not seen by the people of the United States—not known and recognized by them—not touching them as it were in the administration of their high office—not felt, and understood, and realized as part and parcel of this great popular Government; but sitting here alone—becoming philosophical and speculative in their inquires as to law—becoming necessarily more and more dim as to the nature of the law of the various States, from want of familiar and daily connection with them—unseen, final arbiters of justice, issuing their decrees as it were from a secret chamber—moving invisibly amongst us, as far as the whole community is concerned; and, in my judgment, losing in fact the ability to discharge their duties as well as that responsive confidence of the people.[15]

As the country grew, so did the mileage. Consider the estimated travel per Justice in 1838:

Justice	Miles Traveled	Circuit	States in Circuit
Taney	458	Fourth	DE, MD
Barbour	1498	Fifth	VA, NC
Story	1896	First	MA, ME, NH, RI
Baldwin	2000	Third	PA, NJ

Wayne	2370	Sixth	SC, GA
McLean	2500	Seventh	OH, IN, MI
Thompson	2590	Second	NY, CT, VT
Catron	3464	Eighth	TN, KY, MO
McKinley	10,000	Ninth	AL, LA, MI, AR

TABLE 14.1

There were other dangers. Justice Field was assaulted on a train from Los Angeles to San Francisco by a disgruntled litigant. His accompanying Federal Marshall shot the assailant, and both Field and the Marshall were arrested for murder, though they were ultimately released and not prosecuted.

Dreams sometimes come true, and in the Circuit Court of Appeal Act of 1891, Congress reorganized the Federal Judiciary, creating the Circuit Courts and Circuit Judges we know now and making circuit riding voluntary. The Supreme Court's caseload had grown unwieldy and backlogged, so the Act was meant to streamline and give most original appellate jurisdiction to the new circuit courts. Unsurprisingly, once circuit riding was voluntary most Justices chose not to volunteer. The practice was basically abolished in the Judicial Code of 1911.

Solution Number One—Bring Back Circuit Riding

Given how much previous Supreme Courts hated riding circuit this may seem like an inopportune first suggestion for reform. But hear me out. Let's start with the problem. The life experiences of our current Supreme Court Justices have grown narrower and also less diverse. I'll offer the more obvious solution (revive the tradition of nominating individuals from a broad array of backgrounds to the Court) in a minute, but assuming we are stuck with our current version of cloistered and elite meritocracy, let's at least get these Justices out of their chambers and onto the road every year to try cases out amongst the people.

Pause for a second and reread those justifications for circuit riding by members of Congress in the nineteenth century. They sound pretty prescient, no? One predicts a "cloistered court" that has forgotten the "genius and temper of their government." Another warns of a future "political tribunal...far removed from the people." The last foresees Justices that are "philosophical and speculative in their inquires as to law"—"unseen, final arbiters of justice, issuing their decrees as it were from a secret chamber." To reverse this trend, let's re-adopt the original design.

It wouldn't be difficult to accomplish. Supreme Court Justices already get a summer break that starts sometime in June and runs until the first Monday in October. Congress should send these Justices out to the district courts in their circuits for at least two of those months and possibly for the entire time. Each Justice is currently assigned to one or more of the thirteen Federal Circuit Courts of Appeals (some Justices work with more than one Circuit).[16] Their duties in the circuits are both formal and informal, but the current Justices are never required to hear cases, visit any particular district, or really do any of the duties originally involved in riding circuit. Let's require Justices to visit each district court in these Circuits on a regular rotation. The Justices would be required to try cases with district court judges and to interact with the local communities. Congress could even consider reinstating the tradition of the Grand Jury address as an ongoing civics lesson between the Court and the people. Under the Constitution, Congress has the power to set Justice qualifications and their work requirements, within certain constitutional and prudential boundaries. Circuit riding was held constitutional in 1803 in *Stuart v. Laird* and was required for more than a century, so it is hard to believe that bringing it back could be found unconstitutional.[17]

This proposal carries several advantages. First, if the current

Justices have lived lives of relatively narrow experiences, bringing them out into the rest of the country every year could only broaden their thinking.

Second, if the Justices have spent too much time and energy working on constitutional law and the abstruse disputes that end up in our nation's highest court, let's make them learn (or relearn) the rules of procedure and evidence and see what our system looks like from the ground up. If I were actually designing this system from scratch I would make the Justices cycle through some state courts of first instance like family court, juvenile court, or landlord-tenant court, but the founders were loath to mix state and federal courts in that manner, so that suggestion might well be unconstitutional. Regardless, just trying cases in federal courts around the country would provide Justices a crash course in what federal courts actually do, and more importantly, in the people that appear before those courts.

These cases should *not* be especially interesting or novel! The original circuit riding Justices complained bitterly about the travel, but also about the tedium of hearing run-of-the-mill contracts or criminal cases. This is exactly what circuit riding should consist of. The Justices should sit in on motion days. And jury selection. And whatever is on the docket any given day. Asking the Justices to handle cherry-picked constitutional issues would be a waste of their time—they get plenty of that in Washington.

Third, when it is time to replace any current Justice, Congress should demand that the president choose a Justice who is actually from the states within the particular circuits at issue. And by "actually from," I do not mean where the Justice grew up, I mean that the Justice is actually working and practicing in that geographic area.

This is also within Congress's powers. This would immediately solve the problem of geographic diversity on the front end and would also be more likely to fix some other diversity issues, assuming that our most elite credentialed lawyers and judges continue to cluster in and around Washington, D.C., and New York City. Imagine a future in which geographic diversity was required on the Court, and ambitious young lawyers moved to Montana or Missouri to practice *because* they wanted to become Justices.

Fourth, the original problems with circuit riding have been greatly reduced. Because of contemporary amenities such as air travel and comfortable hotels, the Justices will hardly be fording any rivers or sleeping in any "rascally publick houses." Circuit riding died when the Supreme Court's caseload became too large for the Justices to travel and deal with all of the appeals on their docket. But with the current *certiorari* system allowing the Court to control its workload and the Court's current tradition of a relatively light load, there is plenty of time for a summer's circuit ride.

Fifth, as Steven Calabresi and David Presser argued in the *Minnesota Law Review* in 2006, bringing back circuit riding might also force some older Justices to retire, potentially shortening the historically long tenures of our Justices.[18] From 1789 to 1970, Justices averaged about fifteen years on the bench; since 1970, they have averaged about twenty-six years. Calabresi and Presser are quite frank: Supreme Court Justices are staying on the Court for too long because the job is too cushy. The solution? Make it harder. Glenn Reynolds and David Stras (currently a Judge of the Eighth Circuit Court of Appeals) have likewise advocated for a return to circuit riding as a means of avoiding a cloistered Court.[19]

The current Justices might well hate this system for the very reasons earlier Justices hated it. That is sauce for the goose: they could retire. Or they can stay on and learn through suffering. Not all broadening experiences are enjoyable. In fact, most are not. There is an easy solution to fixing an overly cloistered and academic Court: let's get this show on the road.

Solution Two—Sunshine, Political Pressure, and Some Guts

The public profile and salience of Supreme Court nominations and the Court itself have waxed and waned over the years, and it is of course hard to compare eras. Nevertheless, we are undoubtedly undergoing a period of heightened politicization, dissension, and strife over nominations. In 2016, presidential candidate Donald Trump went so far as to release a list of potential nominees in an explicit effort to draw conservative support to his campaign. Then candidate Joe Biden agreed that nominations can be a potent political issue. He pledged to nominate the first female African-American Justice if he became president.

Because the Court has grown in importance, presidents feel enormous pressure to nominate Justices that can both survive an increasingly politicized confirmation process and stay true to their perceived political allegiances once they join the Court. That's a tall order! Given the stakes, it makes sense that presidents have sought to take at least one issue, Justice qualifications, off of the table. Thus the unimpeachable and oddly similar credentials reflected on the current Court. Theoretically this makes confirmation easier and also makes ideological drift less likely, since these nominees have already had years on the bench to drift and have steadfastly chosen not to.

One way to counter this impulse is to raise awareness of its costs. As noted in Chapter One, Justices Scalia, Kagan, and Sotomayor have already started the ball rolling, as have journalists like Adam Liptak and Emily Bazelon, and Senators like Ben Cardin.[20] There have been law review articles on the issue, and of course there's this book. This attention is a start, but we need much more to change the political calculation for future presidents.

Given the relative collapse of faith in our elite institutions, including the Supreme Court, one would think the time is ripe for a frontal attack on the current Justice prototype. On both the right and the left there is a rising disgust with a rigged system run by and for elites. That was one of Donald Trump's campaign themes in 2016 and 2020. Strangely it was *also* the central message of Bernie Sanders in those cycles. Americans on both sides of the aisle have had it with the status quo and the elites who operate it. Compare MSNBC host Christopher Hayes's book *Twilight of the Elites*, a liberal book arguing that elites have failed America, with conservative *Townhall* columnist Kurt Schlichter's book *Militant Normals: How Regular Americans are Rebelling Against the Elites to Reclaim Our Democracy*. Obviously the solutions proposed are quite different, but the underlying diagnosis of the disease is almost identical. Strange times.

Of course, Trump was himself the ultimate personification of America's anti-elite sentiments. He ran as the most anti-elite president since Andrew Jackson. Trump pointedly had a portrait of Jackson moved into the oval office and visited Jackson's Tennessee home, The Hermitage, on one of his first official trips as President in March 2017.

This is why Trump's Supreme Court nominees have been so surprising. We expected Obama to carefully comb the country to choose the "best" nominees for the Court, given that the president himself was a Harvard Law graduate and a former professor at the University of Chicago Law School. What else would he do? But Trump offered new possibilities. It is true that many among Trump's first list of potential appointees were sitting federal judges. But a closer scan showed a number of state supreme court justices and even Mike Lee, a sitting Senator, any one of whom would have changed the Court. The list also reflected more geographic diversity and fewer Harvard and Yale graduates than one might expect. Yet, when push came to shove, Trump appointed Justices from the most elite educational and professional backgrounds possible.

We must also convince voters that the problems on our Court run much deeper than just an ideological split. Glenn Reynolds's *The Judiciary's Class War* is a good start. Here he argues that the elite backgrounds of America's judges influence their decisions, especially at the Supreme Court level. Reynolds notes that these issues are not Left–Right issues, but class issues (or front row/back row issues, to use Reynolds' apt phrasing).

Commentators on the left agree. Adam Cohen's *Supreme Inequality* argues that for a generation the Supreme Court has favored business interests and economic inequality, and not always along the traditional conservative–liberal axis. Cohen argues that the elite backgrounds on the Court lead naturally to decisions that favor corporations.

Likewise, the Supreme Court's radically fractured opinions in *Ramos v. Louisiana* (discussed as an example of a glaring lack of practical wisdom in Chapter One) raised alarm bells on both the left and the right, with *The New York Times*'s Linda Greenhouse calling it a sign of a Court in "crisis" and conservative constitutional law professor Josh Blackmon stating that parts of the decision left him "flummoxed."[21] When I present this work and get to the part about legal complexity I am always heartened by the audience reaction, especially when speaking to non-lawyers. No one is a fan our longer and more complicated opinions, packed with dissents and concurrences. Tying the trend to Justice backgrounds is simple.

Last, I would offer a piece of advice to future presidents. To paraphrase President Trump, "what the hell have you got to lose?"

The focus on elite backgrounds has hardly made the confirmation process smoother. Did Merrick Garland's A+ paper credentials make his confirmation smoother? Did Kavanaugh's? Did it hurt Amy Coney Barrett that she was a Rhodes grad? We are now so polarized that going outside the box may actually make little difference. If Trump had chosen Mike Lee rather than Kavanaugh, some might have squawked, but would it have been worse than what we got?

Takeaway Solution—Go Back to the Future and Make the Court Weird Again

We have redefined our idea of greatness and merit in the last half century, turning away from those with broad life experiences and instead requiring potential Justices to jump through an ever-narrower series of hoops. Fans of this development might note that cronyism and nepotism were more powerful institutional forces before our adoption of this more scientific determination of merit. Bushrod Washington became the twelfth Justice on the Supreme Court in 1799 largely because he was George Washington's favorite nephew. Likewise, many objected to George W. Bush's nomination of Harriet Miers to the Court, suggesting that her appointment was based upon a long friendship and working relationship with the president, rather than exceptional merit.

Yet if a B.A. from an Ivy League school is going to be a *de facto* requirement for joining the Supreme Court, that means the path for future Justices begins to narrow in ninth-grade algebra, which is just too soon. Studying the full arc of the history of the Court gives one a great appreciation for late bloomers. The sheer variety of different kinds of lawyers that have been chosen to sit on the Court is breathtaking. It also gives one an appreciation for the multiplicity of experiences these Justices brought with them to the Court. They lived and practiced all over the country. They fought in wars. They served at the highest levels of the government and at some of the lowest. There was a Postmaster General, and also the postmaster for tiny Cortland, New York. There were police court judges and state supreme court justices. There were Senators, Congressmen, and a former President of the United States along with a Schoolboard member. Let's bring back a Court that reflects American greatness in all of its bizarre variation: geographical, economic, and experiential. Let's make the Court weird again, featuring former mayors and Latin professors and ambassadors and journalists and entrepreneurs. If diversity is our strength, let the Supreme Court reflect the richest version of that diversity.

NOTES

CHAPTER ONE

1 Jesse Byrnes, *Trump: Republicans 'Have No Choice' But to Vote for Me*, The Hill, July 28, 2016, at https://thehill.com/blogs/blog-briefing-room/news/289716-trump-republicans-have-to-vote-for-me-because-of-supreme-court.

2 Mark Barrett, *'Hold Your Nose and Vote,' Graham Tells Christians*, Citizen Times, October 15, 2016, https://www.citizen-times.com/story/news/politics/elections/2016/10/15/hold-your-nose-and-vote-graham-tells-christians/92139852/.

3 Jane Coaston, *Polling Data Shows Republicans Turned Out for Trump in 2016 Because of the Supreme Court*, Vox, June 29, 2018, https://www.vox.com/2018/6/29/17511088/scotus-2016-election-poll-trump-republicans-kennedy-retire.

4 Corey Mitchell, *The Supreme Court Justices Are All Ivy League Law Grads, But What About High School?*, Education Week, July 12, 2018, https://www.edweek.org/ew/articles/2018/07/12/the-supreme-court-justices-are-all-ivy.html.

5 The facts in this paragraph all come from Clarence Thomas, My Grandfather's Son 29-38 (2007).

6 Todd C. Peppers, *Birth of an Institution: Horace Gray and the Lost Law Clerks*, in In Chambers: Stories of Supreme Court Justices and Their Justices 17 (Todd C. Peppers & Artemus Ward eds., 2012).

7 Neil A. Lewis, *Rejected as a Clerk, Chosen as a Justice: Ruth Joan Bader Ginsburg*, N.Y. Times, June 15, 1993, https://www.nytimes.com/1993/06/15/us/supreme-court-woman-rejected-clerk-chosen-justice-ruth-joan-bader-ginsburg.html.

8 Sonia Sotomayor, My Beloved World 258-85 (2013).

9 The remaining facts in this paragraph come from Jessica Gresko, *Fancy Meeting You Here*, U.S. News, August 24, 2018, https://www.usnews.com/news/politics/articles/2018-08-24/decades-of-fancy-meeting-you-here-for-gorsuch-kavanaugh

10 Bryan A. Garner, et al., The Law of Judicial Precedent (2016).

11 David Montgomery, *Conquerors of the Courts*, Wash. Post, January 2, 2019,

https://www.washingtonpost.com/news/magazine/wp/2019/01/02/feature/conquerors-of-the-courts/?utm_term=.5b22f0eea7aa.

12 Michael Kruse, *Trump Reclaims the Word 'Elite' With Vengeful Pride*, POLITICO, November/December 2018, at https://www.politico.com/magazine/story/2018/11/01/donald-trump-elite-trumpology-221953.

13 Michael D. Sheer & Maggie Haberman, *Trump Interviews 4 Supreme Court Prospects in Rush to Name Replacement*, N.Y. Times, July 2, 2018, https://www.nytimes.com/2018/07/02/us/politics/trump-supreme-court-nomination.html.

14 For Gorsuch *see* Orin Kerr, *Trump just said that Neil Gorsuch graduated first in his class at Harvard Law School. Although Justice Gorsuch is super smart, he wasn't first*, TWITTER, September 6, 2018, https://twitter.com/orinkerr/status/1037883011096670208?lang=en. For Kavanaugh, *see* Eliza Relman, *Trump Keeps Repeating False Claim About Kavanaugh's Academic Past at Yale*, BUSINESS INSIDER, October 2, 2018, https://www.businessinsider.com/trump-brett-kavanaugh-yale-1st-in-class-2018-10.

15 ABA, *Ratings*, https://www.americanbar.org/groups/committees/federal_judiciary/ratings/.

16 ABA Ratings, 109th Congress.

17 Robert L. Jackson, *Thomas Rated 'Qualified' for Court by ABA*, L.A. TIMES, August 28, 1991, http://articles.latimes.com/1991-08-28/news/mn-1149_1_court-nominee.

18 576 U.S. 644, 717 (2015) (Scalia, J., dissenting).

19 Adam Liptak, *Sonia Sotomayor and Elena Kagan Muse Over a Cookie-Cutter Supreme Court*, N.Y. TIMES, September 5, 2016, at http://www.nytimes.com/2016/09/06/us/politics/sotomayor-kagan-supreme-court.html?smprod=nytcore-iphone&smid=nytcore-iphone-share&_r=0.

20 Emily Bazelon, *How to Bring the Supreme Court Back Down to Earth*, N.Y. TIMES, February 15, 2016, http://www.nytimes.com/2016/02/15/magazine/how-to-bring-the-supreme-court-back-down-to-earth.html; Adam Liptak, *What Would Scalia Want in His Successor? A Dissent Offers Clues*, N.Y. TIMES, February 15, 2016, http://www.nytimes.com/2016/02/16/us/politics/what-would-antonin-scalia-want-in-his-successor-a-dissent-offers-clues.html.

21 Glenn Harlan Reynolds, *We Should Elect Supreme Court Justices*, USA TODAY, September 15, 2016, http://www.usatoday.com/story/opinion/2016/09/15/supreme-court-garland-scalia-elect-justices-glenn-reynolds/90351964/; Glenn Harlan Reynolds, *Would Trump Nominate Peter Thiel to Supreme Court?*, USA TODAY, September 20, 2016, http://www.usatoday.com/story/opinion/2016/09/20/supreme-court-peter-thiel-trump-scalia-ginsburg-glenn-reynolds-column/90621788/; Glenn Harlan Reynolds, *Supreme Court Picks Need Diversity, Compromise*, USA TODAY, March 17, 2016, http://www.usatoday.com/story/opinion/2016/03/17/supreme-court-merrick-garland-diversity-column/81834920/.

22 NOAH FELDMAN, SCORPIONS: THE BATTLES AND TRIUMPHS OF FDR'S GREAT SUPREME COURT JUSTICES (2010).

23 *Ramos v. Louisiana*, 590 U.S. ___ (2020).

CHAPTER TWO

1 1 JOHN MARSHALL: LIFE, CHARACTER AND JUDICIAL SERVICES AS PORTRAYED IN THE CENTENARY AND MEMORIAL ADDRESSES AND PROCEEDINGS THROUGHOUT THE UNITED STATES ON MARSHALL DAY, 1901, at 207 (John Forest Dillon, ed., 1903).

2 JEAN EDWARD SMITH, JOHN MARSHALL: DEFINER OF A NATION xi (1996).

3 CHARLES EVAN HUGHES, THE SUPREME COURT OF THE UNITED STATES: ITS FOUNDATION, METHODS AND ACHIEVEMENTS 43 (2000).

4 THOMAS S. KIDD, PATRICK HENRY: FIRST AMONG PATRIOTS (2011).

5 BERNARD SCHWARTZ, A HISTORY OF THE SUPREME COURT 16 (1995).

6 9 GEORGE PELLEW, JOHN MARSHALL 301 (1898).

7 HARLOW GILES UNGER, JOHN MARSHALL: THE CHIEF JUSTICE WHO SAVED THE NATION 180 (2014).

8 The facts in this paragraph come from SMITH, JOHN MARSHALL, *supra* note 26, at 1-20.

9 Marbury v. Madison, 5 U.S. 137 (1803).

10 Id. at 177.

11 McCulloch v. Maryland, 17 U.S. 316 (1819).

12 Id. at 406.

13 Id. at 355.

14 Id. at 408.

15 LACKLAND H. BLOOM, DO GREAT CASES MAKE BAD LAW? 39 (2014).

16 LEE EPSTEIN, ET AL., THE SUPREME COURT COMPENDIUM 103-105 (5th ed. 2012).

17 Ogden v. Saunders, 25 U.S. 213 (1827).

18 SMITH, JOHN MARSHALL, *supra* note 2, at 1-20.

19 All of the facts in this paragraph come from 5 THE JUSTICES OF THE UNITED STATES SUPREME COURT: THEIR LIVES AND MAJOR OPINIONS 1916–1922 (Leon Friedman & Fred Israel, eds., 1995).

20 HENRY J. ABRAHAM, JUSTICES AND PRESIDENTS 66 (2nd ed., 1985).

21 JOHN MARSHALL DAY, *supra* note 1, at 118.

22 LYNNE CHENEY, JAMES MADISON: A LIFE RECONSIDERED 434 (2015).

23 SMITH, JOHN MARSHALL, *supra* note 2, at 1.

24 Id. at 21-36.

25 Unless otherwise noted, the facts in this paragraph come from Id. at 21-36; 70-86.

26 Herbert Alan Johnson, *John Marshall, in* 1 THE JUSTICES OF THE UNITED STATES SUPREME COURT: THEIR LIVES AND MAJOR OPINIONS 184-85 (Leon Friedman & Fred Israel, eds., 1995).

27 SMITH, JOHN MARSHALL *supra* note 2, at 37-69.

28 Id. at 144-68.

29 Id. at 144-91. For a detailed and excellent overview of Marshall's involvement

in the purchase and litigation over the Fairfax property, *see* Charles F. Hobson, *John Marshall and the Fairfax Litigation: The Background of* Martin v. Hunter's Lessee, 2 J. S. Ct. Hist. 36-50 (1996).

30 Smith, John Marshall *supra* note 2, at 87-267.

31 Id. at 192-233; 268-81.

32 Montgomery N. Kosma, *Measuring the Influence of Supreme Court Justices*, 27 J. Leg. Stud. 333, 350 (1998).

33 Robert McCloskey, The American Supreme Court 219 (6th ed., Sanford Levinson, ed., 2016).

34 Juan Williams, Thurgood Marshall: American Revolutionary xvi (1998).

35 Mark Tushnet, *Thurgood Marshall, in* 4 The Justices of the United States Supreme Court: Their Lives and Major Opinions 1498 (Leon Friedman & Fred Israel, eds., 1995).

36 Michael O'Donnell, *Thurgood Marshall, Badass Lawyer*, The Atlantic, October 2015, *available at* https://www.theatlantic.com/magazine/archive/2015/10/thurgood-marshall-badass/403189/.

37 *Id.*

38 Michael D. Davis & Hunter R. Clark, Thurgood Marshall: Warrior at the Bar, Rebel on the Bench 37 (1992).

39 Unless otherwise noted by citation, the facts covering Thurgood Marshall's life come from Davis & Clark, *supra* note 38; Williams, *supra* note 34; Mark Tushnet, Making Civil Rights Law (1994).

40 Williams, *supra* note 34, at 34-35.

41 Davis & Clark, *supra* note 38 at 37.

42 Williams, *supra* note 34, at 53.

43 Id. at 57.

44 Davis & Clark, *supra* note 38 at 56.

45 Williams, *supra* note 34, at 63.

46 Davis & Clark, *supra* note 38 at 88.

47 Sandra Day O'Connor, *Thurgood Marshall: The Influence of a Raconteur*, 44 Stan. L. Rev. 1217, 18 (1992).

48 *Id.*

49 Leon Friedman, *Byron R. White, in* 4 The Justices of the United States Supreme Court 1577 (Leon Friedman & Fred L. Israel, eds., 1997).

50 *Id.*

51 Dennis J. Hutchinson, *The Man Who Was Once Whizzer White*, 103 Yale L.J. 36, 43 (1993).

52 *Id.*

53 John Hogrogian, *Byron White's Rookie Season, available at* http://www.profootballresearchers.org/archives/Website_Files/Coffin_Corner/18-06-675.pdf.

CHAPTER THREE

1 Herbert Alan Johnson, *John Jay: Lawyer in a Time of Transition*, 1764-1775, 124 PENN L. REV. 1260, 1260-62 (1976).

2 ADAM SMITH, THE WEALTH OF NATIONS, Book I, Chapter X.

3 HERBERT ALAN JOHNSON, JOHN JAY: COLONIAL LAWYER 144-45 (1988).

4 WENDELL BIRD, PRESS AND SPEECH UNDER ASSAULT: THE EARLY SUPREME COURT JUSTICES 119 (2016).

5 1 HAMPTON L. CARSON, THE SUPREME COURT OF THE UNITED STATES: ITS HISTORY 189 (1892).

6 Herbert A. Johnson, *William Cushing, in* 1 THE JUSTICES OF THE UNITED STATES SUPREME COURT 44-45 (Leon Friedman & Fred L. Israel, eds., 1997).

7 *Id.* at 44.

8 *Id.* at 49.

9 Cushing, William, CQ PRESS—SUPREME COURT COLLECTION, *available at* https://library.cqpress.com/scc/document.php?id=bioenc-427-18166-979174&v=cc86c5b610618229

10 Robert G. McCloskey, *James Wilson, in* 1 THE JUSTICES OF THE UNITED STATES SUPREME COURT 69 (Leon Friedman & Fred L. Israel, eds., 1997).

11 *Id.* at 73.

12 MARY ELLEN SNODGRASS, CIVIL DISOBEDIENCE 285 (2015)

13 H.G. CONNOR, JAMES IREDELL, 1751-99 5-6 (1912).

14 WILLIS P. WHICHARD, JUSTICE JAMES IREDELL 6 (2000).

15 Id. at 27.

16 JAMES IREDELL, SPEECH IN THE RATIFYING CONVENTION, 31 July 1788, *available at* https://csac.history.wisc.edu/wp-content/uploads/sites/281/2017/07/nc_iredell.pdf.

CHAPTER FOUR

1 Herbert Alan Johnson, *Thomas Johnson, in* 1 THE JUSTICES OF THE UNITED STATES SUPREME COURT 96 (Leon Friedman & Fred L. Israel, eds., 1997).

2 *Id.* at 98.

3 LETTER TO GEORGE WASHINGTON FROM THOMAS JOHNSON, 18 June 1770, *available at* https://founders.archives.gov/documents/Washington/02-08-02-0233.

4 Michael Kraus, *William Paterson, in* 1 THE JUSTICES OF THE UNITED STATES SUPREME COURT 111 (Leon Friedman & Fred L. Israel, eds., 1997).

5 Leon Friedman, *John Rutledge, in* 1 1 THE JUSTICES OF THE UNITED STATES SUPREME COURT 35 (Leon Friedman & Fred L. Israel, eds., 1997).

6 ROBERT ERNST, RUFUS KING: AMERICAN FEDERALIST 212 (2014).

7 Both quotes can be found in Friedman, *supra* note 5, at 36.

8 ARTHUR G. SHARP, NOT YOUR FATHER'S FOUNDERS (2012).

9 Irving Dilliard, *Samuel Chase, in* 1 THE JUSTICES OF THE UNITED STATES SUPREME COURT 122 (Leon Friedman & Fred L. Israel, eds., 1997).

10 *Id.* at 123-24.

11 Richard B. Lillich, *The Chase Impeachment*, 4 AM. J. LEG. HIST. 49, 50 (1960).

12 *Senate Prepares for Impeachment Trial, available at* https://www.senate.gov/artandhistory/history/minute/Senate_Tries_Justice.htm.

13 Michael Kraus, *Oliver Ellsworth, in* 1 THE JUSTICES OF THE UNITED STATES SUPREME COURT 137 (Leon Friedman & Fred L. Israel, eds., 1997).

14 1 THE DOCUMENTARY HISTORY OF THE SUPREME COURT OF THE UNITED STATES, 1789–1800 115 (Maeva Marcus, ed., 1985).

15 Kraus, *supra* note 13, at 138.

16 *Id.* at 137.

PART TWO

1 Benjamin H. Barton, *An Empirical Study of Supreme Court Justice Pre-Appointment Experience*, 64 Fla. L. Rev. 1137, 1141-48 (2012).

2 THE FEDERAL JUDICIAL CENTER, THE BIOGRAPHICAL DIRECTORY OF THE FEDERAL JUDICIARY (2021).

3 LEE EPSTEIN, THOMAS G. WALKER, NANCY STAUDT, SCOTT HENDRICKSON & JASON ROBERTS, THE U.S. SUPREME COURT JUSTICES DATABASE (2021), available at http://epstein.wustl.edu/research/justicesdata.html. The study also worked from a less comprehensive print version of similar data, EPSTEIN, COMPENDIUM, *supra* note 40.

4 THE JUSTICES OF THE UNITED STATES SUPREME COURT (Leon Friedman & Fred L. Israel, eds., 1997).

CHAPTER FIVE

1 Olmstead v. U.S., 277 U.S. 438, 478 (1928) (Brandeis, J., dissenting).

2 Unless otherwise cited, the facts in the next few paragraphs all come from MELVIN J. UROFSKY, LOUIS D. BRANDEIS, A LIFE (2009) and JEFFREY ROSEN, LOUIS D. BRANDEIS, AMERICAN PROPHET (2016).

3 Rosen, *supra* note 2, at 33.

4 ALPHEUS MASON, BRANDEIS: A FREE MAN'S LIFE 83-85 (1946).

5 UROFSKY, *supra* note 2, at 71.

6 Id. at 58.

7 Id. at 62.

8 Id.

9 Id. at 63.

10 Samuel D. Warren & Louis D. Brandeis, *The Right to Privacy*, 4 HARV. L. REV. 193 (1890).

11 LOUIS D. BRANDEIS, OTHER PEOPLE'S MONEY AND HOW THE BANKERS USE IT (1914).

12 Louis D. Brandeis, The Opportunity in the Law, An Address delivered May 4, 1905, at Phillips Brooks House, Before the Harvard Ethical Society, *available*

at https://louisville.edu/law/library/special-collections/the-louis-d.-brandeis-collection/business-a-profession-chapter-20.

13 Russell G. Pearce, et al., *A Challenge to Bleached Out Professional Identity: How Jewish was Justice Louis Brandeis?*, 33 Tuoro L. Rev. 335 (2017).

14 *See* George W. Bush Whitehouse Archives, *Chief Justice John G. Roberts, Jr.*, *at* http://georgewbush-whitehouse.archives.gov/infocus/judicialnominees/roberts.html.

15 Michael Grunwald, *Roberts Cultivated an Audience With Justices for Years*, Wash. Post, September 11, 2005, https://www.washingtonpost.com/archive/politics/2005/09/11/roberts-cultivated-an-audience-with-justices-for-years/45dc4932-5045-4037-acbc-7be731a86068/?utm_term=.db49ad4885e9

16 Urofsky, *supra* note 2, at 57.

17 Wayne K. Hobson, The American Legal Profession and Organizational Society, 1890-1930 168 (1977).

18 All of the facts in this paragraph come from Robert Taylor Swaine, The Cravath Firm and Its Predecessors, 1819–1947 138-219 (2007).

19 Joan Biskupic, Sandra Day O'Connor 30 (2005).

20 David R. Stras, *Pierce Butler: A Supreme Technician*, 62 Vand. L. Rev. 695, 704 (2009).

21 Note the difference in scale on the vertical access between Figures 5.1 and 5.2 (0-25 years per Justice) and Figure 5.3 (0-10 years per Justice). The scales are different because private practice has been much more common than service as a government lawyer.

22 Watts v. Indiana, 338 U.S. 49, 59 (1949).

23 United States Att'y Gen. Robert H. Jackson, Address at the Second Annual Conference of United States Attorneys 4-5 (Apr. 1, 1940), *available at* https://www.justice.gov/sites/default/files/ag/legacy/2011/09/16/04-01-1940.pdf.

24 Terminiello v. Chicago, 337 U.S. 137 (1949) (Jackson, J., dissenting).

25 Brinegar v. U.S., 338 U.S. 160, 181 (1949) (Jackson, J., dissenting).

26 Brown v. Allen, 344 U.S. 443, 540 (1953) (Jackson, J., concurring).

27 Massachusetts v. United States, 333 U.S. 611, 639-40 (1948).

28 SEC v. Chenery Corp., 332 U.S. 194, 214 (1947).

CHAPTER SIX

1 *See* Anthony T. Kronman, The Lost Lawyer 53-108 (1993); *see also* Anthony Kronman, *Practical Wisdom and Professional Character, in* Philosophy and Law 203, 208 (Jules Coleman & Ellen Frankel Paul eds., 1987).

2 Id. at 109 (emphasis in original).

3 Edward Mayes, Lucius Q.C. Lamar: His Life, Times, and Speeches 1825–1893 (1896).

4 Arnold M. Paul, *Lucius Quintus Cincinnatus Lamar, in* 2 The Justices of the United States Supreme Court 694 (Leon Friedman & Fred L. Israel, eds., 1997).

5 *Id.*

6 MAYES, *supra* note 3 at 29-30.

7 Paul, *supra* note 4, at 695.

8 *Id.* at 700.

9 *Id.*

10 *Id.* at 700-01.

11 *Id.* at 706.

12 ALEXIS DE TOCQUEVILLE, DEMOCRACY IN AMERICA AND TWO ESSAYS ON AMERICA 313-15 (Gerald E. Bevan, trans., 2003).

13 M.E. BRADFORD, FOUNDING FATHERS: BRIEF LIVES OF THE FRAMERS OF THE UNITED STATES CONSTITUTION (1994).

14 Dan Slater, *Barack Obama: The U.S's 44th President (and 25th Lawyer-President!)*, WSJ LAW BLOG, *at* http://blogs.wsj.com/law/2008/11/05/barack-obama-the-uss-44th-president-and-24th-lawyer-president/.

15 Nick Robinson, *The Decline of the Lawyer-Politician*, 65 BUFF. L. REV. 657, 668 (2017).

16 JENNIFER E. MANNING, MEMBERSHIP OF THE 115TH CONGRESS: A PROFILE 3 (2013), available at https://www.senate.gov/CRSpubs/b8f6293e-c235-40fd-b895-6474d0f8e809.pdf.

17 DENNIS ABRAMS, SANDRA DAY O'CONNOR 49 (2009).

18 *See* JOHN C. JEFFRIES, JUSTICE LEWIS F. POWELL, JR.: A Biography 160-66 (2001).

19 Linda Greenhouse, *Black Robes Don't Make the Justice, But the Rest of the Closet Might,* N.Y. Times, December 4, 2002, https://www.nytimes.com/2002/12/04/us/black-robes-don-t-make-the-justice-but-the-rest-of-the-closet-just-might.html.

CHAPTER SEVEN

1 MICHAEL J. BRODHEAD, DAVID J. BREWER: THE LIFE OF A SUPREME COURT JUSTICE 1837–1910 74 (1994).

2 ABRAHAM, JUSTICES AND PRESIDENTS, *supra* note 44, at 147-48.

3 Arnold M. Paul, *David J. Brewer, in* 2 THE JUSTICES OF THE UNITED STATES SUPREME COURT 50 (Leon Friedman & Fred L. Israel, eds., 1997).

4 U.S. v. E.C. Knight Company, 156 U.S. 1 (1895).

5 James F. Watts. Jr., *Horace H. Lurton, in* 3 THE JUSTICES OF THE UNITED STATES SUPREME COURT 929 (Leon Friedman & Fred L. Israel, eds., 1997).

6 *Id.* at 930.

7 ABRAHAM, JUSTICES AND PRESIDENTS, *supra* note 44, at 165.

8 BERNARD SCHWARTZ, A HISTORY OF THE SUPREME COURT 203 (1995).

9 LISI SCHOENBACH, PRAGMATIC MODERNISM (2014).

10 Glenn Kessler, *Is the D.C. Circuit Last in 'Almost Every Category?,* Wash. Post, June 6, 2013, https://www.washingtonpost.com/blogs/fact-checker/post/

is-the-dc-circuit-last-in-almost-every-category/2013/06/05/a589b186-ce22-11e2-8f6b-67f40e176f03_blog.html?utm_term=.9f8c8026466f.

11 BJS, *State Court Caseload Statistics, available at* https://www.bjs.gov/index.cfm?ty=tp&tid=30.

12 US Courts, *Judicial Caseload Indicators, available at* http://www.uscourts.gov/sites/default/files/statistics_import_dir/mar06indicators.pdf

13 ABA, *Fact Sheet on Judicial Selection Methods*, available at https://www.americanbar.org/content/dam/aba/migrated/leadership/fact_sheet.authcheckdam.pdf.

CHAPTER EIGHT

1 William Lasser, *Justice Roberts and the Constitutional Revolution of 1937 – Was There a "Switch in Time"?*, 78 TEX. L. REV. 1347, 1370 (2000).

2 William E. Leuchtenburg, *When Franklin Roosevelt Clashed with the Supreme Court – and Lost*, SMITHSONIAN MAGAZINE, May, 2005, https://www.smithsonianmag.com/history/when-franklin-roosevelt-clashed-with-the-supreme-court-and-lost-78497994/.

3 Fred L. Israel, *Wiley Rutledge, in* 4 THE JUSTICES OF THE UNITED STATES SUPREME COURT 1316 (Leon Friedman & Fred L. Israel, eds., 1997).

4 Robert Harrison, *The Breakup of the Roosevelt Supreme Court: The Contribution of History and Biography*, 2 LAW AND HISTORY REVIEW 165, 167 (1984).

5 PETER G. RENSTROM, THE STONE COURT: JUSTICES, RULINGS, AND LEGACY 41 (2001).

6 John P. Frank, *Harlan Fiske Stone: An Estimate*, 9 STAN. L. REV. 621, 627 (1957).

7 Harrison, *supra* note 4, at 167.

8 *Id.* at 169.

9 RENSTROM, *supra* note 5, at 41.

CHAPTER NINE

1 All of the facts about John McLean's life in the next three paragraphs all come from FRANCIS P. WEISENBURGER, THE LIFE OF JOHN MCLEAN: A POLITICIAN ON THE UNITED STATES SUPREME COURT (1937).

2 For a description of the challenges of nailing down exact dates, *see* TIMOTHY S. HUEBNER, THE TANEY COURT: JUSTICES, RULINGS, AND LEGACY 51 (2003).

3 The Western Star (Ohio), Wikipedia, https://en.wikipedia.org/wiki/The_Western_Star_(Ohio).

4 Frank Otto Gatell, *John McLean, in* 1 THE JUSTICES OF THE UNITED STATES SUPREME COURT 305 (Leon Friedman & Fred L. Israel, eds., 1997).

5 Act of February 24, 1807, ch. 16, § 5, 2 Stat. 420, 421 ("That the supreme court of the United States shall hereafter consist of a chief justice, and six associate justices, any law to (the) contrary notwithstanding.").

6 Barbara A. Perry, A "Representative" Supreme Court? 4-6 (1991).

7 John S. Goff, *Mr. Justice Trimble of the United States Supreme Court*, 58 Register of the KY Hist. Soc. 6, 26-27 (1960).

8 Weisenburger, McLean, *supra* note 1, at 67.

9 Ohio Supreme Court decisions were not published until 1823, but some newspapers throughout Ohio printed transcripts of several cases. Lunsford's case, *The State of Ohio v. Thomas D. Carneal* (1817), was such a case.

10 Gatell, *supra* note 4, at 303-4.

11 John McLean, Supreme Court of Ohio, available at https://www. supremecourt.ohio.gov/SCO/formerjustices/bios/mclean.asp.

12 Frank O. Gatell, *John Catron, in* 1 The Justices of the United States Supreme Court 372 (Leon Friedman & Fred L. Israel, eds., 1997).

13 New England (ME, VT, NH, MA, RI, and CT), Mid-Atlantic (NY, PA, NJ, DE, and MD), South (WV, KY, TN, VA, NC, SC, GA, AL, MS, AR, LA, and FL), Midwest (ND, SD, NE, KS, MN, IA, MO, WI, IL, IN, MI, and OH), Southwest (AZ, NM, TX, and OK), and West (AK, WA, OR, CA, NV, ID, UT, MT, WY, HI and CO). Supreme Court Justices spent at least a year pre-appointment in each of the following countries: Austria, England, Ireland, Italy, France, Scotland, Spain, Germany, Russia, Turkey, Mexico, and the Philippines.

14 Perry, *supra* note 6, at 4.

15 The other states with no Justices are less surprising: Alaska, Arkansas, Hawaii, Idaho, Montana, Nebraska, Nevada, New Mexico, North Dakota, Oklahoma, South Dakota, West Virginia and the District of Columbia.

CHAPTER TEN

1 The biographical facts in this paragraph all come from Eugene C. Gerhart, America's Advocate: Robert H. Jackson 25-48 (1958).

2 John Q. Barrett, *Albany in the Life Trajectory of Robert H. Jackson*, 68 Alb. L. Rev. 513, 520 (2005) is the source of this quote. That source also supports the facts in the rest of this paragraph.

3 *Id.* at 518

4 *Tuition and Mandated Fees, Room and Board, and Other Educational Costs at Penn 1910-1919*, available at https://archives.upenn.edu/exhibits/penn-history/tuition/tuition-1910-1919.

5 Barrett, *supra* note 2, at 522-23.

6 Gerhart, *supra* note 1, at 34.

7 Barrett, *supra* note 2, at 523.

8 All of the facts in this paragraph come from Gerhart, *supra* note 1, at 34-48.

9 Philip Halpern, *Robert H. Jackson, 1892-1954*, 8 Stanford L. Rev. 3, 7 (1955).

10 Barrett, *supra* note 2, at 530.

11 Gerhart, *supra* note 1, at 34.

12 Id.

13 All of the facts in the next two paragraphs come from Douglass R. Heidenrich, With Satisfaction and Honor (1999).

14 Id.

15 Leon Friedman, *Warren E. Burger, in* 4 The Justices of the United States Supreme Court 1467-68 (Leon Friedman & Fred L. Israel, eds., 1997).

16 *Id.* at 1468-73.

17 *Id.* at 1473.

18 Epstein, Compendium, *supra* note 40, at 416.

19 Michael D. Sheer & Maggie Haberman, *Trump Interviews 4 Supreme Court Prospects in Rush to Name Replacement*, N.Y. Times, July 2, 2018, https://www.nytimes.com/2018/07/02/us/politics/trump-supreme-court-nomination.html.

20 All of the facts in the rest of this paragraph can be found in Albert P. Blaustein & Roy M. Mersky, *Bushrod Washington, in* 1 The Justices of the United States Supreme Court 152-57 (Leon Friedman & Fred L. Israel, eds., 1997).

21 The Supreme Court Justices: Illustrated Biographies 126-29 (Clare Cushman ed., 1993).

CHAPTER ELEVEN

1 All of the facts concerning Justice Bradley's pre-appointment life come from Charles Fairman, *The Education of a Justice*, 1 Stanford L. Rev. 217 (1949).

2 *Id.* at 223.

3 *Id.* at 224.

4 *Id.* at 230.

5 The facts in this paragraph come from Charles Fairman, *Mr. Justice Bradley's Appointment to the Supreme Court and the Legal Tender Cases*, 54 Harv. L. Rev. 977, 981 (1941).

6 Society of Actuaries, *Historical Background*, at https://www.soa.org/about/historical-background/.

7 Miscellaneous Writings of the Late Hon. Joseph P. Bradley x (1901).

8 Id.

9 Id.

10 Daniel R. Ernst, *Legal Positivism, Abolitionist Litigation, and the New Jersey Slave Case of 1845, in* Abolitionism and American Law 103, 120 (John R. McKivigan, ed., 1999).

11 Civil Rights Cases, 109 U.S. 3 (1883).

12 Fairman, *supra* note 1, at 220.

13 Loren P. Beth, John Marshall Harlan: The Last Whig Justice 161 (2015).

14 Andrew A. Lambing, Allegheny County: Its Early History and Subsequent Development 112 (1888).

15 Russell J. Ferguson, Early Western Pennsylvania Politics 188 (1938).

16 James D. Van Trump & James B. Cannon, *An Affair of Honor: Pittsburgh's Last Duel*, 57 Western Pa. Historical Mag. 307, 311 (1974).

17 *Id.*

18 The Pittsburgh Post-Gazette, 1758–2008 14 (2009).

19 T.L. Rogers, *The Last Duel in Pennsylvania, available at* https://journals.psu.edu/wph/article/download/1477/1325/.

20 Michael A. Ross, Justice of Shattered Dreams: Samuel Freeman Miller and the Supreme Court 10 (2003).

21 David L. Hudson, Supreme Court Answer Book 43-45 (2007).

22 Richard Davis, Justices and Journalists: The U.S. Supreme Court and the Media 56-57 (2011).

23 Hudson, *supra* note 21, at 43-44.

24 Id.

25 Irving Bernstein, *The Conservative Mr. Justice Holmes*, 23 New England Q. 435, 436 (1950).

26 G. Edward White, Oliver Wendell Holmes: Sage of the Supreme Court 17 (2000).

27 Mark R. Brewer, Swim, Surrender or Die: The Union Army at the Battle of Ball's Bluff 20 (2019).

28 Id.

29 Susan-Mary Grant, Oliver Wendell Holmes, Jr.: Civil War Soldier, Supreme Court Justice 49 (2015).

30 White, *supra* note 26, at 27.

31 G. Edward White, Justice Oliver Wendell Holmes: Law and the Inner Self 57 (1995).

32 White, Sage of the Supreme Court, *supra* note 26, at 32-33.

33 Oliver Wendell Holmes, The Essential Holmes: Selections from the Letters, Speeches, and Judicial Writings 109 (2012).

34 Id. at 119.

35 Ronald Collins, *Ask the Author*, SCOTUSBLOG, March 28, 2019, https://www.scotusblog.com/2019/03/ask-the-author-the-great-oracle-of-american-legal-thought-revisiting-the-life-and-times-of-justice-holmes/.

36 Andrew Cohen, *None of the Supreme Court Justices Has Battle Experience*, The Atlantic, August 13, 2012, https://www.theatlantic.com/national/archive/2012/08/none-of-the-supreme-court-justices-has-battle-experience/260973/.

37 *Id.*

38 William Gillette, *Samuel Miller, in* 2 The Justices of the United States Supreme Court 508-9 (Leon Friedman & Fred L. Israel, eds., 1997).

CHAPTER TWELVE

1 Richard Kluger, Simple Justice (1976).

2 Id. at 582.

3 Id.

4   ID. at 591.

5   JIM NEWTON, EISENHOWER: THE WHITE HOUSE YEARS 170 (2011).

6   ID. at 170.

7   KLUGER, SIMPLE JUSTICE, *supra* note 1, at 615-16.

8   ID. at 656.

9   ID. at 657-58.

10 ID. at 663.

11 ID. at 659.

12 ID. at 664.

13 ID.

14 ID. at 682-83.

15 ID. at 683.

16 ID. at 697.

17 Brown v. Bd. of Ed. of Topeka, 347 U.S. 483, 495 (1954).

18 KLUGER, SIMPLE JUSTICE, *supra* note 1, at 698.

19 ID. at 707-8.

20 Herbert Wechsler, *Toward Neutral Principles of Constitutional Law* 73 HARV. L. REV. 1, 26- (1959).

21 DAVID EPSTEIN, RANGE (2019).

22 A good entre to Hogarth's work is: Robin Hogarth, Tomas Lejarraga, Emre Soyer, *The Two Settings of Kind and Wicked Learning Environments,* 24 CURR. DIRECTIONS IN PSYCH. SCIENCE 379 (2015). Hogarth's work is covered throughout *Range,* but EPSTEIN *supra* note 278 at 20-21 is the lengthiest discussion.

23 EPSTEIN *supra* note 21 at 21.

24 ID. at 29.

25 ID. at 11.

26 ID. at 108-09.

27 ID. at 177.

28 ID. at 163.

29 PHILIP E. TETLOCK, EXPERT POLITICAL JUDGMENT: HOW GOOD IS IT? HOW CAN WE KNOW? (2009).

30 EPSTEIN, *supra* note 21 at 229-30.

31 Katz, Bommarito & Blackman, *Crowdsourcing Accurately and Robustly Predicts Supreme Court Decisions, available at* https://www.researchgate.net/publication/321744890_Crowdsourcing_Accurately_and_Robustly_Predicts_Supreme_Court_Decisions.

32 EPSTEIN *supra* note 21 at 34.

33 ID. at 76.

34 Dylan Matthews, *How the Good Place Taught Moral Philosophy to Its Characters – and Its Creators,* VOX, January 30, 2020, at https://www.vox.com/future-

perfect/2019/9/26/20874217/the-good-place-series-finale-season-4-moral-philosophy.

35 MICHAEL J. SANDEL, JUSTICE: WHAT'S THE RIGHT THING TO DO? (2009).

36 http://justiceharvard.org/justicecourse/

37 *See, e.g.,* E.M. Anscombe, *Modern Moral Philosophy,* 33 PHIL. 1, 1-19 (1958); Christopher Miles Coope, *Modern Virtue Ethics, in* VALUE AND VIRTUES: ARISTOTELIANISM IN CONTEMPORARY ETHICS 37-38 (2006); ROSALIND HURSTHOUSE, ON VALUE ETHICS (1999).

38 SANDEL, *supra* note 35, at 260.

39 ARISTOTLE, NICOMACHEAN ETHICS, Book VI (W.D. Ross trans., 1908), available at http://www.ilt.columbia.edu/publications/Projects/digitexts/aristotle/nicomachean_ethics/book06.html.

40 ID. at Book VI, Chapter 7.

41 ID.

42 ID. at Book VI, Chapter 9.

43 ID.

44 *See* Laurie Morin & Louise Howells, *The Reflective Judgment Project,* 9 CLINICAL L. REV. 623, 678-79 (2003) ("Notions of practical wisdom and creative problem solving by their very nature depend upon life experience."). Mark Tushnet has similarly argued that the best sign of a Justice's character is his or her experience. Mark Tushnet, *Constitutional Interpretation, Character, and Experience,* 72 B.U. L. REV. 747, 756-63 (1992).

45 ARISTOTLE, *supra* note 39, Book VI, Chapter 7.

46 ID. at Book VI, Chapter 8.

47 ID. at Book VI, Chapter 12.

48 https://www.yourdictionary.com/eudemonia.

49 Lawrence B. Solum, *Natural Justice,* 51 Am. J. Juris. 65, 69-76 (2006); Lawrence B. Solum, *Virtue Jurisprudence: A Virtue-Centered Theory of Judging,* 34 METAPHILOSOPHY 178 (2003).

50 *See* Solum, *Virtue Jurisprudence, supra* note 49, at 202 ("[T]he notion of a just decision cannot be untangled from the notion of a virtuous judge grasping the salient features of the case. Virtue, in particular the virtue of phronesis, or judicial wisdom, is a central and ineliminable part of the story."); Lawrence B. Solum, *A Virtue-Centered Account of Equity and the Rule of Law,* 142-62, in VIRTUE JURISPRUDENCE 142-62 (Colin Farrelly & Lawrence B. solum, eds., 2007).

51 For a classic version of law as craft, see KARL N. LLEWELLYN, THE COMMON LAW TRADITION: DECIDING APPEALS 213-35 (1960). For a more modern overview, see Brett G. Scharffs, *Law as Craft,* 54 VAND. L. REV. 2243, 2274-322 (2001).

52 MCCLOSKEY, AMERICAN SUPREME COURT, *supra* note 57, at 295.

53 *Negative Capability,* POETS.ORG, at https://poets.org/glossary/negative-capability.

54 Richard A. Posner, *Law and Economics Is Moral*, 24 Val. U. L. Rev. 163, 166 (1990).

55 During the 1970s and 1980s the Court's caseload hovered around 170 cases per term. Since the 1990s that number has settled around ninety cases per term. *See* Margaret Meriwether Cordray, *The Solicitor General's Changing Role In Supreme Court Litigation*, 51 B.C. L. Rev. 1323, 1339-40 (2010). For a description of the collapse in the number of *certiorari* petitions granted as an absolute and relative number, see Kevin H. Smith, *Certiorari and The Supreme Court Agenda: An Empirical Analysis*, 54 Okla. L. Rev. 727, 729 & n. 9 (2001).

56 The Court's own Rule 10 suggests that *certiorari* will be granted only for "compelling reasons," based upon an "important federal question" or "important matter" that has divided federal courts of appeals, divided federal and state courts; and has not been decided by the Supreme Court. *See* Supreme Court Rule 10.

57 Richard A. Posner, *The Supreme Court, 2004 Term—Foreword: A Political Court*, 119 Harv. L. Rev. 31, 37-39 (2005).

58 David O. Stewart, *Quiet Times: The Supreme Court Is Reducing Its Workload—But Why?*, A.B.A. J., Oct. 1994, at 40, 43.

59 In 1988, Congress eliminated mandatory appeals from state supreme courts, as well as appeals from any courts that invalidate state statutes. Act of June 27, 1988, Pub. L. No. 100-352, 102 Stat. 662, (codified as amended at 28 U.S.C. §§ 1252, 1254, 1257, 1258 (2012)). *See also* David M. O'Brien, *Join-3 Votes, the Rule of Four, the Cert. Pool, and the Supreme Court's Shrinking Plenary Docket*, 13 J.L. & Pol. 779 (1997).

60 Stephanie Ward, *Clerks Avoid Getting Their DIGs In: They Just Say No to Cert Petitions, as the Court's Docket Shrinks*, ABA J., Mar. 18, 2007.

61 Joshua C. Teitelbaum, *Age and Tenure of the Justices and Productivity of the U.S. Supreme Court: Are Term Limits Necessary?*, 34 Fla. St. U. L. Rev. 161, 164-68 (2006).

62 Kevin Fayle, *Supreme Slackers?*, *at* http://blogs.findlaw.com/courtside/2009/09/supreme-slackers.html.

63 Arthur D. Hellman, *The Shrunken Docket of the Rehnquist Court*, 1996 Sup. Ct. Rev. 403, 409-29 (1996).

64 Richard A. Posner, How Judges Think 323 (2008).

65 *See* John Henry Merryman & Rogelio Perez-Perdomo, The Civil Law Tradition 134-42 (3rd ed. 2007).

66 Karl N. Llewellyn, *Remarks on the Theory of Appellate Decision and the Rules or Canons of About How Statutes are to be Construed*, 3 Vand. L. Rev. 395, 399 (1950).

67 Adam Feldman, *Empirical SCOTUS: An Opinion is Worth at Least a Thousand Words*, SCOTUSBlog, April 3rd, 2018, at https://www.scotusblog.com/2018/04/empirical-scotus-an-opinion-is-worth-at-least-a-thousand-words/; Ryan C. Black & James F. Spriggs II, *An Empirical Analysis of the Length of U.S. Supreme Court Opinions*, 45 Houston L. Rev. 621, 632-38 (2008).

68 *See* Henry J. Abraham, The Judicial Process 221-27 (1997) (noting the trend away from unanimous opinions and towards increased use of dissents and concurrences); Feldman, Empirical SCOTUS: Amid Record-Breaking Consensus, the Justices' Divisions Still Run Deep, SCOTUSBlog, February 25th, 2019, at https://www.scotusblog.com/2019/02/empirical-scotus-amid-record-breaking-consensus-the-justices-divisions-still-run-deep/.

69 Ryan C. Williams, *Questioning Marks: Plurality Decisions and Precedential Constraint*, 69 Stan. L Rev. 795, 799-800 (2017).

70 Suzanna Sherry, *Our Kardashian Court (and How to Fix It)*, 106 iowa L. Rev. 181, 183 (2020).

71 Laura E. Little, *Hiding With Words: Obfuscation, Avoidance, and Federal Jurisdiction Opinions*, 46 UCLA L. Rev. 75, 126-27 (1998).

72 Joseph Goldstein, The Intelligible Constitution: The Supreme Court's Obligation to Maintain the Constitution as Something We the People Can Understand 17 (1992).

73 Robert Nagel, *The Formulaic Constitution*, 84 Mich. L. Rev. 165, 165 (1985).

74 *See, e.g.*, Louise Ellen Teitz, *Complexity and Aggregation in Choice of Law: An Introduction to the Landscape*, 14 Roger Williams U. L. Rev. 1 (2009).

75 *See, e.g.*, Barry Friedman , *The Wages of Stealth Overruling (With Particular Attention to Miranda v. Arizona)*, 99 Geo. L.J. 1 (2010).

76 Stephen M. Johnson, *the Changing Discourse of the Supreme Court*, 12 U.N.H. L. Rev. 29 (2014).

77 *See* Posner, *A Political Court, supra* note 57, at 38-39 ("Last Term [2004], 80% of the Court's primarily constitutional decisions were by split vote, compared to 63% of its other decisions, and a split decision is more likely to attract attention than a unanimous one, in part by generating more—and more contentious—opinions in the case. Although only 38% of all the Court's cases were primarily constitutional, 44% of all opinions (including concurrences and dissents) were issued in such cases.").

78 *See Kevin J. Burns, Chief Justice as Chief Executive: Taft's Judicial Statesmanship*, J. Sup. Ct. History, March 12, 2018, available at https://doi.org/10.1111/jsch.12165.

79 Felix Frankfurter, Felix Frankfurter on the Supreme Court 487-88 (1970).

80 Nancy Scola, *Courts 'Choose' to Lag Behind on Tech, Says Chief Justice Roberts*, Wash. Post, January 2, 2015, http://www.washingtonpost.com/blogs/the-switch/wp/2015/01/02/courts-choose-to-lag-behind-on-tech-says-chief-justice-roberts/; *2014 Year-End Report on the Federal Judiciary*, https://perma.cc/87EQ-B8HU.

81 *2014 Year-End Report on the Federal Judiciary, supra* note 80, at 11.

82 *Remarks of the Right Honourable Richard Wagner, P.C., Chief Justice of Canada, Access to Justice: A Societal Imperative* (2018), *available at* https://www.scc-csc.ca/judges-juges/spe-dis/rw-2018-10-04-eng.aspx.

83 For an overview of these powers and their historical development, *see* Paul

M. Bator, et al., Hart and Wechsler's The Federal Courts and the Federal System 749-65 (3d. ed. 1988).

84 Paul D. Carrington, *Learning from the Rule 26 Brouhaha: Our Courts Need Real Friends*, 156 F.R.D. 295, 297 (1994); *see also* 28 U.S.C. §§ 2074, 2075 (2012).

85 Thomas F. Hogan, *The Federal Rules of Practice and Procedure*, available at http://www.uscourts.gov/RulesAndPolicies/FederalRulemaking/RulemakingProcess/SummaryBenchBar.aspx.

86 Bell Atlantic Corp. v. Twombly, 550 U.S. 544 (2007); Ashcroft v. Iqbal, 129 S. Ct. 1937 (2009); *See* Kevin M. Clermont & Stephen C. Yeazell, *Inventing Tests, Destabilizing Systems*, 95 Iowa L. Rev. 821, 823-31 (2010).

87 Elizabeth C. Burch, *There's a* Pennoyer *in My Foyer*, 13 Green Bag 105, 115 (noting that "the old [Rule 8] has not been amended at all" but the Court's interpretation changed nonetheless).

88 *See* Lisa Eichhorn, *A Sense of Disentitlement: Frame-Shifting and Metaphor in* Ashcroft v. Iqbal, 62 Fla. L. Rev. 951, 967 (2010); Judy M. Cornett, *Pleading Actual Malice in Defamation Actions After* Twiqbal: *A Circuit Survey*, 17 Nevada L.J. 709 (2017).

89 Stephen B. Burbank & Sean Farhang, *Litigation Reform: An Institutional Approach*, 162 U. Penn. L. Rev. 1543 (2014).

90 Michael Orey, *The Vanishing Trial*, Bloomberg Businessweek, April 30, 2007, available at, http://www.businessweek.com/magazine/content/07_18/b4032047.htm.

91 Pew Research Center, *Negative Views of Supreme Court at Record High, Driven by Republican Dissatisfaction*, July 29, 2015, http://www.people-press.org/2015/07/29/negative-views-of-supreme-court-at-record-high-driven-by-republican-dissatisfaction/.

92 Justin McCarthy, *Americans Losing Confidence in All Branches of U.S. Gov't*, Gallup, June 30, 2014, https://news.gallup.com/poll/171992/americans-losing-confidence-branches-gov.aspx.

93 Jeffrey M. Jones, *Trust in U.S. Judicial Branch Sinks to New Low of 53%*, Gallup, September 18, 2015, https://news.gallup.com/poll/185528/trust-judicial-branch-sinks-new-low.aspx.

94 Megan Brenan, *Confidence in Supreme Court Modest, but Steady*, Gallup (July 2, 2018).

95 Lydia Sadd, *Supreme Court Enjoys Majority Approval at Start of New Term*, Gallup, (October 2, 2019), https://news.gallup.com/poll/267158/supreme-court-enjoys-majority-approval-start-new-term.aspx.

96 Justices Breyer, Gorsuch, and Kagan all earned scholarships to study for a year or more at Oxford (Breyer and Gorsuch earned Marshall Scholarships and Kagan a Daniel M. Sachs Scholarship).

97 Justices Kagan, Alito and Roberts worked in the Solicitor General's Office. Justice Ginsburg argued several cases before the Supreme Court while working for the ACLU Women's Rights Project.

98 *See* Douglas Adams, The Restaurant at the End of the Universe 38 (1980).

CHAPTER THIRTEEN

1 The caption for this photo reads: Formal group photograph of the Supreme Court as it was comprised from 2010-2016. The Justices are posed in front of red velvet drapes and arranged by seniority, with five seated and four standing. Seated from left are Justices Clarence Thomas and Antonin Scalia, Chief Justice John G. Roberts, Jr., and Justices Anthony M. Kennedy and Ruth Bader Ginsburg. Standing from left are Justices Sonia Sotomayor, Stephen G. Breyer, Samuel A. Alito, and Elena Kagan.

2 The caption for this photo reads: February 23rd, 1867: Formal group photograph of the Supreme Court as composed under Chief Justice Salmon P. Chase between 1865-1867. The Justices are seated in a semi-circle at the photographer's studio in downtown Washington. The room is plain, with darkened windows on either side and lit from above. The Clerk of the Court, D. W. Middleton, is standing on the far left. Seated from left to right are Justices David Davis, Noah Swayne, Robert C. Grier, and James Moore Wayne, Chief Justice Salmon P. Chase, and Justices Samuel Nelson, Nathan Clifford, Samuel Miller and Stephen Field.

3 Benjamin H. Barton & Emily Moran, *Measuring Biodiversity on the Supreme Court with Biodiversity Statistics*, 10 J. EMP. L. STUD. 1 (2013).

4 National Institute for Mathematical and Biological Synthesis, *About*, http://www.nimbios.org/about/.

5 Unless otherwise noted the facts in this paragraph come from MIKE J. JEFFRIES, BIODIVERSITY AND CONSERVATION (1997).

6 ARISTOTLE, THE BASIC WORKS OF ARISTOTLE 7-40 (Richard McKeon, ed. 2001).

7 Edward H. Simpson, *Bayes at Bletchley Park*, SIGNIFICANCE, June 2010, http://www.medicine.mcgill.ca/epidemiology/hanley/bios601/ch10Bayes/SimpsonBayesatBletchleyPark.pdf.

8 Edward H. Simpson, *The Interpretation of Interaction in Contingency Table*, 13 J. ROYAL STATISTICAL SOC. 238 (1951), http://www.epidemiology.ch/history/PDF%20bg/Simpson%20EH%201951%20the%20interpretation%20of%20interaction.pdf.

9 Edward H. Simpson, *Measurement of Diversity*, 163 NATURE 688 (1949), http://people.wku.edu/charles.smith/biogeog/SIMP1949.pdf.

10 Simpson's diversity, D, ranges from 1 (when all individuals are in the same category) to 0 (when all individuals are in different categories), and is calculated as follows:

$$D = \sum_{i=1}^{N} p_i^2$$

where N is the number of subcategories (for example, species within a site), and *pi* is the proportion of individuals in each subcategory. There can be "open" categories without representatives, but these categories do not count (that is, the result is the same if there is one category without representatives or five categories without representatives).

Because it is more intuitive to have the larger number represent higher diversity, statisticians and demographers often use 1- D, called the Index of Diversity or $\tilde{D}$. So, to calculate the Index of Diversity or $\tilde{D}$:

$$\tilde{D} = 1 - \sum_{i=1}^{N} p_i^2$$

The Index of Diversity represents the probability that two randomly chosen individuals belong to two different subcategories. We use this version of the statistic here.

11 Josh Blackmon, et al., *FantasySCOTUS: Crowdsourcing a Prediction Market for the Supreme Court*, 10 NORTHWESTERN J. TECH. & INTELL. PROP. 125 (2012). For an overview, *see* Oliver Roeder, *Why the Best Supreme Court Predictor in the World Is Some Random Guy in Queens*, FIVETHIRTYEIGHT, November 17, 2014, http://fivethirtyeight.com/features/why-the-best-supreme-court-predictor-in-the-world-is-some-random-guy-in-queens/.

12 Kimberly D. Krawiec, et al., *Diversity and Talent at the Top: Lessons From the Boardroom, in* DIVERSITY IN PRACTICE: RACE, GENDER, AND CLASS IN LEGAL AND PROFESSIONAL CAREERS 92-93 (Spencer Headworth, et al., eds., 2016).

13 James A. Fanto, Lawrence M. Solan & John M. Darley, *Justifying Board Diversity*, 89 N.C. L. Rev. 901 (2011).

14 TAYLOR COX, CULTURAL DIVERSITY IN ORGANIZATIONS: THEORY, RESEARCH, & PRACTICE (1994); Taylor Cox & Stacy Blake, *Managing Cultural Diversity: Implications for Organizational Competitiveness*, 5 ACAD. MGMT. EXECUTIVE 45 (1991).

15 ANTHONY P. CARNEVALE & SUSAN CAROL STONE, THE AMERICAN MOSAIC: AN IN-DEPTH REPORT ON THE FUTURE OF DIVERSITY AT WORK (1995).

16 David A. Carter, Betty J. Simkins & W. Gary Simpson, *Corporate Governance, Board Diversity, and Firm Value*, 38 FINANCIAL REV. 33 (2003). This finding has been controversial, and other studies disagree. Renee Adams & Daniel Ferreira, *Women in the Boardroom and Their Impact on Governance and Performance*, 94 J. FIN. ECON. 291 (2007).

17 Carole J. Buckner, *Realizing Grutter v. Bollinger's Compelling Educational Benefits of Diversity – Transforming Aspirational Rhetoric Into Experience*, 72 UMKC L. REV. 877 (2004); Nicholas A. Bowman, *Promoting Participation in a Diverse Democracy: A Meta-Analysis of College Diversity Experiences and Civic Engagement*, 81 REV. ED. RES. 29 (2011).

18 ACRITAS, DIVERSITY REPORT (2016), available at http://www.acritas.com/diversity-insight; INSTITUTE FOR INCLUSION IN THE LEGAL PROFESSION, THE BUSINESS CASE FOR DIVERSITY: REALITY OR WISHFUL THINKING? (2011), *available at* http://www.theiilp.com/resources/Documents/IILPBusinessCaseforDiversity.pdf.

19 Anne Sasso, *Group Diversity: Mock Juries Reveal Surprising Effects on Diversity in Groups*, SCIENCE, May 5, 2006, http://www.sciencemag.org/careers/2006/05/group-diversity-mock-juries-reveal-surprising-effects-diversity-groups.

20 Samuel R. Sommers, *Effects of Racial Composition on Jury Deliberations*, 90 J. PERSONALITY & SOC. PSYCH. 597 (2006).

21 *See, e.g.*, FEDERALIST no. 83.

22 Adrian Vermeule, *Should We Have Lay Justices?*, 59 STANFORD L. REV. 1569 (2007).

23 Lee Epstein, Jack Knight, and Andrew D. Martin, *The Norm of Prior Judicial Experience and Its Consequences for Career Diversity on the U.S. Supreme Court*, 91 CAL. L. REV. 903 (2003).

CHAPTER FOURTEEN

1 All of the facts in this paragraph come from the Judiciary Act of 1789, ch. 20, 1 Stat. 73.

2 JOURNAL OF WILLIAM MACLAY, UNITED STATES SENATOR FROM PENNSYLVANIA, 1789-91, *available at* https://memory.loc.gov/ammem/amlaw/lwmj.html.

3 For a longer overview of these arguments, *see* Joshua Glick, *On the Road: The Supreme Court and the History of Circuit Riding*, 24 CARDOZO L. REV. 1753 (2003).

4 English Translation of the Magna Carta, *available at* https://www.bl.uk/magna-carta/articles/magna-carta-english-translation.

5 Maeva Marcus & Natalie Wexler, *The Judiciary Act of 1789: Political Compromise or Constitutional Interpretation?*, *in* ORIGINS OF THE FEDERAL JUDICIARY: ESSAYS ON THE JUDICIARY ACT OF 1789 21 (Maeva Marcus, ed., 1992).

6 2 THE DOCUMENTARY HISTORY OF THE SUPREME COURT OF THE UNITED STATES, 1789-1800 122 (Maeva Marcus, ed., 1985).

7 See Letter from George Washington to the Chief Justice and Associate Justices of the Supreme Court (Apr. 3, 1790), *reprinted in* 2 DOCUMENTARY HISTORY OF THE SUPREME COURT, *supra* note 385, at 21.

8 Ralph Lerner, *The Supreme Court as Republican Schoolmaster*, 1967 S.CT. REV. 127 (1967).

9 For an outstanding overview of these grand jury charges, *see* David J. Katz, *Grand Jury Charges Delivered by Supreme Court Justices Riding Circuit During the 1790s*, 14 CARDOZO L. REV. 1045 (1993).

10 2 DOCUMENTARY HISTORY OF THE SUPREME COURT, *supra* note 385, at 27.

11 Lerner, *supra* note 8, at 133.

12 All of these facts come from WHICHARD, IREDELL, *supra* chapter 3, note 14, at 199-214.

13 33 ANNALS OF CONG. 125-26 (1819) (statement of Sen. Smith).

14 2 Reg. Deb. 932 (1826) (statement of Rep. Buchanan).

15 Cong. Globe, 30th Cong., 1st Sess. 596 (1848) (statement of Senator George Badger).

16 The Supreme Court of the United States, Circuit Assignments, https://www.supremecourt.gov/about/circuitAssignments.aspx.

17 5 U.S. 299 (1803).

18 Steven G. Calabresi & David C. Presser, *Reintroducing Circuit Riding: A Timely Proposal*, 90 Minn. L. Rev. 1386 (2006).

19 Glenn Harlan Reynolds, The Judiciary's Class War 41-42 (2018); David Stras, *Why Supreme Court Justices Should Ride Circuit Again*, 91 Minn. L. Rev. 1710 (2007).

20 Benjamin Cardin, *Diversity Matters on the Supreme Court*, The Hill, October 7, 2010, http://thehill.com/blogs/congress-blog/judicial/123191-diversity-matters-on-the-supreme-court-sen-benjamin-l-cardin.

21 Linda Greenhouse, *A Precedent Overturned Reveals a Supreme Court in Crisis*, N.Y. Times, April 23, 2020, at https://www.nytimes.com/2020/04/23/opinion/supreme-court-precedent.html?referringSource=articleShare; Josh Blackman, *5 Unanswered Questions from Ramos v. Louisiana*, Reason, The Volokh Conspiracy, April 21, 2020, at https://reason.com/2020/04/21/5-unanswered-questions-from-ramos-v-louisiana/.

INDEX

Note: Page numbers followed by *f* indicate figures or photographs. Page numbers followed by *t* or *n* indicate tables or notes.